COXSWAIN IN THE NORTHERN CONVOYS

COXSWAIN
IN THE
NORTHERN CONVOYS

S.A. Kerslake

Foreword by
Vice Admiral B.B. Schofield CB, CBE

WILLIAM KIMBER · LONDON

First published in 1984 by
WILLIAM KIMBER & CO. LIMITED
100 Jermyn Street, London, SW1Y 6EE

© S.A. Kerslake, 1984
ISBN 0-7183-0508-6

Typeset by Tellgate Limited, Shaftesbury, Dorset
and printed and bound in Great Britain by
The Garden City Press Limited
Letchworth, Hertfordshire, SG6 1JS

Contents

List of Illustrations

Foreword
by Vice Admiral B.B. Schofield, CB, CBE

I am pleased to write this Foreword as I know what valuable work
these trawlers performed during World War II. Painfully short of
Escort ships as this country was at the outbreak of war, fishing
vessels were requisitioned by the Admiralty, converted to Anti-
Submarine ships and employed as Convoy Escorts.

Mr Kerslake, an ex-fisherman, was no stranger to the fog, snow,
ice, storms and mountainous seas between Norway, Iceland and on
to the White Sea, but in wartime there were the added dangers of
enemy torpedoes and mines. He has written a fascinating account of
his four years' service in AST *Northern Gem*, of around 600 tons and we
must be grateful to him for persevering over a period of seven years to
do so. War histories cannot concentrate on the individual so we must
rely on memoirs of the men who took part. They all added a chapter
to our Naval History of which this country may be justly proud.

B. B. Schofield

First and foremost, I must dedicate this book to my wife Gladys, and to my two sons, Brian and Michael, not forgetting of course my daughter Carol. They have all for years badgered me into writing my experiences down on paper, with the view to getting them published. Now peace reigns once more.

Secondly, I dedicate this book to the members of the Fleetwood Branch of the Royal Naval Patrol Service Association, of which I am a member. Also to all officers and men of that service wherever they may be, for they came from all parts of the world, to serve in the 'small ships', the mine-sweeping and anti-submarine trawlers, and the corvettes, to fight not only the common enemy, but the sea in all its moods.

Many of these small ships were not as lucky as the *Northern Gem*: many were sunk with a great loss of life. The Royal Naval Patrol Service, for its size, lost more ships than the Royal Navy, and had more casualties than any other service, so great was their loyalty to their King and country. They shirked nothing, no matter what the odds against them were. They were, like me, ex-fishermen, or men of the Merchant Navy, or in the latter years of the war, Hostilities-Only men, some of whom had never seen the sea before, let alone a ship of any kind. This book is my story, and my story is theirs, for they all went through similar situations at some time or other, during the long hard slog of those wartime years.

We Remember Them.

S.A.KERSLAKE
Fleetwood, Lancashire

CHAPTER ONE

The Beginning

On 3rd September 1939 I was sitting on the edge of the table in the kitchen of my parents' home, in Campion Avenue, Kingston-upon-Hull; my father sat in his chair, and my mother busied herself on the preparation of the Sunday dinner. We were all waiting for the Prime Minister's speech, which was to be given on the radio, at 11 a.m. that morning, as were millions of ordinary people in their homes in Great Britain, and in the Commonwealth, in fact in every country of the world, in particular Germany I expect, where Adolf Hitler and his gang of thugs awaited the British response when no reply was received to their ultimatum.

At 11 a.m. precisely, the staid tones of Big Ben in London rang out the hour, and the announcer introduced the Prime Minister, Mr Neville Chamberlain. I do not remember his actual words, but it came down to the fact that Britain was now at war with Germany, and after Mr Chamberlain had been through his explanations, (many of which I myself did not understand at the time) the announcer gave out a list of directions for men of all service reserves to report immediately to their nearest depot or Mercantile Marine office.

Being a Royal Naval Reservist, I had to report to the Mercantile Marine office in Hull.

After a mix-up over my call-up papers, I arrived at Lowestoft after a terribly tiring journey, made my way to the Sparrow's Nest, and reported in; I was given billets – mine was in a house on London Road South. I am certain there were about a hundred sailors already in digs there; if not there certainly appeared to be so. The liveliest things in the place were the other occupants of my bed. I was covered in flea bites when I woke up that first morning, and I resolved there and then that I would not stay in Lowestoft any longer than I had to do. At the Nest that morning, I started asking how one got a draft to a ship, and what was the best way to go about getting one.

I was told in no uncertain terms that I must be mad to want to get on a ship and out of a cosy place like the Nest, but I had made my mind up. I had been ashore for five or six weeks, the longest spell I had on terra-firma since I first became a 'Decky Learner', and 'Liver Boiler' some four and a half years before.

The drafting office was my main concern, I kept as close to it as possible; from there most messages went out over the tannoy to all parts of the grounds of the Nest, such messages as: one cook, two stokers, etc. wanted for such and such a draft. I haunted that office at every opportunity, and was sent away disappointed scores of times. But on 16th September, just three days after I had arrived there, a call came over the loudspeakers for four seamen, one cook, one leading seaman – in fact for a full crew. I was in one of the pavilions when I heard it, and I ran like the wind to the office and saw the drafting CPO. I said that I would like to go on this one, and he asked how long I had been at the Nest. I told him and my heart stopped when he answered, 'Sorry, lad, but there's hundreds of men before you yet to go. Anyway what's your hurry?' I told him and after a bit of bantering, he finally relented and said, 'Right, if you're so keen to go, get your name on this bit of paper, and here's your orders' etc.

I was over the moon, I was out of the Nest, and on 17th September 1939 I found myself on a train with the rest of the crew, bound for Barrow-in-Furness, to join His Majesty's Ship 194. It turned out to be the armed escort trawler, *Northern Gem*, which I had seen several times before the declaration of war, on the northern fishing grounds of Iceland, Bear Island, the Spitzbergen grounds, and the White Sea, which is in fact the Barents Sea, off the North Russian Coast, for the White Sea proper is inside the confines of the Russian coast-line.

Little did I know then that within the next four years I would be one of many fighting for survival in those self-same waters. I must say here and now that I have not many memories of any of the ports we visited on our travels on the *Gem*, as I was not one for going ashore too much, only at odd times such as celebrating the wetting of babies' heads, and on shipmates' birthdays, plus the odd dance here and there. So it was at Barrow. I remember that I went to a cinema once or twice and as we were then the only ship of war in the port, the local council and the residents gave the crew an open invitation, which meant in effect that we did not have to pay. We used to go ashore in dungarees with our Navy hats perched on the back of our heads, and we were accepted by the good people of Barrow.

Our first glance around the *Gem* gave us a picture of complete shambles. Everything seemed to be in pieces, with gear of all shapes and sizes lying about all over the place, decks were cluttered up as were the alleyways, the compartments and the engine room. I believe the only compartment that hadn't been turned out was the crews' quarters. On this type of trawler these were on a level with the deck and directly under the bridge structure, and were entered by a watertight storm door on both the port and starboard sides of the casing. It was quite roomy compared to my previous ships, in which the 'deckies and firemen' slept in bunks below the forecastle, right in the fore part of the ship, and under the whale-back, where in strong head winds you were literally lifted or heaved some 20 or 30 feet upwards with the violent motion of the vessel, owing to the effect of the huge seas passing forcefully under the forefoot. One moment you were being transported up to the 'gods'; then suddenly the deck, or the bed if you were lying in it, would drop and leave you suspended in the air for a fraction of time. Then you would come down with a thump and carry on down until the whole process was repeated again and again and again until the weather moderated, or the course of the vessel was altered.

The armaments on board consisted of one 4-inch quick firing gun of World War I vintage, set on a platform just above the after end of the whaleback, and behind the windlass which was used for hauling in the anchor, or in some cases hauling the ship alongside the quay by means of the head rope. Amidships, on either side of the Skipper's cabin, was a sort of half round platform on each of which there was situated a twin Lewis gun. Further aft and actually on top of the galley and in between both the port and starboard lifeboats there was another twin Lewis gun. Apart from the depth charge rails right in the stern, and the single depth charge thrower on the deck at each side of the galley, these were the only weapons with which we had to go off to war and take on all comers. Looking back, I suppose one could say that they were more than inadequate for the jobs we were eventually given to do during the course of the next four years.

On finishing a look around my new ship, I came to the conclusion that apart from the guns, an extra top bridge, and the depth charge throwers and rails, nothing much had changed on the vessel since she had fished in the same seas in which she was now going to fight for her survival. The sea and its moods would be the same enemy that she had been up against then, but now there was the extra enemy, the Germans and all that they stood for against our way of life. This ship we were going to take out to sea to stand up to the enemy, was one of fifteen ships that had been built in Germany in 1935, in Bremerhaven, as a reparation against some debt or other that the Germans owed to this land of ours. They were marvellous ships, and as trawlers go, were somewhat larger than the ordinary run of British fishing vessels, being able to catch and bring home something like 4,000 10 stone kits of fish. Those that I had been going to sea on for the past five years were 'full up' with just 2,500 x 10 st. kits, and even then I've known us have to jump on the wooden hatch covers to get them into their proper place to enable us to batten them down properly, ready for the run home to catch the market.

The starting off point for our war, Barrow-in-Furness, is just across from Fleetwood where I now live with my wife, and my daughter, so for me the past but for a few miles has almost caught up with me. Three years ago I sailed back into Barrow for the first time since leaving it in September 1939. This time it was not on a trawler, but on a friend's yacht. The seas outside were still the same, but there were no mines or U-boats, nor were there any dive-bombers or spotting planes, those nose-to-sea blood-hounds that haunted the convoys to Russia, to pass on the position of their enemy to their base on the Norwegian Coast. But as I stood at the helm of the yacht I could still see and feel the *Gem* leaving Barrow, and the thoughts that flashed through my mind were overwhelmingly clear, and a sense of nostalgia came over me as I remembered those times and happenings all those years ago. Now I can put them down on paper.

*

From being a young boy at school, I had always had a yearning to go to sea; all the comings and goings of the uncles on my mother's side of the family, who followed this occupation of deep sea fishing had excited me in the past. My own father, though he never went to sea, was in the fish trade on the wholesale side, buying on the quayside the fish landed by the trawlers and sold by the salesmen of the different trawling companies. He also did the curing of the fish for his employer in Hull, eventually becoming the manager, and looking after the running of the small fish house, selling all of their products either fresh or cured. In the early thirties, he followed the herring shoals around the coast, going to each port in turn as the herring shoals and fleets moved around. It was to the port of North Shields that I used to go and join him with my mother, when the school's summer holidays started in Hull at the middle of July.

The family was in rooms in North Shields one year, in the house of a man who was a fisherman on a small herring drifter, and many times I went down to see him off, walking past the old wooden dolly as I did so, and waving to him from the edge of the jetty, as the drifter made its way out to sea between the long arms of the moles of the harbour entrance. Each time I returned to the house I pleaded with my father to ask this man to take me for a trip with him, but he always tried to put me off. However I was so adamant that one day my wish came true, and he took me down to the jetty and saw me onboard.

He waved me off on the drifter, and I in turn waved goodbye very excitedly as my long fought-for trip began. It was, I remember, a lovely day; the sun was shining, the sky was a deep blue and the sea from the inside of the harbour looked like a park boating lake. But I could smell the nets and the stench of the remnants of the last catch that hadn't been taken properly from the nets, and once the drifter got clear of the moles and into the open sea, my happy world turned into a nightmare of sea sickness, during which I became aware that I was lying on the floor of the very small wheel-house, on some wooden gratings which were covered by a layer of coconut matting. I was wedged up against the side of the wheel-house by wooden pound boards from the fish room, to stop me rolling about and hurting myself. I saw the sea once when I was coaxed to stand up and have a drink of tea from a mug almost as big as myself and almost as filthy, and a piece of jam sponge cake. This made me very ill again immediately, and I really wished that I were dead, or back home with Mum.

I never ventured to sea again until I was thirteen years old, and once again it was during my summer holidays. I asked an uncle of mine who was a skipper sailing for the Marr Steam Fishing Company to take me for a trip in his trawler the ST *Maretta*, a Fleetwood vessel sailing out of Hull. He agreed to take me, and off I went, not for a thirty-six hour trip into the North Sea fishing for herrings this time, but for a three weeks' voyage to Iceland looking to catch cod, haddocks, and plaice, two thousand kits or so of the stuff. Although I was sick once again, I was nowhere near as bad as I had been on that drifter, because the *Maretta* was three or four times bigger than the drifter, and did not throw herself about as much; she had a different motion.

On this trip, fishing off Langaness, a long promontory that sticks out like a sore thumb into the North Atlantic, inside the Arctic Circle, we had a bad storm, the first one of its severity that I had experienced, and it was then I suffered my first bad fright. I went to the toilet which was situated on the deck, right on the stern. It was a small steel cubicle perched on the port quarter, two steel half doors opened forward, instead of a full one. When you were in position with the top half of the door latched open you could see right along the deck, and on to what lay ahead of the ship. On this occasion I could not get the bottom half of the door to close properly. I was watching the seas coming at the ship from head on, and was fascinated by the way she lifted her head up and climbed over the top of them, but I was also having to try and concentrate on keeping myself on the seat as the stern of the ship dropped down over the top of the same wave, after it had swept under the full length of her. However I was more than fascinated when the *Maretta* failed to get her head up in time for one of the larger seas, and I sat firmly riveted to the toilet seat as I watched it come green over the whaleback, and race foaming along the deck at the speed of a train, and straight for where I was sitting.

Before I could do anything I was completely submerged in freezing, icy green water, and I was struggling to stay in the toilet to save myself from being dragged out of it, and over the stern by the terrific force of water that had pushed the door open. My trousers were down around my ankles, and I was a very very frightened boy. Eventually, I plucked up the courage, and my trousers, to make a dash for the galley and then on to the mess deck below, where I stripped off and dried myself down, and changed into some dry clothing. While I was doing this, I had to suffer quite a bit of joking from the men who were down there at the time, and I decided for the second time in my short life that once I got my feet on to dry land, that was my lot with the sea as far as making a living at it in the future.

However one unguarded moment on the part of my uncle when my father met us at the quayside at the end of the trip, made me change my mind. My father asked uncle, 'How has he been?' and the reply was, 'He'll never make a sailor as long as he has a hole in his bottom.' When I heard that, I was determined to prove them both wrong, and I did that just before my fifteenth birthday.

I had made friends with a lad of my own age, called Tommy Nightingale whose eldest brother Bill was the skipper of the trawler *St Gatien*, she was owned by the Hamling Steam Trawling Company of Hull. It was not long before I found myself, along with my friend Tommy, bound for Bear Island up in the Arctic Circle, on what was termed for boys on these occasions as a pleasure trip. We had to sign articles before we left for the sake of insurance, and we were paid a nominal sum of one shilling per week, for which we worked very hard, in the hope that when the trip was over we might have a chance to sign on properly as one of the crew. We both did two trips as 'pleasurers', then on the third one, Tommy went as the 'Decky Learner', and I signed on as the Liver Boiler. I spent fourteen months in that capacity, and very hard-working but happy months they were. I think that I enjoyed my first working spell at sea in her as much as I did in any other ship that I sailed in, up to the outbreak of the war. She had a young crew, and as good a working crowd as you would find anywhere. They were full of fun, but in those days each one of us knew that you had to work damned hard to stay in a ship; if anyone did not pull his weight, then he was soon on the beach walking about, waiting for hand-outs from pals who were still in a ship. Yes, you quickly got turfed out in those days if you did not suit, or if your face did not fit.

On the way out to the fishing grounds, when the weather was suitable all the deck crew with the exception of the men who had just gone below off watch, turned to and got the trawl ready for shooting away for when we arrived at the fishing ground. Sometimes a full brand new trawl would be installed alongside and fixed to the big iron balls or bobbins that would become the bottom part of the mouth of the trawl; these would, along with round flat-sided wooden bobbins, roll along the bottom of the sea bed, over the top of any boulders or rocks that were in the way. The top of the mouth, or the upper lip as one might call it, was kept open by the fixing of aluminium or glass floats to the headline as it was called. During the installation of the trawl, Tom and myself had to keep all the men supplied with full needles of twine, either single or doubles, depending on which part of the net they were working on. This made our hands sore but soon hardened them off for the much harder work that was to come later on in the trip. Once this job was completed to the satisfaction of the mate or the skipper, the watches converted back to their normal work of steering the ship and keeping look out. Those off watch and the day-men if there was no work for them to do settled to a game of cards down in the forecastle, solo being the favourite. It continued from leaving dock until the ship reached the fishing grounds, or vice-versa on the way back, once they had got their sleep in and their bellies full once more.

Once the first haul of fish had been dropped on the deck and the trawl shot away again, the men started to gut the fish. As they were opened up, the livers were thrown into baskets, and then I would come into my own. I would have the steam on ready in the liver house, and once the baskets were full, a great shout would go up to call me to the fish pounds, where I would lift the full baskets over the pound boards and onto the deck alongside of the trawl winch, stick an 'S' shaped net hook into the handle of the basket, and drag them along the deck all the way aft. If there were any seas coming over the ship's rail, I was expected to look after the livers with my life, for they could be turned into oil, and the oil could be sold for money when the trip was over. This money was then shared out between the crew, and was used to pay for the cigarettes and tobacco etc. that we got out of the bonded stores once outside the three mile limit. On many trips if there was an abundance of fish being landed in the port of Hull, the liver money, as it was known, was the only cash that we picked up for all of our hard and dangerous work, so every liver, and each drop of oil had to be well looked after.

The weather of course is a natural hazard of seamen all the world over, and during one trip to the Bear Island fishing grounds in the *St Gatien*, there was a terrific gale blowing along the Norwegian Coast. The ship had reached a position somewhere abeam of the rocky area of Andalsnes when she took a very heavy sea. Before she could clear herself of this one, she took a heavier one, and lay right over to starboard and on her beam ends. We all thought that our last moments had arrived. Those of the crew who were down in the forecastle took their lives in their hands making the effort to get aft when the Skipper shouted for everyone to get down into the bunkers where the coal had shifted or been thrown over to the starboard side when she took the second sea.

By the time we had all got below, water was forcing its way under the closed galley door and dropping down into the engine room, and for what seemed like hours we shovelled the coal frantically back to the other side of the bunkers. It was a very frightening experience as we were expecting her to roll completely over and take us all down with her, at any second.

But like us humans she fought for her life, and finally somehow she came back onto an even keel and a more stable attitude. We counted ourselves very fortunate indeed as several trawlers during the years preceding this had vanished from sight without trace, and one can only assume that a similar thing had happened to them and that they had been overwhelmed before the crew could do anything to save themselves. I don't think I can explain the feeling that one gets in a situation of that kind, and the thoughts that go through one's mind, except to say that one is very, very scared at the time, and when it is all over, there is a period of great relief and a tendency to religion in the fisherman's way, to say Thank God!

I spent thirteen months on the *St Gatien*; then I got the urge to see if I could get a job as spare hand, which was one step up the ladder, and would put my weekly wage up to two pounds seventeen and six pence per week, and would also give me a poundage of twopence in the pound back on the value of the catch – this was of course after the owner's and ship's expenses had been deducted. Bill Nightingale could not take me on as he had a full crew of good men who seldom left him, so I had to take a chance of leaving myself.

Berths were hard to come by, and I started walking around the dock going to each trawler office in turn, but having no luck, I was beginning to think that I would never get back to sea. Then one day one of my uncles who was mate of the *Kingston Sapphire* landed a catch of herring. The next day I went down to see him off, and found out to my surprise that I was still onboard when she got out into the river. I kept out of sight until she cleared Spurn Point, then I went up on to the bridge to see the skipper who wasn't at all put out to find me there.

As it turned out, I had done myself a bit of good, for no sooner had I signed off the *Sapphire* than George Watkins the runner offered me the chance to go as decky on the *Kingston Cameo* for one trip so that the chap whose place I was taking could have a trip off. Then on the day after I got home from that trip, I signed on the *Kingston Chrysolite* as spare hand bound for the White Sea; it was the first time that I had been off the North Russian coast, and it turned out to be a very hard trip, with every variation of weather it could throw at us, gales of wind, snow, ice, and the dreaded 'Black Frost' which came off the sea like a mist and when the ship passed through it everything froze up. I could watch the frost forming on the ship's rails and the rigging, I likened it to desiccated coconut from the way it looked, and the other men told me that once in that stuff it froze an inch a minute, and I could well believe it.

After that trip we had our usual day and a half in the dock then left once again for the same fishing grounds. The trip out across the North Sea was quiet, as was the run from Lodingen to Hammerfest once we had got into Vest Fiord. The bright lights of the towns and small villages, and of the odd farmhouses dotted here and there both on the shore line and up in the mountains, were a pretty sight, twinkling away in the dark frosty air of the night and reflected in the calm still waters of the fiords. The fishing went off pretty well; we got in a fairly quick catch and made our way back to Hammerfest, through the fiords and back to Lodingen. Alongside there was another ship of the same firm named the *Amethyst*; they were all named after precious stones or jewels.

I was on the mate's watch from midnight to four a.m., after we had gone below from our previous one at eight p.m. The sea was getting up and so was a terrific wind from the south-west. We had got a few miles ahead of the *Amethyst* by this time, and I think that we all knew that this was no ordinary gale that was brewing up, for the wind was reaching a great speed, and heavy seas were continually sweeping over the forecastle and along the full length of the ship. Those of us who were already aft stayed either in the galley, or in the mess room down below, as it was becoming more and more hazardous to try to venture forward to turn in to one's own bunk. At midnight when we relieved the watch, I took first spell on the wheel trying to keep her head to the wind and sea. The bridge windows were being hit by bullet-like spray from the seas coming over the whale-back. The skipper, the mate and the other man on watch were keeping a good look-out, or as good as they could in all the water that was being thrown about. The skipper had already eased the speed down considerably to stop her knocking herself to pieces. He later went to his cabin to get a bit of a rest, leaving orders that he was to be called at a certain time, or if there was an emergency of any kind, and as it happened this was not long arriving.

It came shortly after one a.m. The wireless operator had been keeping a listening watch for anything coming over the air. We had listened to the BBC midnight news just a short time earlier, and my thoughts had strayed to those at home, tucked safely up in their nice warm beds snug and dry, and not being tossed about as we were on a sort of mad and demonic roller coaster. Suddenly our thoughts were interupted by a call of, '*Chrysolite*, *Chrysolite*, come in please, *Amethyst* calling. Are you there please? Over'. The voice sounded urgent, and before we had a chance to call him, the skipper was up the ladder and into the wireless room, '*Amethyst* . . . *Amethyst*, *Chrysolite* here. Go ahead'. 'Sam, we are in trouble, the boiler has shifted and we've got a hell of a list, the lads are on the deck now trying to get a door over the side on a warp for a sea anchor to bring her back head. . .' Then there was silence except for the atmospherics in the background.

Both the skipper and the operator called repeatedly for what seemed like an eternity, but there was no reply. With the boiler shifting causing her engines to come to a stop, she would immediately come broadside on to the wind and sea, and at that moment her transmission stopped. She must have been overwhelmed, turned over completely and gone straight down taking with her the whole of her crew. With what was now a hurricane blowing over the North Sea, they would not have had the chance to get a trawl door over the side shackled onto a warp fed from the winch through the fore gallows, so as to lower the door well into the sea, which would have had the effect of an anchor, and brought her up head to wind. In this way she might have been able to ride out the worst of the storm until help of some kind or other could have got to her, but it was not to be. Whatever had happened to her, had done so with such rapidity that it cut off her skipper's call to us.

It was a black night with the wind shrieking through the rigging like a frenzied demon, accompanied by heavy rain and sleet squalls; the seas were mountainous. Anyone who has not been to sea in this type of weather cannot begin to conceive just what the world seems like on a vessel of this size in these conditions. To begin to describe them properly, one could be accused of stretching the old imagination out of all proportion, but, believe me, they would be doing no such thing.

The skipper gave orders to turn the ship round to go to their assistance, but as soon as the ship's head came off the wind she began to take green seas over the side and to lay over until there was a danger that we too would capsize. Then came the struggle when we were told to get her head back into the wind. The force of it was such that it was like a barrier holding the vessel back. However we made it, and the Skipper decided to wait until daylight came before attempting the manoeuvre again.

When daylight did come, it brought with it no respite from the hurricane; the winds were the same strength, but the seas looked much worse in that we could now see the great big waves breaking and coming at us with evil intent. At night in the dark you could only see the area in the small circle of light made by the deck lights aft side of the bridge, to enable the bridge watch to see what was happening in that area of the deck. No light at all was allowed to shine forward of the bridge because it was reflected back by the spray and this reduced the distance that the watch could see from the bridge. Several times that morning the order to turn the ship round to go back and look for the *Amethyst* was given by the skipper, but each time she filled herself up to the rails on the weather side, and another fight would develop to get her back into the wind. After I had eaten my breakfast, nothing would induce me to go below decks, and with one or two of the others of the crew I stood in the entrance to the engine room, or in the galley looking out through the porthole, watching the seas racing past us with the speed and roar of an express steam locomotive; they were frightening. The old cook who had been going to sea since he left school many years previously said that never before had he been through anything like that, and many of the other men agreed with him. Frightened I was and vowed again that once I got my feet on the shore, there would be no coming back – that was, of course, if we ever made it back to the shore again.

There was also now something else to worry the skipper. The chief engineer told him that he was getting very low on coal, and the decision was made that we could do no more towards helping the *Amethyst*. Other vessels were coming up from astern on their way home, which had a better chance than we had as they were going to pass through the area. I think that all of us knew that from the moment *Amethyst*'s message was cut off so abruptly, we could have done nothing at all. So we slowly made our way towards the River Humber and home, but before we reached the safety of the river, we had to feed the furnaces with pound boards and anything else that would burn to keep steam up long enough to allow us to bring this sad voyage to an end.

When we got alongside St Andrew's Dock I saw my father step aboard. His first words to me were that if I went back to sea after this trip, I deserved a medal as big as a frying pan. On arriving home, my mother asked me if I was going back and I said 'No', so she decided not to wash my sea bag. She had received a bad shock on the day that the *Amethyst* was lost, the paper boy had pushed the evening paper through the letter box, and it had fallen in such a way that it was laid on the floor showing for her to read as she picked it up, '*Kingston Chrysolite* lost with all hands'. When she had pulled herself together, and had summoned up the courage to open up the paper, she saw that the full headline was, '*Kingston Chrysolite* searches for sister ship presumed lost with all hands'. She told me this with a full heart, and was glad, very glad that I was not going back again.

Well, the next morning, I went down the dock to see what I had to pick up after the trip had been sold. I do not remember what we received for our troubles, but it would not be much – it never was. However as I walked into the office, George Watkins, who was ship's husband at that time (the man who signs up the crews for the ships), asked me if I was going back in her, and without thinking, I said yes, and that was that. I didn't dare go back on that answer then, for I knew that I should be walking about for many months if I did so. I went home and told Mother who immediately got out my sea bag to wash without saying a word, and took her anger and dismay out on it, so that it would be ready for the next morning.

So it was back to the old routine once more – the frost – the hard work, and the lack of sleep, the things that we always grumbled the most about, but we still came back for more. To my surprise, I found that I was really beginning to like the life and the danger that went with it, and realised that regardless of what my Uncle George had said, I had made a sailor, and I had still got a hole in my bottom.

By and large, being a deep sea fisherman before the war was a hard life and not a very rewarding one. It was, on looking back, a kind of slave labour, but jobs onshore were hard to come by and once you got caught up in the life at sea, you found it very difficult to give up as I did. If you were a bad boy, or upset one of the office staff ashore, or as I have mentioned before if you did not pull your weight to the satisfaction of the skipper or mate, or even if it was just your face that didn't fit, you were sacked and kept walking about the dock until you had either learnt your lesson, or had served the sort of sentence that had been given to you. Even skippers and mates were not immune from this kind of thing. If a skipper landed a couple of small catches on the trot, he was 'rested' for as long as the gaffers thought necessary. Mates, as they said, were ten a penny, and if the fish they landed did not come up to the owner's satisfaction, then they too joined the skipper on the beach, unless they could get a berth as a bosun or third hand or even as a common decky, which is what the majority did. The dole money was a mere pittance; one just existed on it, and many men were reduced to waiting for hand-outs from their pals who were still lucky enough to be still in a ship. The cameraderie amongst fishermen was a great thing to behold, and was second to none. They deserved much more out of life than they ever received.

Many trawlers were lost in the period in which I was fishing pre-war. Hull, Grimsby and Fleetwood seemed to take their turn each winter to lose one or several ships, either from running themselves aground, or from causes due to bad and indifferent weather. Some sailed and were not heard of again and no wreckage was found, but in the years to come between 1939 and 1946, the trawlers lost in the service of their country were to be many, many more. Many fishermen now in uniform were to be lost with these ships at sea in action against the enemy, or by the cause of enemy action such as the laying of mines around the coast of the British Isles and in other parts of the world, which these ex-fishing trawlers, were now having to sweep up to keep the channels and the sea lanes clear, to enable or allow more freedom of movement for the merchant ships, and the larger naval ships, to enter or leave the ports. All this to me in 1938 was a thing that I never thought could happen. I believe that the first impact it had on me was in the July or August of 1939 when the newspaper and radio reports became more concerned with a German called Hitler.

In 1938 I decided to have my first holiday with my parents since I started to go to sea some three and a half years previously; I had a trip off to enable me to accompany them to Skegness for a week at Butlin's holiday camp there. We set off from Hull by ferry across the River Humber to New Holland; there we got onto the old steam train which was to take us to Skegness. On the way we stopped at Grimsby to allow more passengers to board the train; into our carriage came a family of three, a girl of sixteen and her parents. During the journey, I got talking to Gladys as I found her name to be, and during the whole of the week's holiday, both of our families seemed to go everywhere together. As far as I can remember we had a great week together; eventually after a few partings, and at one stage losing track of each other, Gladys and I were married at St Nicholas Church in Gipsyville, Hull, but not until the war with Germany was over and the peace was becoming a reality once more.

CHAPTER TWO

The Northern Gem Sails

September 1939 found me then at Barrow-in-Furness, onboard the AST *Northern Gem*, an ex-fishing trawler, now being fitted out as a convoy escort vessel, but with many other roles to play in the coming years, as we were to find out: patrol vessel, rescue ship, you name it we were destined to do it.

The crew consisted of a skipper lieutenant, a coxswain, a leading hand, four or five seamen, a chief and second engineer, two firemen or stokers, a cook and a gunner, the latter being a retired Navy man from London. I was to strike up a great friendship with this man who although we did not know it at the time was to become the *Northern Gem*'s first fatal casualty. This was the tragic happening that brought me for one, and I am sure the rest of the crew, to the horrible conclusion that we really were at war with the people of the country where our ship had been built, and that people could really be killed or maimed. Until this death occurred, we must have been living in a make-believe world. We did not want to believe that the bad things we read about could happen to us; also we had the feeling in those first few months of the war, that peace would soon be with us once again, that we were immune from bad things, and that soon we should be home and back at the job we liked doing, fishing. What an illusion that was!

And so the time came for us to leave the safety of Barrow, and make our way to join up with the other four ships who were to make us up into a flotilla; they were the *Northern Dawn*, the *Northern Wave*, the *Northern Spray*, and the *Northern Pride*, all built in the land of our enemy at Bremerhaven, all almost identical to each other, but to me the *Gem* was the best of them all. Our destination was Milford Haven, which was to be our base for the next three months. I suppose we were important in that area; a vast amount of shipping was passing along that part of the coast at that period. I can remember the times when just three or four trawlers escorted up to fifty or more merchant vessels, up that part of the coast, through the Irish Sea, and the North Channel, and saw them off into the Atlantic Ocean, where they made their own separate ways to their destinations. The

Royal Navy were short of destroyers for escort duties, and were to remain so for many months to come.

Out at sea life was very relaxing; nothing much was happening at all for it was the period of the Phoney War, at sea as well as on the land fronts in France. Most times after a trip we dropped the anchor in the haven, and anyone who wanted to go ashore did so by tender, only when the ship required coal or water, or any repairs done did we enter the dock.

After Milford Haven we were ordered to the Clyde and Dunbarton where we were given leave starting on Boxing Day 1939. We had been given a reception by the Mayor and Council of this friendly town on Christmas Day, and a great meal was enjoyed by all. We were well treated and well looked after during the whole of our stay in Dunbarton. We did not know what they were going to do to the ship, only that she was going to have an extensive refit. The weather was the coldest for ages; I remember that even inside the railway carriages taking us home there were icicles hanging from the roof, and we were all perished from the cold, but at least we were on our way home, our first leave of the war.

On arriving back onboard the *Northern Gem*, we were to find absolute chaos. The after fishroom had been torn apart, and a mess deck had been built into it. This was to be the seamen's quarters; the firemen were still living down in the mess deck over the rudder and propeller. What had been our living quarters under the bridge was now turned into officers' quarters. There were two small berths for the two extra officers that we were to 'acquire', and they now had a proper officers' wardroom there as well. Apart from the officers, our crew had been increased with the addition of a signalman, a wireless operator, an officers' steward and a couple more seamen.

Next time our move was northwards to Scapa Flow, from where we made several trips out on the Northern Patrol, scouring the seas between the Shetland Islands and the Faeroes, keeping a look-out and a listening watch for U-boats, or ships trying to get back into German waters. Needless to say we had no joy there, but on one of these trips we suffered some appalling weather and were, I believe, given up for lost as we were some days overdue. It was always a relief even to get back to Scapa Flow where there was an abundance of mountain goats and sheep, but very little else. This was a monotonous part of the job, and one that we wished would end with our being sent to the South once more, for a bit of life, but it was not to be. Other things and other places were in store for us.

Early in the morning of April 9th, the Phoney War came to an end as Germany invaded Denmark and Norway. Denmark surrendered that same day but Norway resisted for some weeks. By the 3rd May however it was all under German control. The important port of Narvik was captured after fierce fighting on 9th April, just forestalling a British naval force sent to prevent it. In the First Battle of Narvik early on 10th April, a destroyer force under Captain Warburton-Lee sank two German destroyers and damaged five ships, and on leaving the scene the destroyer Havock *sank the ammunition ship* Rauenfels. *In the Second Battle of Narvik two days later HMS* Warspite *and nine destroyers under Admiral W.J. Whitworth sank eight enemy destroyers and one U-boat, in return for the destroyers* Eskimo *and* Cossack *which suffered heavy damage. On 28th May the Allies retook Narvik, but abandoned it a few days later after Dunkirk and the imminent fall of France.*

Suddenly in April 1940, after coming in from one of those lonely patrols, we were coaled and watered in double quick time, food was dumped onboard, and we were given orders to join a convoy of troop ships and merchant ships. Rumours were rife. Finland, France and several other places were mentioned, but as it turned out we were all bound for Norway. We arrived at Harstadt without any incidents. Once again I was retracing my steps of pre-war days, but now there were added dangers of mines, bombs, and torpedoes; there was sudden death lurking about. I think that it was about now that we saw just how serious war could be, for bombs had fallen and a lot of places had been hit. Wooden houses and chalets had been burnt to the ground, people were dead and others were homeless. To me it seemed tragic indeed; it was a lovely country and the people had always been very friendly towards us fishermen and it was sad to see what was taking place now.

After a day or two being ferry boat, running troops and stores ashore and surviving the odd raids by German aircraft, we were sent further south to Lodingen in the Lofoten Islands. We were to fill up with coal and water here just as I had done in the old fishing days. I met one or two old friends on the coaling jetty, recognition was almost mutual. It was while we were alongside this jetty, that we saw our first air fight, between what we assumed was one of our fighters and an enemy plane. Most of us at the time were below in the mess deck, some playing crib, others writing home, myself and another Hull man, an Asdic operator, were making Xmas decorations out of silver paper and cardboard – why at this particular time of the year I cannot remember, but I do know that I took those that I had made home with me, and I think that my mother still has them after all these years.

However there we were, pre-occupied by our various occupational therapies, when the alarm bells started to ring out the air attack warning; they put the fear of God into you. At first for a second or so you froze into your seats or bunks or wherever you were at the time, you felt a heavy thumping in your chest, from your heart working overtime, getting the adrenaline going; your chest felt constricted and your breathing got harder, but believe me after that first second or so you moved. If you can imagine some fifteen or twenty men, all moving as one, grabbing tin hats and lifejackets at the same time as they were all moving towards the one ladder that led up on to the deck, then you can understand what panic it must have looked and felt like. Don't forget this was the first real action call and we had all been caught down below in the mess deck. We didn't know what we were running into. It turned out to be two aircraft, the British plane chasing the German plane up and down the fiord, the engines roaring like mad and the machine guns chattering away. They waltzed about for a few minutes and then the German seemed to fly straight into the side of a mountain. Whether the pilot had been hit or had just made the mistake of his life, we never knew, but how we cheered, and waved and jumped for joy. Suddenly it was all quiet again, and no one mentioned that a man had just died in a huge explosion and a big ball of fire.

We were paired with the *Northern Spray*, and our patrol area was Ofot Fiord, the scene of the two great destroyer battles that had taken place a short time earlier. We were not allowed to go up the fiord as far as Narvik; we each took one side of the fiord, and our job was to patrol up and down, keeping up an asdic watch for any enemy submarines that were trying to get up to Narvik with supplies for the German troops who were still holding the port. Also we were there to stop any surface vessels 'of any kind' trying to leave that area, for many German destroyers and some of their troop transports had been sunk or damaged in Romsbak Fiord during the battles. Many of their troops and sailors had been killed and wounded in the action and though they still had a foothold, it was thought for a time that they might try to evacuate the area. What two armed trawlers of our size could have done in the event of such a breakout I don't know, but I am sure we would have had a go at something or other; after all that is what we were there for.

On our side of Ofot Fiord, was a German ammunition ship, the *Rauenfels*. Her fore part was right up on the rocks, and she looked as if she had been hit right in the stern by a torpedo from one of our destroyers, because the rear end of her wasn't there any more, and we could see right inside her. The after part of her deck had been blown upwards and right over the top of her bridge. It looked quite a shambles. One day as an exercise in abandoning ship, or getting one of our small boats away as quickly as possible, the Skipper let some of the crew go over to have a look at her. They boarded the vessel and had a walk around as far as they could, but there wasn't much left, two or three long gun barrels, and what seemed like many hundreds of 'Horse Shoes'. I've often wondered what became of them.

Days on patrol up and down the fiord were many and varied. Mostly it was a dull routine job, keeping an anti-submarine watch in case the enemy tried to get supplies up to their troops by U-boat. There were the odd Norwegian (puffers) fishing boats, that came along which we stopped and searched, all of which were on lawful trips. Some were full of women and children being moved to safer places; it was tragic to see them and to have to examine their few belongings, but it had to be done.

There were times when we could see troops moving about in the distance on some remote mountainside amongst the snow, and we had to stand to. On several occasions we spoke to troops on the shore line, as far as I can remember some of them were part of the South Wales Borderers, and equipped with skis. Others we spoke to were French Alpine troops, I believe. They all told us of the several skirmishes that they had had, and they also gave us the positions of the German troops in the area. It seemed incredible to us at the time that we could have been scrutinised by them, and the possibility of a sneak attack from the shore by an enemy patrol, armed with rifle and machine guns, or even something heavier did not escape our notice or make us feel any easier in our bunks. The war was definitely catching up with us.

The weather was changeable. Some days we had brilliant warm sunshine, on others we had rainstorms and gales of wind, but on the majority of those April days we got frequent snow squalls, some of them very heavy at times. It was on one of these days that we got a hell of a fright. We were doing our normal sweep on the south side of the fiord when an urgent signal was received over the radio by both the *Gem* and the *Wave*, warning us that several unidentified warships were entering and proceeding up Ofot Fiord under cover of the snow squalls. All hands were placed on the alert and all guns were manned: our First World War four-inch gun, our three vintage twin Lewis, and even rifles and some revolvers were issued, though what we were going to do against these or any other warships, in the confines of an enclosed and rocky fiord in such bad visibility, made the mind boggle.

All hands were now in a cold sweat and eyeing the quickest way to the shore should the need arise – that was with one eye, the other one was keeping watch in the direction of the entrance to the fiord, and straining to penetrate the falling snow, with all sorts of thoughts running through the minds of each man. Charlie Keen, the signalman, was at his action station on the top bridge with the CO; he had his Aldis lamp at the ready, and was concentrating on the challenge signal for the day, and also on the reply that he was then hoping to get back from them. But if the powers that be had sent a signal to say that unidentified warships were proceeding towards Narvik, who else could they be but German naval forces. . . . Well, we would soon find out, for at that moment coming out of the swirling snow and into our view came a destroyer, and a short distance away another one appeared. Out went the challenge from Signalman Keen, then again, until after what seemed like an eternity to us all, back came the answer that he and the rest of us had been praying for. They were ours, and we thanked God for that, for also into view came HMS *Warspite*. Hell, didn't she look huge and majestic, especially in that sort of visibility; she and her destroyers were tramping along at a great rate of knots, and they were pushing ahead of them great bow waves which turned the placid and still waters of the fiord into what was a heavy sea to us on the *Gem* and *Spray*. We heaved up and down like ships in a gale of wind until the wash from her and her escorts had passed out of sight and were lost in the snow once more.

As it turned out, the *Warspite* and her flock of attendant destroyers, were on their way to bombard Narvik in an attempt to stir things up in that area, and to let the Germans know that they had not got things all their own way yet.

This run of the Navy kept up day after day. Along the fiord they would come, and not long afterwards we would hear the *Warspite*'s big guns firing off their salvos in a 'salute' to the enemy garrison. Intermingled we could hear the sharp crack of the destroyers' lighter guns. It sounded as if all hell was being let loose, and it was a good boost to our morale. Our 'beat' did not seem so lonely now, and we

(*Left*) The author in 1940. (*Right*) Gunner Fred Powell, recalled to the Service after being 'time served', was killed in action on 8th May 1940 at Ae Fjord, Norway.

At anchor in Reykjavik — crew painting ship at midnight in order to win a bet for the CO, sometime during the Arctic Summer of 1941. Note the painted bow-wave to give the impression of being under way even when stopped in the water.

(*Left*) Sitting on left – Skipper George Loades, centre – Skipper George Spindler who won the highest award from the Norwegian Government in the trawler *Arab*, right – First Lieutenant Skipper Jack Pooley, 1940. (*Right*) Practice shoot 1940, on right 'Ginger' Innes.

(*Left*) Author as best man for the daughter of the Belfast family he was billeted with in 1940. (*Right*) William Edward Young, the author's uncle, was killed at Dunkirk 1940.

who were there to see this great flotilla pass by in those grand surroundings, were very thankful to know that they were in the area, and also it made us very proud to be a part of the British Navy, albeit just a very small part.

And so all through the month of April and into May we kept up our patrol and Asdic search of Ofot Fiord. While on patrol in the fiord, we would sometimes lie close up to the shore, with the engines stopped, the Asdic operators keeping a listening watch with their hydrophones, on which they could pick up any underwater sounds, such as the noise of a U-boat's engines and propeller while travelling submerged. This was the time for us to get out our fishing lines and endeavour to catch ourselves some fish for dinner or tea, even for breakfast on odd occasions. Whichever meal it was for, it was a change from the eternal tinned sausage and Red Lead, (tomatoes), corned beef and pilchards, and the inevitable Chinese Wedding Cake, (Rice); meals got monotonously repetitive at times, though this was no fault of the cook's; he always did his best with the food he had, and we often got freshly baked bread, onto which we spread lashings of Ticklers Jam to 'tickle' our palates. However the days went by, and then came 8th May 1940.

This day was to be a memorable one for some of us, myself included, but for one of our crew and one of the *Spray*'s, it was to be their last. The next forty-eight hours were to become a sort of nightmare. I know that they turned me from being a naive sort of youth into a man, and made me realise that in war one could get killed or maimed as easy as falling over a matchstick.

The morning started off in much the same way as usual. The different watches had their breakfast, look-outs were changed, the day men scrubbed the decks down and gave the ship its general clean up. Then at 11.30 a.m. Up-Spirits was called which was when all the men who were entitled to a tot of navy rum were issued with their ration; they were given 'neaters', pure rum, not adulterated by water – some ships' crews were given 'one and one', others 'two and one'. This meant that they were getting a tot of rum with either one or two tots of water added to the rum – the issue much depended on the CO or the 1st Lieutenant of the ship. When the lads had taken their rum ration, it was time for dinner, and a change of watches, and during the afternoon, I suppose we would have had a few practice shoots, sometimes with rifles and at other times with the Lewis guns, firing at objects floating past as we continued up and down, or on occasions at some prominent rock that had been picked out as the target. On one or two days we were allowed to have a go at the shattered remains of the *Rauenfels*, as we could not do her much more harm. This particular afternoon passed away quietly enough, but when we were sitting in the mess deck aft having our tea, the alarm bells went off on their deathly racket, a series of short rings that told us that it was an air attack warning.

Everyone went off at their top speed to their own particular action station. Mine was to take up a position on the deck armed with a rifle to repel boarders in the event of it happening. A German plane was overhead, and it had a trail of smoke coming from it. Our gunners had only the chance to get off one burst of fire at it, before it went out of our sight, disappearing over the land on our starboard side. We learnt from the watch on deck that the aircraft had appeared from over the mountains on the other side of the fiord; the *Northern Spray* immediately opened fire at it. The plane was already smoking then so there was no doubt that it had been in a fight before it came into our sight, and it was obvious that it had been hit and was in trouble. However it was now lost from our view, so we all stood down, and went back to the mess-deck to finish our tea.

An hour or so later, a Norwegian fishing boat was observed going alongside of the *Spray*; after a time it left them and made its way over to us. On its deck were six or seven of the *Spray*'s crew, and all were armed with rifles. The officer with them went up on to our bridge to talk with our CO who shortly afterwards called for some volunteers to go on this fishing boat, with one of our officers in charge of the party. The ones who stepped forward were: Charlie Keen the signalman, Jack Sullivan Asdic operator, the gunner Fred Powell, along with myself and another seaman rating. We were given rifles and ammunition, and the gunner took a Lewis gun and several of the circular magazines of ammunition for it. When we got on the 'puffer', and she was making her way down the fiord, our officer gathered us all around him on the deck, and began to explain to us what it was all about. He told us that the owner and skipper of the boat we were on had seen a German aircraft come down in Ae Fiord, an offshoot of Ofot Fiord, and had gone to the *Spray* to report its crash. He had then agreed to take a party of armed men to the position of the crashed plane and put them ashore to see if there were any survivors or information by the way of documents that had been left on it. Our officer then went on to tell us what we were going to do when we arrived at Ae Fiord; half of us were to go onshore with him, and the remainder, including our gunner, were to stay on the boat keeping a good lookout around the surrounding hills or mountains.

Fred Powell was to set up his machine gun in the bows of the fishing boat, to be in a position to open fire in the event of our being attacked when we reached the shore. We steamed or as we said at the time 'puffed' our way to Ae Fiord. These Norwegian boats had a small funnel that bent itself around the small wheel-house and the end of it came just above the top, and as they went along they made a noise which sounded like 'puff-puff-puff-puff' hence the name that we gave them. The funnel also emitted dark black smoke rings some two or three feet into the air above the wheel-house. As we went along we were beginning to wonder what we had let ourselves in for. One of the last things that my father had said to me, was, 'Whatever you do, lad, don't go and volunteer for anything'. Now I'd done just that.

The boat nosed its way into Ae Fiord around a headland, and almost immediately we saw the aircraft. The pilot had made a pretty good piece of work of the landing; he had put it down on a flattish bit of beach covered with shingle and a few small rocks. We could see that the tip of the port wing was in the water, and there really did not appear to be much damage. None of us could tell what sort of plane it was, but with hindsight I suppose that we should have guessed. As we closed in to the shore we could see that the door on the port side of the cabin was missing, and there was no sign of any of the occupants. This in itself should have made us more wary of the situation than we were. There was a lot of gear strewn about, and we assumed that the crew had got away and were now hiding in the fir trees higher up on the mountain slopes, as these trees were abundant all around the snow-covered fiord.

Still our officer said that we would go in as planned and investigate the aircraft. Looking over the bows and into the water we soon found that we could see the bottom very easily, but the clear water made us underestimate just how deep it really was. So over the side we went. Jack Sullivan who was about five feet four inches in his stockinged feet found himself up to his armpits, and gasping for breath; the water was freezing cold. One after another the rest of the shore party followed him in: our officer, the coxswain, Chris Wilson, myself and four others. We forged our way to the beach where we stamped our feet and jumped up and down to try and warm ourselves up. I remember that we had a good giggle about paddling and getting paid for it, when suddenly the Lewis gun that was set up in the bows of the boat, opened up, and we saw tracers going over our heads. What we didn't know at this time was that Fred Powell had seen some movement in the fir trees above us and had pointed this out to the *Spray*'s officer, who was in charge of the men left onboard. He told Fred to fire a burst over the heads of whoever was up there as an invitation to get them out in the open to show themselves. Instead we onshore found German tracers coming back on a reciprocal course to those of ours from the boat, and we were aware that we were in between.

We had all dropped to the ground as soon as the firing started, and got under or behind what bit of cover there was. We hugged the ground a bit closer, and noticed the Lewis gun on the boat had stopped firing. Turning to look at the boat from where we lay on the ground, we saw that it was moving full astern out of the fiord, with the German fire hitting it all over the place and chopping it to pieces. From where we lay it looked a shambles, and we feared for our shipmates' lives; but we had to think of ourselves now and of the position that we found ourselves in.

My own concern now was whether I could get any better cover. I was between two large rocks which were slightly apart. There was some sort of plant life around them, and I realised that there was a trickle of water coming through between them and I was right in it. I know that I wet myself then, whether from fear or fright I can't be sure as I honestly at that time did not feel I was unduly afraid. Looking up towards the trees, I could see a German soldier standing out clear of a tree, so I lined his chest up in the sights on my rifle and pulled the trigger. Nothing happened and I found that in the excitement of the last few minutes, for that's how fast the time had gone by, I had forgotten to open the cut-off and put a bullet up the spout.

I did not get a second chance, for Jackie Sullivan who was lying alongside of me said, very quietly:

'Don't look now, Sid, but there's a dirty big Jerry behind you'.

I let go of my rifle and turned over, and sure enough there was. He stood over the top of me with his rifle and the bayonet attached to it, held steady a couple of inches from my back. We all stood up and put our hands over our heads, and that was that. We were now captured and were prisoners of war.

The German troops herded us all together by waving their rifles at us in a hostile kind of way, and a couple of them picked our rifles up and threw them into the waters of the fiord, where I suppose they still are to this day, maybe to be found in many years' time by some future generation. I would like to go back there to see if I could find them myself, and to see those beautiful fiords once more. As we were being herded together, we noticed that our officer was not amongst us. We could not see his body lying about in the vicinity, and we were at a loss to know just what had happened to him.

However once we had been gathered together, we along with the German troops, who by now had stopped shooting at the boat, watched her going stern first out of the fiord. We wondered how many of those that we had left onboard were still alive, and at that moment as these enemy troops ordered us up the mountainside, we counted ourselves very lucky to be in their hands and still alive. So we started to climb up in the direction that they indicated to us. By this time we were all chilled to the bone, for our clothes were wet through and we were not dressed for this sort of caper. I myself had come ashore as I had been dressed at the time on the *Gem*; I had on a pair of fisherman's fearnoughts, which were trousers with a drop down flap, similar to the normal sailor's trousers, but an off white colour and made of a heavy woollen material, which I was now finding out was holding the water that they had soaked up. I also wore a fisherman's abb wool jersey, and a muffler around my neck, my tin hat, and just a pair of slip-on walking out shoes that were handy for walking about on the deck of the *Gem* when the weather was dry. Underneath, I had on long johns and a thick woolly vest, so apart from looking anything like a British sailor, I was feeling pretty soggy, and most uncomfortable, but I am pleased to say that I was not on my own in my piratical rig-out. I think that there were only two dressed in the proper rig of the day, our coxswain and signalman. The latter's watch had stopped at 10.20 p.m., through its immersion in the salt water so at least we knew the exact time of our paddle in the fiord, and the time that we were taken prisoner.

The higher that we climbed up the mountain the colder it became, and we were soon knee-deep in snow to add to our discomfort, as our clothes were beginning to freeze on us. We eventually arrived at a sort of base camp that the German troops had set up on an escarpment. There they had two fires alight in no time at all. One they built into a huge bonfire, and instructed us to strip off all our clothing; with some odd thoughts going around our heads at the time we did as we were told. To our surprise they then made us lay our wet gear on the floor around the fire, and even helped us to do it; as we stood shivering the 'enemy' gave us their greatcoats to put on whilst our clothes dried.

These soldiers were part of a Jäger battalion, crack Alpine troops, who had been on their way to Narvik in the plane, which was a troop carrier. It had been fired at from above by a British fighter. They told us that their pilot had been wounded in the legs, but had managed to make that wonderful landing on the edge of the fiord. He now lay well wrapped up, and laid on the door of the aircraft which we had noticed was missing earlier from it; it had been put to use as a stretcher to move him up to the camp site. There were about thirty-five soldiers and air-crew as far as we could see, and there were lots of guns and ammunition and equipment laid around; they did not seem to be short of anything, except transport.

Soon our clothing was dry and we were told to get dressed, also we were ordered to keep on the greatcoats that we had been wearing. We were grateful for this as it was freezing up there once you moved away from the fire, and the snow was, as I have said before, knee deep. Talking it over later, we decided that the idea behind this generosity of theirs, was that if we were sighted at all, should anyone be looking for us, dressed like that we should make their party look larger than it really was. There were other reasons running through our minds also, but at this moment our main worry was that if we were going to do any climbing or marching, we only had thin dress shoes on.

Time was lost to us now, and we managed to sleep for the odd minute or two. After what seemed like hours, there was a flurry of commands and movement, and the German troops started to dash about. The fires, which had been allowed to die down once our clothes were dry, were put out with great alacrity, gear was being stowed into containers, and we were told to stand up and prepare to move off. All of us were given something to carry. I had belts of ammunition for their Spandau machine guns flung over my shoulders and around my neck, and was also given two metal boxes containing ammunition to carry. Jack Sullivan was given the Spandau and was told in no uncertain terms to take good care of it. We were wondering what all the sudden panic was about, when one of our party said quietly, 'Look down there', and pointed down the mountainside. We saw a fine sight, a British destroyer, or so we thought at the time. From the height and distance we were from her, we did not recognise our own ship, the *Northern Gem*! No sooner had we had time to look at her than we were told to move away on the trot to get away from the area, and we had no choice but to do as we were told, but our hopes were raised now with the thoughts that we may soon be rescued, for one of our party said that there had been 'soldiers' coming ashore from the 'destroyer'.

The next few hours were full of frustration and despair, with mixed thoughts of being taken into captivity, and of being rescued. We were being marched along over mountains; sometimes we were waist-deep in snow, then we were ploughing through icy cold streams of melting snow rushing down the mountainsides to the fiords below. We were not used to this kind of exercise after being cooped up on a trawler for so many months, with nothing more strenuous to do than scrubbing decks, coaling ship, or painting. We thought that we were on the mainland, but as it turned out we were actually on an island. One of the Germans told us that they had fired on the Norwegian fishing boat that had dropped us off, because they wanted to capture it for themselves to use to get off the island. When this was denied them, their only other alternative was to make their way to the only village on the island, and there find a boat to make their escape in.

During our forced march, at one time I began to feel thirsty, so I stopped at a pool of clear ice water cupped my hands and prepared to drink some of it, but my hands were knocked away from my mouth by one of the German air-crew, who then advised me not to drink as this water would give me severe stomach cramp. He then took from his pocket a tin from which he took two tablets, passing them to me for me to put in my mouth. They tasted like sugar, and probably were, but at least they got rid of my thirst.

This man and myself then carried on a conversation as we walked along; he spoke good English, and told me that he liked England very much, and that he had flown there several times before the war, as one of the crew of a passenger plane. He asked me why I was fighting in this war. I told him that as a deep sea fisherman, I was also a reservist, I could do little else as it was my duty to do so once our government had called us up. As we were walking along, I said to him at one time that I would have to stop to pull up my long johns, indicating that the loops which went around my braces had broken, and my johns were down to my knees and were making it difficult for me to walk, let alone climb. He told me that he would give me one minute only, after that time he said that he would have to shoot me, for if he didn't, the Nazi would come along and do it for sure, and that he himself would be put on a report. Apparently there was one of these Nazis with each group of soldiers, or other services, and they were fanatical; the one with our group, whom he pointed out to me, was a fierce-looking fellow and his eyes seemed to be all over the place the whole time. It may have been my imagination working overtime, but I can assure you that I had my long johns hoisted into place and secured to my braces with a couple of half hitches in fifteen seconds flat, I'm certain that may have been a record under any other circumstances.

Some time later after marching, climbing, clinging to rock faces and bits of moss and lichen, we eventually arrived at a point overlooking the small village of Underulet; it sat on the edge of a bay, which was surrounded by steep cliffs, and a promontory on either side of the bay which pointed out into the fiord. Under guard we rested here while the remainder of the party went down into the village to see if there was anyone left around in the village or not; from where we sat we could see no signs of movement other than that of the Germans who were trotting from house to house, nor was there anything that looked like a boat in the bay or at the side of the small jetty. The German troops were soon lost from sight amongst the buildings of the village. It was an hour or so later that they eventually returned, and when they did so, after a few minutes' discussion, the whole group of us moved down the mountainside and into the village, where we from the *Gem* and the *Spray* found ourselves being pushed into one of the houses along with the pilot who still lay on the door of his plane, and had been carried the whole of the way by his comrades. He was put down in a corner of the room, and we rested wherever we could. We were very tired indeed, and the bottom halves of our bodies were chilled to the marrow, through our clothing being once again soaked through by fording streams, and by the melting snow. At the same time the tops of our bodies were sweating from the exertions of our marching.

Taking a look through one of the windows, one of the seamen shouted that he could see people coming round the headland and along the edge of the sea, making their way into the village. We all got up to have a look, and as they got closer we saw that they were wearing khaki, and then into the bay steamed the *Northern Spray*. Going over to the other side of the house, we could see the Germans running back up the way we had come from. The *Spray*'s antique four-inch gun started to fire and we saw the explosions of the shells near to where the Germans now were looking for cover amongst the rocks. Back again to the other window, we could now see that the khaki-clad figures were in fact British Marines, who were now charging along and shouting at the top of their voices towards the village of Underulet. What a smashing sight it was to us in the house.

They then surrounded the house we were in, and we could hear one of them shouting:

'Some of the bastards are still in there'.

Charlie Keen opened the door answering as loudly as he could over the racket that the Marines were making, 'We're British sailors' just as a Marine lunged at him with a rifle and bayonet, pulling it back in time. It's a good job that they didn't throw in a couple of hand-grenades through the windows.

A feeling of relief came over us now that we had been rescued, and our exhaustion went from us for the moment as we stepped outside the house, and gathered up bits of equipment that the Germans had left behind in their haste to get away from the Marines. We wanted to keep them as mementoes and souvenirs of our two days of captivity. I went all out to try and get hold of a cine camera with which one of the group had been taking photographs of us during the march, but I was much too slow, and one of the Marines got hold of it first.

Once the Germans had been rounded up and our positions had been as you might say reversed, we saw them lined up. The pilot had been carried outside on his makeshift stretcher, I don't think that there had been any casualties amongst them, or the Marines, for by running back up the mountain, the enemy troops had run right into the arms of those 'soldiers' that had been seen being landed from the ship in the fiord at the place where we had been captured. These soldiers were in fact more Marines, and they had followed the tracks of our flight; apparently they had at times seen us and could have opened fire, but with finding no bodies (ours), as they came ashore near to the ditched aircraft, they guessed rightly that we were in the group. They were not sure however who were the Germans and who were the sailors, for all they could see were a group of men dressed in German army uniforms, so they held their fire, thank God. However as the German troops broke from the village of Underulet, they ran into the trap that had been set for them, and gave themselves up. The last time that I saw them was as they were all being taken aboard the *Spray*, for passage to HMS *Resolution*, the Royal Navy vessel that the Marines had come from.

We were taken back aboard the *Northern Gem*, and as we climbed back over the ship's rail, we were greeted with shouts of, 'Glad you're back', and 'It's your watch now'. We were taken below and given a couple of tots of rum, and then after a short explanation of what had happened to us over the last two days, we were allowed to have a bath to get rid of some dirt, and then get turned in and sleep off the exhaustion that had taken us over once again. The 'Neaters' rum was having a great effect on our empty stomachs; we were told what had happened to the fishing boat and those on it, but none of that sank in to our very tired minds. Later after a good sleep and feeling better for a decent meal of sorts, we started asking questions.

Gradually we were told the story of those we had left on the boat when we had gone ashore in Ae Fiord. One, our gunner Fred Powell, who had served his time in the Navy from being a boy, retired, and had been working as a postman in London, until he had been called back, had been killed in that first exchange of fire from the German Spandaus. He had been hit in the head and had known nothing about it; he had died instantly with his head shattered. He had been my 'Oppo', rather like a father figure to me; the last sight I had of him had been as he was knelt down in the bows of that fishing boat, checking over his Lewis gun once more. I was filled with a sense of grief for his loss.

Harry Peake, a fisherman from my home port of Hull, had died of wounds just after being taken onboard the *Northern Spray*, his ship; all the rest of those onboard the boat had been wounded in some way during the exchange of fire, but whoever had been in the little wheelhouse of the boat, must have had sufficient control to get her out of the fiord stern first, as we ourselves had witnessed. He got her alongside the *Spray*, where everyone was taken onboard as the *Spray* made full speed in order to find some Naval vessel which had a doctor on to give better aid to the wounded. Trawlers in those days did not even warrant a sick berth attendant in their crew, and had to rely on what the skipper or anyone else knew about first aid.

The *Gem*'s officer, whom we had realised was missing when the Germans surrounded us and took us into their 'care', had apparently, when the shooting started, been near to the water's edge, so he dropped to the ground and immediately rolled into the water, then crept around the rocky shore, still in the water and unseen by the enemy, until he reached the outside of the fiord and got within hailing distance of the *Northern Gem*. He was picked up and taken on the *Gem*, where he was stripped off and filled up with gin while he told them his side of the story. The *Gem* with Lieutenant-Commander Scarlett RNR as CO then made haste to the *Northern Spray*, which was now tied up alongside the HMS *Resolution* where she had put her wounded. A conference was then held on the *Resolution*, and a plan to put the two parties of Marines ashore from the two trawlers, was formulated there once that it was realised that the Germans were on an island, and that it was possible that some of those who had dropped to the ground, as the *Gem*'s officer had done, when the firing had started, might still be alive, in which case they would have been taken prisoner. This plan I have explained in the simple terms of an ordinary seaman, without frills and in the language that all can understand.

After we had finished giving the story of our side of the action, and we had such a lot to tell, we picked up once more the routine of the ship, and slipped back into our original watches, and were then left each of us with our own individual thoughts. But this calm and peace was not to last for long. We were sent a replacement gunner for Fred Powell. I think that the coxswain was the only man of the ship's crew to know this man's name. No one else really got the chance for some twenty-four hours later he too was dead.

The morning following our return to the ship, our skipper received orders to proceed to the village of Underulet, to see if any of the Germans had been missed, so off we steamed keeping our eyes open for any enemy aircraft on the way. However we arrived in the bay, without our seeing one at all. As the village came into view, we saw a small fishing boat made fast alongside the jetty. There had been none there on the previous day, so we made our way slowly towards it. All of our guns were manned, and every man on board was on the alert. The occupants of this fishing boat had seen us arriving in the bay, for they immediately cast off their ropes from the jetty, and made all the speed that they could to the far side of the bay on our starboard side. It was obviously a move to avoid contact with us. In spite of signals, and warnings shouted over the loud hailer, plus the fact that we had quite a bit of armament showing, they took no notice so Lieutenant-Commander Scarlett ordered a shot to be fired across his bows as a stronger warning to stop, in true naval fashion; that seemed to do the trick for when the four-inch shell landed and splashed in the water ahead of them, the boat slowed down and turned towards us.

When it got closer, it was ordered to come right alongside the *Gem*, and eventually made fast with her port side up against our starboard side, with two ropes out, one from forward and one from aft. There were four men on the deck, and wheelhouse, all dressed in the garb of Norwegian fishermen. Our CO asked who they were and why hadn't they stopped when we first signalled them to do so. Not one of them answered, and they looked surly and very suspicious, so the officer who had made his escape from our landing party some two or three days previously, took the two men nearest to him on the deck of the *Gem*, saying, 'Come on follow me.' They were a seaman from Stornaway, and the new replacement gunner who had only come on board the day before and they climbed over onto the deck of the fishing boat. All three were armed with revolvers, and spread out to make a search of the vessel. As they did so the man in the wheelhouse shouted something out; at once the boat started going full ahead, the ropes holding both ships together became taut and the men fore and aft cut the ropes with knives. All this happened in the blink of an eye, and was so sudden and unexpected.

In the space of a couple of minutes she was a good distance away from us, and we could see a fearful struggle going on on her deck. Our officer was grappling with one of the men, when one of the others came up behind him and hit him with an axe; he fell to the deck with the axe still lodged in his back. The gunner was being stabbed repeatedly with knives, but both he and the other seaman had the presence of mind to jump over the side and into the water. Up to that time we had dared not to open fire in case we hit one of our own men, but now that they were off the boat, and as far as we knew, our officer lay dead where he had fallen, everyone opened up with whatever they had their hands on, rifles, machine guns, revolvers. Within minutes she was stopped dead in the water with no sign of life to be seen anywhere on the deck.

First we stopped to pick up our two men out of the water, where the seaman was supporting the gunner. Myself and another seaman reached over and pulled him upwards so that others could get a better hold of his arms and his clothing to heave him inboard. As we got him over the ship's rail we could see the blood pumping out of the rents in his clothing; blood and salt water ran out of his seaboots and onto the deck like miniature rivers. It was tragic that as we laid him on the deck he gave us a great big grin, then he died. I have seen this happen in my mind's eye many times since then, but I am sorry to say that I never even got to know his name, his membership of the crew had been so short. Our other seaman was unscathed.

We now went alongside the fishing boat, and several of our men then jumped onboard her and made her fast once again. Others had run to our officer who still lay where he had fallen. The axe was still buried in his back, he was still alive but unconscious and was lifted up very gently and taken to the wardroom on the *Gem*. Here he was made as comfortable as possible. No one had the knowledge to treat such a wound so time was of an essence to get him to a doctor.

In the meantime some of our crew had looked at the crew of the boat. All four were dead, two had been shot at close range by revolver shots, the other two were riddled with machine gun bullets. The wheel house was a shambles, the engines were shattered, she was taking water in rather quickly from the bullet holes in her hull, and how she hadn't caught fire no one knew. The seaman peering down the forecastle shouted that he could hear someone down there; he shouted down the hatch for whoever it was down there to come up on a deck, once, twice, and a third time, and as no one appeared he fired a couple of shots down into the deck below the hatch. This brought a response straight away, but imagine our surprise when up the forecastle ladder and onto the deck, came an old man of about seventy years of age, followed by a young woman with a small baby in her arms, then came an old lady. None of them was hurt at all, but they were all in a state of shock, and when they saw what had happened on deck and the four bodies laid there, the two women burst into tears. The sight the bodies and the deck literally running with blood as it was must have stayed with them for the rest of their lives, as it has with me. They must have been terribly frightened for themselves at that minute.

We ourselves were stunned and just couldn't believe our eyes. Two men who had gone down the forecastle to have a look round came back up and reported that there was no one else below, but that there were holes all over the place and water was coming in. In their own words it was like the inside of a colander down there.

The old man, the two women and the baby, were taken onboard the *Gem*, the ropes were then cast off, and a few four inch shells were fired into her hull. As she settled deeper into the water, we in the *Gem* set off once more to seek out the *Resolution* to get medical aid for our wounded officer, and to land the bodies from the foredeck.

In the warmth of the *Gem's* after mess deck, as she steamed along, some of us were still wondering at the miraculous survival of these people. They were now being given hot drinks and a good meal, the sympathy of the British sailor now coming to the fore as it always seems to do in cases like this. It was really heart-warming to see a big six-foot stoker who hailed from Grimsby, rough and ready, and just in his vest and trousers, off watch, and handling the baby as if he were the mother of the child, feeding it with diluted Nestles milk in warm water with a spoon, and making a damn good job of it. As the time passed and the remaining three people relaxed a bit, we learnt from them that the old couple were man and wife and also the grandparents of the baby. The four who died on the boat were friends and relations, including their son, the young woman's husband and the baby's father. Apparently the day before they had seen what had happened at their village of Underulet; the boat had been out on a fishing trip and when it arrived back, they had decided that it would be best if they left the village for a time and went to stay with friends further north. They had just got ready to leave when they saw this ship, (the *Northern Gem*), come into the bay, and thought it was a German one that had come back to take revenge for what had happened to their troops. This was understandable to those of us who had been fishermen, as the *Gem* was German-built, and she looked like many of the German trawlers which passed through the fiords in peace-time making their way to the White Sea fishing grounds.

The big White Ensign which we were flying had meant nothing to them as they had not seen one before, and even when they were alongside us and hearing our skipper questioning the men on deck, they still thought that we were German. That was why the ropes had been cut away and the engine put on to full ahead to get away from us. Instead their four men were all dead and now lay with our dead gunner under the whale-back, and our officer was in the ward-room with severe if not fatal wounds. When eventually we arrived at the *Resolution*, and these unfortunates had to go onboard her, they didn't go empty-handed, for they took with them a substantial amount of money in Norwegian kroners, given very willingly by every member of the *Gem*'s crew to help to make up for the loss of their relatives and friends.

After this episode we were sent for a rest to the small port of Svolvaer in the Lofoten Islands. I remember the day well – there was a brilliant blue sky, with hardly a cloud to be seen and the sun was shining and there was not a breath of wind, with the surface of the Vest Fiord looking like a huge sheet of glass. All hands except the lookouts and those on watch on the bridge were finishing off the job of cleaning up the ship. The last traces of blood and the empty cartridge cases had been erased from sight. We were about three or four miles from Svolvaer and we could pick out the individual buildings, houses, the church all cluttered around the foot of the mountains around the port. The town itself we could not see properly, only the tops of the fuel storage tanks near to the docks. It was at this point that an aircraft was reported coming towards us. At the moment it was just a speck in the sky but getting larger every minute. Soon it was close enough for one of the lookouts to identify it through his binoculars as a Junkers 88, but we weren't too sure as we hadn't seen one before. He was making straight for us at a height of about two to three thousand feet.

The alarm had sounded and every one was closed up at their action station. We had no gunner onboard now, and what was worse we only had star shells to fire from the four-inch gun now. As it was not much use against aircraft, there did not seem to be much point in manning it but the guns crew did so. The gun was elevated to its highest point and a star shell was fired in the general direction of the plane; when the shell exploded in our puny effort to put him off, he turned away, but then made two more attempts or passes at us, each time a star shell was fired off towards him. After the last one he veered away from us and went out of sight without making a determined effort to carry out a proper attack on us, for which we were all very grateful. If he had come back we did wonder what would have happened because we had not much to throw back at him. However we all stood down, with one eye on the far and distant horizons as we went on with our work again, and the ship's head pointing once more towards our destination, the port of Svolvaer.

On our arrival there we were quite surprised to see a crowd of the local people on the quay-side, all clapping their hands and shouting to us in Norwegian, with the odd bit of English here and there. They were headed by the mayor or whatever he was of the town, and it was only when he came onboard to welcome us that we found out why most of the population of Svolvaer were here to greet us. It seems that some one had seen us making our way down the fiord, and had then got sight of the plane making towards us, word had gone quickly round, and everyone had made for the shore line on the edge of the fiord or some other vantage point. They had watched us shooting at the aircraft and from the way they were behaving had thought that we had fought him off. It's probably as well that they did not know what had really happened.

Opposite the *Northern Gem*, on the other side of the dock, lay the destroyer *Eskimo*, which had been torpedoed in the fore part. It looked as though the whole of her bow right up to the bridge had just completely disappeared, compartments and all. Her fore deck had dropped down into the water over the remains of the lower part of the hull; the bulkheads had held and saved her from sinking, but until the day before we arrived there they had not been able to get at their dead shipmates who had been trapped in the debris. On that day they had buried them out in the deep water of the fiord, and we were told that they had buried our two gunners and the lad from the *Spray* in a sailors' grave in Vest Fiord not far from the lovely town of Svolvaer.

When I heard this, I broke down and cried for Fred Powell my late friend. I shall never forget Bill Maitland chief engineer of the *Gem*, a trawler engineer from Aberdeen for he put his arm around my shoulder and talked to me like a father; it was he who made me realise that this sort of thing was now a part of our lives. It would get worse, he said; until the war ended we must expect these things to happen. I really grew up that day in Svolvaer. I'd had my twentieth birthday just five weeks before, and although I had been through many storms, and had several escapes while fishing I did not think that I could go through much worse than I had been through in the previous few days. Along with a couple more of the crew Bill took me down to his cabin, where I had more than a few glasses of rum and whisky. Later I was dropped into my bunk in the forward mess-deck, and there I had the best and longest sleep of the whole time we were in Norway.

All too soon like all good things, the time arrived when we had to leave this lovely town of Svolvaer and its hospitable people. Back to Ofot Fiord we went to continue our patrolling in the same monotonous way, except that there now seemed more and more German aircraft flying overhead. We were much luckier than our compatriots further south at Namsos, though we did not know that then.

We carried out our patrols for another week or so, and then we got an urgent signal telling the skipper to make for Harstadt together with the *Northern Spray*. When we arrived all seemed utter chaos, and there was a sense of frantic urgency. Small boats were dashing about all over the harbour, and the town seemed in ruins from the constant air raids that they had suffered. Now we knew where all the German aircraft had been making for; they had been after bigger game than a couple of trawlers, for in the fiord at Harstadt there were large merchant ships and troop transports. The job we were given was to ferry out the troops for as long as it took. Many smaller trawlers were made fast alongside the quay; these were having a field day collecting up all sorts of goods and stowing them aboard their ships, motor bikes. Some even had cars on the fore decks, not just one but two or three. Quite a lot of new furniture was vanishing into the bowels of the trawlers, and we were told that one of them had in the seamen's

Coaling ship Norway 1940.

At Ae Fjord, Norway May 9th, 1940. Marines being put ashore to rescue men taken prisoner by German Jäger Battalion troops. The men were a landing party from *Northern Spray* and *Northern Gem* and included the author.

(*Left*) Chief Engineer Bill Maitland who was like a father to the author, 1941. (*Right*) The author as coxswain of HMT *Northern Gem*.

HMT *Northern Gem* at anchor in Reykjavik harbour between convoy duties. Painting ship at midnight in the light of the midnight sun, summer 1941.

mess deck below fitted carpets, and a grand piano complete with potted palms, and from what we saw going on, we could quite believe that story. From what we could see this was the end of our stay in Norway, for ships full of troops had been pulling out for days. It looked as though the trawlers or what was left of them were going to act as rearguards, and we wondered what our role was to be.

The Chief said that we had enough coal to get us back to the UK; from somewhere we were given an Oerlikon gun, and we had to go on shore and procure two railway sleepers; they had to be made into the shape of a cross, and then they were bolted to the deck on the port side forward. Once this was finished the Oerlikon was then bolted into place in the centre of the cross, on its stand and we finished up with a do-it-yourself gun platform. With the Oerlikon came a navy gunner and plenty of ammunition, which was a good job because we could get none for our four-inch gun; not one vessel had any to spare and there was none on the jetty amongst other supplies. Maybe the powers that be thought we could spit at the Germans, or did they think that it would be a waste of supplies giving such things to trawlers? It seemed like nothing short of a suicidal one way trip for us in the *Gem* and the vessel that we were to act as escort for.

A Norwegian passenger cargo vessel named the *Ranen*, had been taken over by the British, and been re-named the *Raven*. She was now to start on the journey back home. Her crew was a mixture of men from different services, RN and RM, and some men from the Army units in the area, volunteers from the Royal Scots Guards and the Royal Welch Fusiliers I believe. If I am wrong on that score then I must apologise for my error.

The *Northern Gem* was to accompany the *Raven*, and both ships were to make their way out through the Vest Fiord, which was now virtually enemy-held territory. As far as we were told in the *Gem*, the task given to our minute force was to steam down the fiord and shoot up anything in sight, telephone lines, oil tanks, in fact to destroy anything and everything that we could, and then make our way out into the North Sea and make directly for Scapa. None of us on the *Gem* fancied our chances at all, and wondered why we were picked; it must have been that someone somewhere either did not like us, or they thought that we were the best ones for the job. But we knew that we had to do it and the sooner the better as far as we were concerned. Before we left Harstadt we saw many more refugees fleeing to get away from the now quickly encroaching German forces; they were Norwegian men, women and children coming along the fiords in boats of all types and sizes. Some looked as though they'd had to get out of bed quickly, and had no time to get dressed as they were still in their night clothes. It was a pathetic sight and one that made us forget the dangers on our forthcoming trip, and even more determined to get home.

Soon we were on our way, the *Gem* and the *Raven*, along Vest Fiord, where we turned onto a course that would take us towards the North Sea and home. We kept watch for any signs of the enemy, while along the way we were constantly taking long distance shots at telephone lines, and any other small targets that we saw. Whether we did any damage at such a distance is anyone's guess. Very shortly we were approaching Svolvaer, where we had enjoyed our few days' rest with the good and generous people of the town. Was it only three weeks ago? As we got closer to the port, we saw what we on the *Gem* took to be an armed trawler of some description close in under the land. She was flashed the recognition signal of the day but did not answer, so the CO of the *Raven*, told us to open fire with our four-inch gun! But the men on the four-inch – and I was acting trainer on this occasion – managed to hit the target three or four times, including one shot that landed slap bang on the bridge, starting a fire. He turned away to starboard as the fire took a hold, and both *Gem* and *Raven* were steaming straight for him, when suddenly he laid smoke and vanished from sight.

Even now it still isn't clear as to where he got to. The *Raven* went right into Svolvaer, whilst we went along the coast looking into the rocky inlets around the area, but neither we in the *Gem*, nor those in the *Raven* ever saw him again. We were certain that the vessel had not sunk, as the star shells alone would not have been sufficient to cause that amount of damage, so her vanishing trick remains a mystery to this day. While the *Raven* was inside Svolvaer she shot up the oil tanks and installations, and also the telephone exchange and put that out of action. I was glad in a way that it was not us who had gone in to do this bit of dirty but necessary work after the way we had been treated by the inhabitants of the town.

Once this destruction had been carried out, we both turned onto a course which would take us out into the North Sea, a matter of fifty or sixty miles or so away in a south by east direction. Once we saw the island of Vaeroy we could come round to starboard and onto a south-westerly course which should take us home to that great base of the British Navy, Scapa Flow. After leaving those burning oil tanks on the island of Ostvaagoy behind, we had seen no sign of either enemy aircraft or shipping. We were hoping that it would carry on in this way until we got to safety in the UK, but it was not to be like that at all.

At dawn on the following morning, we were called to action stations by the sound of the alarm bells giving out their warning of aircraft in the vicinity. Every one of us was up on deck in next to no time at all, to find that we were being circled by some eight or ten enemy bombers. From the start it looked as though we in the *Gem* were going to be the main target, and that the *Raven* was going to be left alone. Talking about the attack later, none of us could remember there being one attack on her.

On this particular morning in 1940 we learnt a new lesson in survival from air attack. The planes came in at us singly after breaking away from the circle going around overhead; the first one came in from ahead and dropped a full stick of bombs. We were pleased to see them all explode some distance off our starboard side. A second one too came in from straight ahead. He also dropped what we thought was a full stick, which again went well over to starboard before dropping into the sea. Then the pattern of the attack changed: the rest of the planes took turns in coming in towards us from different directions, sometimes two came in in such a way that as the bomb from the first one hit the water and exploded, the second plane was releasing his above us. They only dropped one bomb at a time and it seemed to go on for an eternity.

It was fascinating to watch these black objects leaving the bomb bays under the aircraft and to watch them getting larger and larger by the second. It was anyone's guess where they would land, for with the movement of the ship as she rolled and owing to the Skipper's instructions shouted to the coxswain at the wheel, the bombs seemed to be wavering all over the place, and I'm glad to say that none of them came near enough to do any damage. I can't say how long it took them to get rid of all their bombs, but when they had done so they formed up quite leisurely as though they were out on a training mission, which they may quite well have been, with the first two showing the others how to do it. Once they had all joined up in formation, they turned and went off in the general direction of Southern Norway, much to our relief.

I think it was about this time, that our CO Lieutenant Commander Scarlett decided that he was taking the *Gem* to Aberdeen, and not to Scapa Flow as he had been instructed; he then advised the *Raven* of this decision, and was reminded that the *Gem* was to follow the *Raven* into Home Fleet's anchorage at Scapa. Skipper Scarlett repeated that he was making for Aberdeen; he shouted to the *Raven* that once you got into Scapa, you never got out of there without difficulty, and anyway they only made trawlers into glorified liberty boats. After a few more exchanges both vessels parted company, and went their different ways.

Steaming along as fast as the engine and the propeller would take us on our way to the Granite City of Aberdeen, we sighted a huge plane coming towards us from the direction of England, and as it came closer we realised that it was a Sunderland flying boat. He challenged us and was given the correct reply; then our signalman Charlie Keen told him about our being attacked an hour or so earlier by those German aircraft; the reply from the Sunderland was, 'The bastards. I'm going over there now and I'll look you up on the way back.' We could see under his wings some large red and yellow cylindrical objects, which we took to be bombs of some kind or other, and off he went on whatever job or work he had been sent off to do. We did not see him again, and I can only hope that he did arrive back at his base safely.

About the time we thought that this Sunderland would be on his way back, all hands were on the deck keeping a look out, when up from over the horizon from astern of us came a plane towards our starboard quarter, flying low down as near to the surface of the sea as it could possibly get without hitting it. As it got closer we started to wave and shout, for we had been waiting eagerly and watching for the Sunderland coming back. We soon found out that we had made a big mistake about the identity of this particular one, for he manoeuvred himself around until he was on our starboard beam and then came in like a rocket. He was now just above mast height and the gunner must have had his foot hard down on the trigger of his gun, for we could see the water being churned up in fury as the row of bullets hit it and came nearer.

Jack Sullivan and myself were near to the stern, so we ran towards the iron ladder which led up to the top of the galley where one of the twin Lewis was situated, but this pair of guns was out of action so we took what shelter we could, shoulder to shoulder at the side of the steel mizzen mast. Each time the plane came in at mast height and shooting, we stood on the opposite side to the one he was coming in from. On each side of us were the lifeboats in their davits, and we watched great big chunks of timber being knocked out of them as the bullets blasted their way through from one side to the other; water pipes started spouting water out of holes that suddenly appeared in them, and ropes and rigging were being cut as though by an invisible knife. Jointly Jack and I decided to wait until after his next attack and then make for a safer place – if we could find one.

During the whole of the time that he was attacking the Oerlikon gun on our foredeck had been having a go at him on each of his passes; his next one was from port to starboard and once he had gone over, we ran forward along the casing towards the funnel and ventilators. The explosive bullets that he was hitting us with were making a right mess of the galley top and the boats and boat deck, and as we thought that discretion was the better part of valour, away we went running as fast as we could go. On arriving at the area around the funnel we stopped to have a look to see where he was. He was just completing his turn and now started to make a low run towards the front of the ship. We just had time to step onto the veranda which led to the W/T Office, the CO's cabin and bathroom, when with a terrific roar he hedge-hopped over the whale-back. As he did so he released what looked to us like a cigar-shaped object, silverish in colour and about eight or ten feet long. It dropped towards the whale-back, and as the ship rolled to starboard as the wheel was put over, it slid down the port side of the bow, and into the sea alongside without exploding, thank God.

We got back on to the veranda to find the crew cheering, for shells from the Oerlikon gun had been seen to hit the plane as he turned away. Now he was going back towards Norway with black smoke pouring out of his port engine, and leaving a long trail behind him. We watched as he seemed to us to be getting lower and lower, but he finally went out of sight below the horizon. The next few hours went by without further trouble and we arrived in Aberdeen. We tied up alongside the fish quay, where quite a number of people stood watching us in.

Everyone wanted to know where we had come from, and how we had got ourselves damaged in such a way. After the last attack by the single twin-engined aircraft, we had gone around the deck picking up little steel darts which had apparently come out of the bullets that had been fired at us from the plane; as the bullet had hit something, its outer casing had opened up and the little steel dart had carried on in the original direction, making great holes in whatever it had hit. Fortunately we had not suffered one casualty aboard the *Gem*, which amazed us when we worked out how many times the plane had come in firing at us.

Amongst the crowd on the quay was my Uncle Harry, he came aboard for 'sippers', a drop of the old navy rum. He was one of the crew of a trawler minesweeper out of the port, and it was he who broke the news to me about the death of his brother and my favourite uncle, Ted, who had lost his life on the way to Dunkirk. He was then a member of the crew of a wooden drifter sweeper named the *Frons Olivae*, which had left Ramsgate to go to the rescue of the troops from Dunkirk, when they were evacuating from France. Apparently the crew had all been ashore when the urgent message came for them to put to sea, and once they had been rounded up from pubs or cinemas, or other places, and the ship had left the harbour, those not on watch had congregated aft. They were sitting on the ship's quarterrail yarning, when suddenly Ted lost his balance and fell over backwards into the sea. He was a very strong swimmer, but he must have been drawn into the propeller by the suction, and was, so I was told later, killed instantly. It was not until I went home on leave that the news really sank in and I felt the full shock of his death.

Some months later we arrived at a port the name of which I have not been able to remember, and I saw tied up to the quay astern of us a wooden drifter. Just out of curiosity I climbed onto the quay and went over to have a look at her; to my amazement I found that she was the *Frons Olivae*. There was a quartermaster on the gangway, and I asked him if he had been aboard her when she went to Dunkirk. He wasn't, but he said that he thought the motor mechanic was with her then, and told me to shout down the engine room hatchway. This I did and shortly afterwards a CPO engineer came on deck wiping his hands with the inevitable bit of oily waste, which all men who work below in the bowels of the ship seem to carry about with them.

He asked who I was, and when I explained to him what I was interested in, he told me that after falling over the side, my uncle Ted had come to the surface, and that he, the engineer, had immediately dived into the sea and gone to his aid; but he realised as he got hold of Ted, that unfortunately he was already dead, having been killed by the propeller. I thanked him for telling me this and for what he had tried to do; it takes some guts to dive into the sea and I appreciated this fact.

Back in Aberdeen once all the visitors had gone, we sat down to a good meal which we all enjoyed, mainly due to being able to sit and eat it without being disturbed. Like many of the crew I then went ashore to see if I could find a telephone, so that I could get in touch with home, and let them know that I was safe. I decided that I would phone my father at his place of work, and when I did so he sounded very surprised and happy that I was back in Britain again. Yet it was myself who got the biggest surprise of all when he asked me straight out of the blue:

'Just tell me one thing, while you were in Norway were you ever taken prisoner at all?'

When I replied, 'Yes,' he said, 'Your mother was right then', and he would tell me more when I arrived home on leave.

CHAPTER THREE

Making Ready for War

Two days after we had tied up at Aberdeen, we were sent home on fourteen days leave; the *Gem* was left in the hands of the repair gangs, and the one or two crew members who had to stay to keep an eye on things.

When I arrived home I suppose I felt rather like a returning hero of sorts, and enjoyed being made a fuss of by all and sundry. I was back home again for my first leave after some six months since my last one at Christmas 1939. This time I had come home after seeing quite a bit of action one way or another. On my first day home I was having tea with my parents and thinking how good it was to be at home with them again, when the alarm clock on the mantelpiece in the kitchen decided to go off. As it did so, my heart all but stopped beating. I felt myself go white, like a sheet, and before either of my parents could say a thing, I was out of my chair, through the door and into the back garden. Rather sheepishly I went back into the house when I realised where I was, feeling ridiculous, and apologised to both of them for startling them as I had done. After explaining my reason for dashing out as I had, they said that they understood. This little episode proved one thing to me – that my reactions had certainly got much quicker during the last few months and that the will to survive was still with me.

On this leave on our return from Norway, one of the first questions my mother asked me was, 'Is it right you were taken prisoner in Norway?' and when I said yes, she replied that she had known it was so; that about the second week in May, they were having a cup of tea before going to bed, when she suddenly said to my father, 'Our Sid has been taken prisoner'. He told her not to be silly, but how true her premonition had turned out to be. Did she in some way receive some of my thoughts during the time it was all happening, because I had thought about my home and all who were there, and whether I should see them again, when we were transfixed to the ground under the cross fire from the Germans and from the fishing boat? I've tried several times to reason this thing out but it just remains a mystery. I have read of similar things happening to other people, but I still find it very hard to accept.

Back at Aberdeen, I found that a number of changes had taken place. Skipper Scarlett had gone, and in his place was Chief Skipper Mullender. He was a short stocky man, as tough as they come; he was an ex-trawler skipper from Lowestoft, who had also been the skipper of a collier (a ship running coal) between Lowestoft and Methyl for a number of years before the war. This was brought about by the way in which the fishing industry had deteriorated in the nineteen thirties, resulting in so many fishermen being on the dole. We were to find later that he was a fair man and a very good skipper, quite unflappable, even under the most extreme and provocative circumstances. He was to become a sort of idol to me, and a great friend until he passed away in 1977. I would have sailed anywhere in the world with him at any time as I had all the confidence in the world in him. He had apparently been one of several brothers, and had suffered some serious illness as a child and did hardly any schooling as a result. His parents were told that he would not live. His father was a fisherman on a smack sailing out of Lowestoft, and 'Billy' had asked if he could go to sea with him. His father must have taken him out of compassion. Skipper Mullender told me that he was too weak and too ill to help himself; he just lay on the deck and that it seemed just a matter of time before his young life came to an end. But fortunately he and his father persevered, and after two or three trips, breathing in the strong salt sea air of the North Sea into his lungs, they suddenly realised that he was getting very much stronger. He eventually took up the sea as his life's work, taught himself to read and write and took examinations for first his bosun's ticket, then his mate's, and later his skipper's. I have never before or afterwards served under anyone like him.

The coxswain of the *Gem*, Chris Wilson, who was from my home town of Hull, had contracted an illness not long after we returned from our leave, and would not be coming back. I was called in to the wardroom and introduced to Skipper Mullender for the first time, and he told me that he could not get a replacement for the coxswain, and that he had been told to upgrade one of the crew to be acting coxswain until such time as a replacement could be sent onboard. He said that he had been through all the records and that he had decided that I was to be the one, as I had more actual sea time in than any of the others. When I mentioned that there was a leading seaman on board, he said that until he joined the *Gem*, the leading seaman had very little sea time in, and even less experience of the sea as he had been working as a diver on the lochs in Scotland. Of course I could not refuse the chance; I took it with both hands. I was told to move my gear into the berth vacated by the ex-coxswain. I could hardly believe it, a berth of my own. I sat in this, the then previously Holy of Holies and wondered why I should be so lucky.

My berth was at the foot of the wooden staircase leading down to the petty officers' quarters, just on the right as you reached the bottom. It had a single bunk with two blue draw curtains, and had a reading lamp fitted in to it. Underneath the bunk there were two good sized drawers, which could be pulled out to clear a seat locker which was covered in a blue leather, the same colour as the draw curtains. There was also in one corner a fitted wardrobe, and on the right as I walked in through the door, there was a mirror fixed onto the bulk head over the top of a desk, the lid of which lifted up to reveal a wash basin with hot and cold water taps. These did not always work properly, but this did not matter because just at the top of the staircase was a petty officers' bathroom and toilets and of course these I was now allowed to use. The whole of the cabin was lined out with a beautiful and well-polished wooden panelled mahogany lining.

My job as acting coxswain now consisted of everything to do with the running of the seamen's side of the ship under the new first lieutenant, Ordinary Skipper Jack Pooley, also of Lowestoft. He was built a bit on the small side, a thin, almost always worried looking man, easy to get on with, and he did eventually leave most of the organising and working of the ship to me; he only got on my back if there was anything special in the wind.

I found myself ordering all of the food, and doing all of the victualling, the issuing of the rum ration, making sure that the ship was kept clean at all times, at sea or in harbour, weather permitting of course; in fact I was doing all the things that a coxswain of a ship was supposed to do, and many others that he was not. I've heard that lots of strange things happened on other HM trawlers that had RNR officers in command, and ships with Wavy Navy Officers (RNVR). The majority who at the early part of the war had little or no authority of the sort required were I am told sticklers for naval protocol. Some seemed to think that trawlers were destroyers, manned throughout by three badge Killicks,. It's surprising how when some people get a bit of authority thrust upon them, take on the mantle of the Almighty, and it happens just the same in peace-time.

Personally I would rather be a happy man with moderate means, rather than have to struggle in the rat race of today. These people today don't realise the honesty of the comradeship as we knew it; it has gone by the board and such comradeship will never come back, ever. I suppose there are as good lads amongst these today, as there were amongst the RNVRs of our wartime days for since then I have found out that there were some jolly good ones, good fighters and damn good sailors, who became excellent officers; others, of which I am certain there were a minority, acted like God; yet whatever they were, or whatever they became, many gave their lives for their King and their country, and many of these have no known grave but the sea. Without them all, comradeship such as ours would not have survived.

Once the dockyard people had left the ship, the task was to get her back to looking like a minor war vessel again. The damage that had been done by that lone German aircraft while on our way back from Norway had been put right, a few small alterations had been made, and we found that we had lost our Oerlikon gun. It had been sent down to the south to do its duty in what was to become the Battle of Britain, though we did not realise this at the time. A lot of other trawlers lost armament that they had gained by one means or another. Our stock of high explosive shells for the four-inch gun was back to the normal amount. The twin Lewis which had been on top of the casing aft, had been taken away, and in its place was a new weapon, a Holman Projector, a steam-powered piece of equipment not unlike a bit of fall pipe that comes down from the guttering of a house to allow the rain to find its way to the drains.

We were to find out that this was all that it was fit for. Its crew was supposed to put down this pipe an ordinary hand grenade which nestled in a tin; the lever from the grenade came through a slot in the metal container and was held down by a pin in the safe position on the outside of the container. The drill was that when the crew were going to fire this 'thing', first they had to make quite certain that there was enough steam pressure on the gauge to project the grenade out of the pipe. They then took the pin out of the grenade, dropped the grenade still in its container down the spout of the pipe, banging their foot down on a pedal at the base of the pipe, and at the same time aiming the 'gun' at the target. If the target was a plane, the grenade was supposed to go off in the vicinity of the plane after parting company with the container as it left the mouth of the pipe. In theory I suppose that this was quite a legitimate description of its action if the steam pressure applied to the projector was correct; if it wasn't, the grenade and its container had a nasty habit of just managing to climb out of the end of the pipe, and dropping onto the deck where they separated, rolling about until they either exploded where they were, and fragmented amongst those of the crew who were panicking to throw them over the side, or in the sea out of harm's way if the crew had been successful in doing what they had set out to do.

Most ships' crews found as time passed by that the best use for the Holman Projector was for throwing potatoes or empty cans at their 'chummy ships' as they passed by them in a channel. To be used for the job for which it was really intended was thought to be more dangerous to those actually firing it than to the aircraft supposed to be at the receiving end. Eventually, I believe, these Holmans were taken off most if not all ships.

Before our leave from Aberdeen, the crew's bedding, bed covers, sheets and pillow cases, had been sent ashore to be cleaned and even repeated visits to the laundry did not get it back onboard by the time came for the ship to leave, and we had to sail without it. Our destination this time was on the west coast of Scotland, Tobermory, in the Sound of Mull. Tobermory was a training school under the command of a bewhiskered old commodore, who had no qualms about sending a whole ship's company back to their depots if they were not up to his expectations. None of us was looking forward to this visit, for even officers were not immune from his wrath and could be replaced. However there was no way that a ship could, once it had been ordered to report to the HMS *Western Isles*, get out of the visit unless of course the invasion of Britain was taking place; even then I'm not certain that it would have constituted an excuse.

We arrived in the Sound of Mull, during the course of an afternoon. I cannot remember now if there were any other ships at anchor when we arrived, apart from the old inter-island boat, the *Western Isles*, which was the headquarters of Commodore Stephenson. Everything seemed placid enough at the time, with no suggestion that it could, and did more often than not, turn into a hive of intense activity, with everyone feeling shattered and broken. We were preparing to drop anchor when the signal lamp began to flash from the base ship.

I was on the forecastle with Mr Pooley at this time, along with one or two seamen. The CO shouted from the wheelhouse that we were to shackle up to a buoy. None of us had ever done this before, even Mr Pooley, but the operation had to be carried out to the best of our ability. In the middle of it, I was ordered to go to the seamen's mess-deck on the double, as the commodore was there and wanted to see me.

I dropped everything, and with my mind full of all sorts of thoughts as to what he could want to see me for, I shot down the ladder leading off the whale-back, and onto the deck, made my way quickly to the top of the companion way, and 'dropped' down the ladder. Here I saw that an inspection was taking place. Our CO was talking to the commodore, and as he saw me, motioned with his hand for me to come forward. The commodore turned towards me, so I came to attention and saluted him, 'You sent for me, Sir.' He looked me up and down, walked right around me, and then said, 'Who the bloody hell are you? I sent for the coxswain.'

I was dressed in fisherman's clothing, by now off white thick woolly fearnoughts, a mottled grey and white abb wool jersey, I had a red muffler around my neck and on my head an ordinary working man's flat cap. By the way that he was eyeing me, I thought 'By hell, I'm for it now', and my heart dropped all the way down to the bottom of my fisherman's thigh boots. I stood waiting for the terrific blast that I was now expecting.

With his eyes staring right into mine, he said, 'Right then, coxswain, where is the bed linen for all the bunks on this mess deck?' Without taking his eyes off me, he listened as I explained. He heard me out without interruption and then said, 'At 0530 hours tomorrow morning, I want your ship's boat alongside the gangway of my vessel; you yourself will be in charge of it, and everyone will be in the rig of the day. I want to see the boat handled properly, as I shall be watching your approach from the head of the gangway, and if the operation is not carried out in the way that I think it should be, then heads will roll, and I do not care whose they are. So don't forget you will arrive alongside my ship at precisely 0530, *not* 0528, or 0532, do you understand? Now, then, coxswain, how many sets of bed linen do you require?'

Of course I felt uptight about this, but fortunately I knew just how many sets of bed linen that I required, so I replied, 'Yes, Sir, I understand. 0530 at your gangway, and I shall require 52 sets, that's one for each bunk, and one spare set for each'. At that he turned away and gave a chuckle, as he said, 'It's a good thing that you asked for spare sets as well, coxswain. They will be ready for you to collect in the morning.' He went up the ladder and onto the upper deck with the CO, and I breathed a sigh of relief and lit a cigarette to steady my nerves. We saw him often during our ten days' stay there, but I never came into contact with him again on a personal level.

From that moment on, every one of the crew wore rig of the day – he was not going to catch me out again if I could help it.

At 0500 hours the next morning the boat's crew and myself, stood on the deck along with Skipper Mullender and the Ist Lieutenant, waiting for the time to get into the boat, and pull over to the HMS *Western Isles*. The distance between the two ships had been seriously calculated, and the seamen had been told what to do to make it look good, for none of us had ever practised the art of tossing the oars upright in a boat when approaching another ship in the proper Purser manner. We had seen it done, but now was our chance to have a go at doing it properly the first time. We checked our watches, and with a shout of good luck, the skipper and Mr Pooley retired to the top bridge as we pulled away from the ship's side, to watch the proceedings, hoping that nothing would go wrong. As it turned out things went well, I'm not going to say that we were perfect, but we got ourselves into a position for the last few yards' run in to the gangway ladder; the oars were raised to my order, out of the water, and with just enough way we touched at the correct time.

As soon as we did so the sentry challenged us, and I stated the purpose for our being there, and was told to come onboard, the boat was made fast, and I ran up to the top of the gangway, turned aft and saluted. There was no officer to be seen about, but that did not mean that there was not one there. At the top of the gangway lay several bundles for which I signed after first checking them over. There were fifty-two sets of bedding as the commodore had promised, and we got them into the boat and cast off, once again going through the right drill as we moved off. By this time in spite of the sharp cold morning air, I was sweating profusely as were the other lads in the boat. Theirs was brought on by rowing the boat, but mine was from worry as to whether we should be called back to the *Western Isles* for something that I had forgotten to do, or which had not pleased the commodore or his duty officer, neither of whom I had caught a glimpse of the whole time, though I have no doubt that they were keeping their eyes on us throughout the trip there and back. Nevertheless we arrived back at the *Gem* with no sign of any signals, much to our relief.

Our training programme got under way: without any warning the Commodore would come alongside in his boat and step aboard, have a little walk up and down the deck, and suddenly say, 'That buoy over there! It's a U-boat surfacing after being depth charged, she's going to scuttle herself. What are you going to do about it?' There was a panic then to get a small boat away with a crew in it armed to the teeth with rifles and revolvers, and a pocket full of potatoes for use as hand grenades. Those in the boat along with the First Lieutenant at the helm had to pull quickly to the buoy that he had indicated as being the U-boat, Mr Pooley, the 'Jimmy', and one of the men had then to jump onto the buoy, pretend to lift up the hatch to the conning tower and throw down grenades to immobilise the U-boat crew and stop them scuttling the boat. After much fiendish shouting and not a little gymnastics, they would then pull back to the *Gem*, only to be told that they were all dead and what a bloody shambles it had been; the sub was still going to scuttle, and someone had to go and stop it, and as they were all dead and had to stay where they were, others had to go in their place to see what they could do.

Guns crews and depth charge gangs had to go through their drill time after time, discharging and reloading the depth charge throwers. This was a back-breaking job, with three-hundred pounds of amatol in each charge having to be hoisted time and time again back into the thrower day after day, until the gunnery officer from the *Western Isles* who had been timing them with a stopwatch, was satisfied with their timing.

Mock fires were fought, aircraft had to be repelled, so had boarders as they tried to get on deck to take the ship over; on occasions several things were timed to happen at once. Air attack, U-boat on the verge of surfacing, fire somewhere below or under the whale-back, it would be all hell let loose, and woe betide any slack attempts at putting things right. During these battles, my action station was as always in the wheel house, steering the ship and answering orders from the top bridge, so while I was up there I managed to keep out of the most hectic situations that cropped up. My main concern was whether my books were in good order; there was a crew list to keep up to date, account books. The book in which I kept the tally of Grog issued each day and what stocks were still down in the spirit room was the most important; it had to be spot on, neither too much nor too little of the rum left in the gallon jars down there. Either way it was a crime, and a serious one at that. I think that it was the chief writer who came into my cabin to check up on my work, but luckily apart from one or two minor things, I was OK, and was in fact given a few good tips to make the keeping of books and records much easier.

There were many times at night as well as during the day, when we had to drop our mooring buoy and put out into the submarine exercise area between Tyree and Iona. Then the Asdic operators got their chance to find a real live submarine. Even though it was only an exercise, and the crews in the submarines were learning also, it was almost like the real thing, except that for safety's sake those of us on the bridge could see where the sub was because they used to tow small metal floats called 'buffs', to indicate their position. The Asdic operators could not see these and had to rely on picking up the submarine on their sets, which sent out a beam of sound. If it happened to hit the sub, then it would rebound back to the set where the operators had to decide quickly whether it was the sub or a shoal of fish or even a tide rip. If it was the sub then they had to make an 'attack', guiding the ship towards the target. The officer on the bridge would then let the CO know if it could be confirmed as a hit, and if so we would drop a small five pound charge over the side to let the submarine know that she had been attacked. I don't think that I remember our reaching that stage, but we may well have done so. Once this exercise was finished, it was back to Tobermoray and the task of mooring up to the buoy again, unless old 'Fiery Whiskers' had something else for us to tackle, such as fireworks and flares being thrown aboard while you were tying up to the buoy; this was presumably to indicate that we were now being attacked by some invisible E-boat. Like the submarine exercise we had to keep going until the attack was properly repulsed, or until the 'enemy' got fed up and went home to tea.

It certainly did us no harm, but quite a lot of good; we were not so slow, and not so complacent, and we were much more aware of what the enemy could and did do. Our reactions were very much quicker, and this was what it had all been about. I think that most of us realised this and had enjoyed it for all the lack of sleep, and the hard work that we'd had to put up with. But even so, when the time came for us to leave, and we realised that we had come through it all unscathed, the entire crew including the officers too took a deep breath of relief and were pleased that no one had been sent back to base.

And so we left Commodore Sir Gilbert Stephenson, the HMS *Western Isles* and the Sound of Mull behind. Ever since my meeting with him on that first day, I had felt a great respect for the commodore. The way in which he spoke to me in spite of how I was dressed in the garb of a deep sea fisherman amazed me greatly, but at

(*Left*) Atlantic convoy 1941. Left to right: Radio Operator, Yeoman Signaller Charlie Keen, Stoker. (*Right*) Londonderry 1941. Left to right: Not known, Signaller Charlie Keen, Skipper Lieutenant Mullander, Not known, Mrs Keen, Skipper Loades, Mrs Loades.

(*Left*) From left to right: L/Seaman Tim Coleman, Stoker, Ernie Thain, 'Yorkie' and 'Darky' Bob. 1941. (*Right*) From left to right: Seaman Ernie Thain, Skipper George Spindler, Leading Asdic Operator Jack Sullivan, and two unidentified: 1941. Skipper George Spindler was awarded the Norwegian Victoria Cross for valour during the Norwegian campaign while on the trawler *Arab*.

The Balloon site in Hull where Gladys worked. She [is] on the left of the group.

Fishing Trawler *Ocean Kn[ight]* the only ship the author wa[s] discharged from in pre-wa[r] days. 1938.

Steam trawler *Kingston Cornelian* another of the fishing trawlers the author served in during his pre-w[ar] occupation of deep sea fishing. The majority of the[se] ships were taken over by [the] Admiralty at the outbreak [of] war for duties as convoy escorts or minesweepers [and] many were lost in the cour[se] of these duties.

that time I was rather young, and tended to be overawed at the sight of any officer with straight rings around his arm, and had certainly not been in a position to speak to another officer of his rank in the Royal Navy. His understanding of us ex-fishermen must have been first class; he knew what sort of men we had been, and he also saw the sort of men that we could turn out to be given half a chance. He sorted the wheat from the chaff, and the wheat respected him for it. Since I became a member of the Royal Naval Patrol Service some years ago, I have spoken to captains and commanders, and one vice-admiral who were still on the active list, and it has been an honour to have found out at least that they themselves, had some respect and not a little admiration, for the way the trawlermen conducted themselves during those hostile years and afterwards, when the minefields had to be cleared to make the seas safe for the passage of all vessels, even when peace arrived.

Once we were released from the confines of Tobermory, the sailing orders were for us to make our way to Belfast, where we arrived at the beginning of August 1940. We were based on HMS *Caroline*, and joined the 27th A/S Group if I remember correctly. From Belfast we were sent on a variety of jobs, patrols, convoy escort and the like. We did several stints to Iceland and the Faeroes to patrol the seas around these islands, and often we found ourselves on our own in the Denmark Straits. This was a weird place, as those who have been there will agree, especially if you had no chummy ship to keep you company. There was nothing to see for days on end but the wide unfriendly ocean, that stretch of dangerous water between Greenland and Iceland.

The sea could be calm for a day or two, and then within minutes it could change to mountains of aquatic fury, driven on by hurricane force winds, bringing with them snow and sleet from the mountains and plateaux of ice-covered Greenland. At certain times of the year huge icebergs would drift down, shrouded in thick fogs after starting their journeys by breaking off from some remote glacier. You got so that you could smell them if the ship was down wind of them, but they never failed to excite me or strike me with awe at their majestic size, and sometimes at their breathtaking beauty. One always had to be on the alert looking out for them as they could be very dangerous in the darkness of the night, and of course more so in fog. We carried no radar at the time I was a member of her crew. It was possible to get an echo from one on the Asdic, but in fog one had to be certain what the echo was from as the skipper could not send the vessel charging forward thinking the object returning the echo was a U-boat, when in fact it could be an iceberg, for the bottom could be ripped out of the vessel in no time. Of course these icebergs were not the only unfriendly things in these waters, and being on a small trawler, even though she was one of the largest in the country at six hundred gross tonnes, alone for days on end, did not do the nerves of those onboard very much good whatsoever.

To illustrate my point, on one such occasion during May 1941, the German warships *Bismarck* and *Prinz Eugen*, left Norwegian waters to break out into the Atlantic to do what damage they could to the ships in the convoys, which were crossing from the new world to the old and vice versa. At about the same time the *Northern Gem* was acting as an escort and rescue vessel on an outward bound convoy. It was the practice at this stage of the war for the escorts to stay with their convoy of merchant ships until the halfway stage was reached, including convoys leaving America, Halifax or St John's Newfoundland, and bound for England. At a prearranged spot, the escorts handed their charges over to each other, in other words changing convoys. The outward-bound escort then became the inward one making its way back to England, and once this had been accomplished we felt that at least one part of the job had been done, and that this second part was taking us nearer and nearer to our home base.

On this particular trip, we on the outward bound leg had been having a quiet time for once, but the buzzes that came down from the bridge and wireless room told us that the convoys we were to exchange with were having a tough old time and that many ships had been sunk by repeated attacks from U-boats. It was going around the ship that if it kept up in this way there would soon be no convoy for us to take back to the UK. The weather in their part of the Atlantic had been pretty bad, though not severe enough to keep the U-boats down, but it was said to be getting better. Some time later we were ordered to leave our convoy and make for the last reported area of the sinkings, to make a thorough search for any survivors who might still be around in small boats or rafts. It was a forlorn hope for one ship searching in this way, but nevertheless it had to be carried out to the best of our ability. The orders were what we should make our way back along the convoy's estimated course, and make square searches as we went along. This we learned would take us the biggest part of the way across the Denmark Straits all on our own, just one lone armed ex-fishing trawler, now a very small part of the Royal Navy, the crew of which were not relishing the next few days by any means. But we knew that it had to be done, and that many men were probably fighting for their lives somewhere out there in those wild wastes of water.

On the evening of the first day's search, as it got darker and the Northern Lights began to spin their web of beauty across the Arctic skies to the north of us and on our starboard side, we saw ahead of us, and in the distance, the glow of a huge and fierce fire reflected on the clouds. The skipper ordered the slight alteration of the *Gem's* course which put the ship's head pointing straight towards it. Down below in the bowels of the *Gem*, the chief engineer and his staff of firemen were banging coal onto the fires and the engines began to pile on the revs. We could feel her shaking as if with excitement, as if she herself was trying to get us to the scene as soon as was possible.

Even moving along at twelve or thirteen knots was pushing it for the old girl, and it was almost dawn before we saw the cause of the blaze at a distance of some six or seven miles ahead of us. It was easy to make out that the fire was on a tanker, and even though the flames appeared to be dying down a bit as we closed up to it and the smoke was being blown away over her stern, we could see that her hull was red hot, white hot in some places, that she had been ravaged by the fire from end to end and that there would be no hope of finding anyone alive onboard her.

Skipper Mullender decided that he would make a wide sweep in a big circle right around the burning vessel to see if there were any U-boats waiting in the area, waiting to put a torpedo into any unsuspecting ship that came along, for this is what they used to do. We were all wide awake; there had been no need to call all hands on deck, for they had been at their action stations for most of the night cat napping where they stood and keeping a good look-out by spelling each other. I myself had taken over the wheel and throughout the night had spelled it with Tim Coleman, until we got close to the casualty; then I took over and stayed at the wheel for some considerable time, which helped to keep me from thinking too much about what could happen in a situation like the one we were in now.

Two wide Asdic sweeps were made of the surrounding area, with no sign of either the enemy or small boats or rafts with survivors in, so we ran in to have a look at the derelict and burning tanker, ostensibly to see if we could put a name to her. But no name could be seen; all the paint had been burnt off her and she was still red and white hot. As the ship rolled in the swell, and the hot glowing plates touched the water, we could hear them 'hissing' and see the steam rising from them. There was a hole in her port side, just forward of amidships that two double decker buses could have been driven through side by side. It amazed us that she was still afloat, and our thoughts were that the crew must have all died instantly in the first blast of the scorching heat created by the explosion of the torpedo. They must have been incinerated without having a chance to get away in their small boats and rafts. What a horrible death this must have been, yet a much quicker end than the lingering one of being adrift in open boats or rafts for days on end, dying one by one through the cold, hunger, thirst or through the loneliness of it all. I'm pretty sure that none of us in the *Gem* looking at that sight would have swapped places with a tanker man. In our opinion they must have had some guts to sign on for the long and ever dangerous trips that they made. I have seen tankers carrying aviation fuel, when they were hit by a tin fish, just vanish in a puff of smoke, one minute a ship moving along in station with others, then an open space with just a pall of smoke drifting away over the sea.

The skipper was satisfied that we would learn no more about her, and said that we would carry out a further search for survivors, though he thought that it was unlikely that we should find any. He used the burning tanker as a fix, and we carried out our search by going in ever widening circles around her. This we did during the whole of that day, until we could see her no more and until darkness came upon us again.

The following dawn broke out over a dull grey sea. It looked greasy as we used to say. There was a long heavy rolling swell, of the type that if we had another ship in our company, would appear to swallow one of us up, while the other looked as if it were about to be marooned on the top of a moving mountain. This was the morning of 24th May 1941, and unknown to the ship's company, throughout the night heading towards us at a speed of some thirty or more knots, were those two big ships of the German navy.

The wireless operator had known but had been told by the skipper not to spread it around. Then after breakfast he let it be known that the pride of the British Navy, the HMS *Hood*, while chasing the *Bismarck* and the *Prinz Eugen* through the Denmark Straits had been sunk, and that from reports coming in, they were being shadowed by other ships of the fleet. I doubt if any of us would have slept so soundly if we had known of this. I'm certain that I would not have done, but like the others when darkness had come and many of us were allowed to go below, I was finding it very difficult to keep my eyes open owing to staring at the compass card for most of the day, and the horizon through binoculars for the rest of it on the lookout for some sign of survivors.

I slept fully dressed as always when at sea, with the old blown up sausage-shaped lifebelt fastened around my waist, and in my pockets packets of cigarettes and a few bars of chocolate. If we had to abandon and we got the chance to get away, these things would have come in handy. I think we all knew that if a tin fish were to hit us from some U-boat short of a bigger target, not many of us would stand a cat in hell's chance of getting away from the ship. Those who were caught down below would stay there and go with her on her last trip, that's for sure. However on this 24th May 1941, we had the news broken to us about the loss of the *Hood* and that these two ships were heading at least in our general direction. From what the wireless operator passed on to us in the wheel house, the Admiralty were continually sending out coded signals as to the course and position of the *Bismarck*, and this was why we were altering course every so often.

I was ordered to take the leading seaman with me and to check over the two small boats and the rafts, put extra blankets and water in them, as well as some more food and a jar of rum. My thoughts at this point were that if we were going to lose the *Gem*, then it was no good losing all of the crew with her. Surely some of us would have the chance to survive even if we saw the *Bismarck* in the distance though I believed that a near miss from one of her salvos would have turned the *Gem* over.

It was passed down from the top bridge that a signal had been sent to the *Gem* from HMS *Suffolk*, ordering the *Northern Gem* to close the *Bismarck* on such and such a course, and to attack her at all costs. In spite of all that the signal implied we all burst out laughing; to us it was like setting a push bike against a Tiger tank. We would not have got close enough to let off our vintage four inch gun at such a big target. The mind boggles at the thought and yet it helped to cheer us up no end that day.

We talked of the loss of the mighty *Hood*, and the possibility that our end could be near. I think we all made our peace with our Maker in our own individual ways. The men of the sea are a religious lot regardless of what they say in public. I have myself thanked God many times while at sea both in peace and war, and believe that a prayer at the right time of stress has brought me through many of the frightening incidents that I have been involved in. I am not a deeply religious man, but faith was all that we had to hang on to, and on this occasion, I truly believe that it brought us and the old *Gem* through once again, because we were told later that the *Bismarck* that day passed some fifty or so miles away to the east of us. Soon after this we were ordered to make our lonely way back to Belfast. Apart from the burning tanker, we did not see another vessel from leaving the outward bound convoy, until we got near to the Irish Coast. We had been at sea for eighteen days, twelve of these being spent all on our own.

This had been a trip when nerves and imagination played a big part, and strong wills had been needed to conquer the fear that was akin to us all if the truth was spoken. Not only on this trip but on many others during my four years on the *Gem*, I have lain on the bunk in my cabin, and thought to myself as I heard the water gurgling past the ship's plates, what would I think or feel for the few seconds or so, before the explosion of a torpedo that came through the ship's side and into my berth. Would it leap in and fall across me before it went bang? I would probably have died of fright instantly. Then there were the mines, which were no respector of ships or persons; they either waited for you to come along, in 'fields' like balloons filled with gas, which floated just below the surface of the sea and were packed with explosives, waiting for your ship to run onto them with some part of the hull, or they just floated partly submerged after breaking from their moorings. If there was a bit of a lop on the surface of the sea they were difficult to notice, and many ships were sunk by floating mines as well as the moored ones.

These thoughts were not always on one's mind, but were hidden away in the back somewhere, and only surfaced when you were tired and had been at sea for a long time. After two or three weeks out there you got to thinking that your luck could not last much longer. Being on watch at night time was a bad period, for you often saw things that were not there, particularly if the ship was on a lone patrol.

During 1941, we were to do many patrols, and go on quite a few convoy escort jobs both up to Iceland and out into the wide open spaces of the Atlantic. The weather in the North Atlantic could be anything, from being like a mill pond, to a savage and ruthless killer, with huge mountainous seas, flinging ships all over the place with no regard for their size. They could overwhelm a large and well founded merchant ship suddenly without warning, and without any other vessel in the vicinity being aware of what had taken place. Even if the calamity had been seen, nothing much could have been done because every vessel in that area would be fighting desperately for its own survival. If the weather moderated in reasonable time then one rescue vessel might be sent back to see if they could locate any of the crew, but in these sorts of cases more often than not, nothing at all would be found, not even a bit of floating wreckage. Yes the sea could be at times more dangerous than the U-boats and the mines, it could be tranquil and also treacherous – a proper Jekyll and Hyde.

Hurricanes seemed to be abundant and prolific, especially in the middle three years of the war, 41, 42, and 43, with howling winds and huge rolling seas seemingly miles high accompanied by frequent rain hail and snow which felt like bullets as it hit you. On watch one was constantly wet through even though you had on several layers of clothing, on the top of which you had oilskins and sea boots and a souwester on your head, with a towel wrapped around your neck to keep out the water and stop it from getting down to the inner layers. Coming off watch proved to be just as bad. Trying to get your wet clothing off while being thrown from one side of the cabin or mess deck to the other was a nightmare at times, and on many of these occasions you just could not be bothered to try. You just turned in to your bunk as you were, oilskins and all.

When you got into your bunk fully dressed or not, it was sometimes difficult to stay in it let alone get off to sleep; it was a fight to wedge yourself in by jamming the knees up on one side and the back against the other. When it came to sleep, I was more fortunate than most due to my previous years of experience in this type of ship. Provided I was tired enough I could get all the sleep that I required to recharge my batteries. Being somewhat used to the unpredictable motions of the vessel helped, but even so it did not make the situation any more pleasant.

On the other hand of course the weather could be very beautiful, the sea calm and apart from the obvious dangers of the war, it could be a grand way of life. I suppose I have always loved the sea in my own way, and I still do to this day, getting out in a yacht or an inshore fishing boat for the weekend with some friends.

Of course we had a light side to our lives, like the time when a few of us went ashore at Belfast, to celebrate some now long forgotten event. We'd all had a few too many to drink, and eventually staggered onboard, and it was some time later when a wet and bedraggled Charlie Keen came down to the mess deck. No one had

missed him as he slipped into the space between the ship's side, and
the wall of the dock and into the water. When the rest of us had gone
below and it was quiet on the deck, the sentry on the dock side,
walking up and down on his beat, heard Charlie shouting his head off
down there in the darkness. He got some help from passers by and
got the 'drowning' man onto the deck, cursing and swearing. Charlie
had apparently when he fell into the water, grabbed hold of a wire
that was hung down over the side of the *Gem*, and attempted to climb
up it. All that happened was that the more he tried, the more wire
was coming over the side; this was because it was coming off a reel
fixed to the casing of the *Gem*, under the starboard small boat. You
can imagine what happened when everyone heard about this, they
all fell about laughing. At least he had sobered up a lot quicker than
the rest of us, and later when he realised the predicament that he had
been in and saw it in the light that we had seen it in, he had a good
laugh himself, but of course with the *Gem* being the inside ship of a
trot of four, it could have had a tragic end; he could have been
crushed between the dockside and the ship very easily, and if it had
not have been for the sentry no one else would have been aware of his
very dangerous position. Charlie Keen is still alive and kicking to
this day, and I hope that if he reads this he will remember and have a
good laugh over it again.

The year of 1941 drew to a close, and we were told that the *Northern
Gem* on completion of this convoy that we were now escorting would
go into the dry dock at Belfast for a boiler clean and a refit, and that
all hands were to go on leave. This cheered us up no end, we had been
at sea on and off for the whole year, with just the odd few days in
either Belfast or Londonderry between each voyage. Nerves tended
to get strained a bit after such long periods, because by being at sea
you were sort of in the front line during the whole of the time, the
enemies being not only the U-boats and the mines, but also the vast
North Atlantic and its variable weather and moods.

And so we went on leave, and when we returned to Belfast, we
were put in digs with various families in the town. After a month it
was time for us to pack our bags and leave these good people to
return to the ship in order to get back into the fray once more, and I
must say that it was very hard to say goodbye to people who were
almost in tears at the thought of our near departure, so close had we
all become.

Several times during the last month I had been down to the ship to have a look around to see what was happening to the old girl. At first it was difficult to make out just what was going on – all the men who have in the past seen a ship being pulled to pieces during a major refit will understand. It was a shambles of machinery, cables and wires, and parts of the ship were laid about all over the decks and on the quayside, where also lay the two small boats and their davits just where they had been dropped. The inside of her looked like an empty shell, apart from lots of junk piled up here and there; it was enough to make one weep with despair when you thought back as to how she looked before she was handed over to all these perfect strangers who were clambering about, chipping and painting, hammering and cutting pieces out of her here and there with oxy-acetylene torches. It always has been and always will be a mystery to me as to how they managed to stick all the bits back together again to create order out of such chaos, but they did, and this time was no exception as we were to find out.

CHAPTER FOUR

Convoy PQ17

The first noticeable alteration to the *Gem* was the small boats, which previously had been located one at each side of the casing containing the after mess deck, the davits being attached to the casing. They had been in that position ever since she had been built, and this may have been the correct place for them when she was at her normal job of deep sea fishing, for here they were out of the way of the working of the trawl gear. The times for the boats to be used when fishing were very few and far between, and in the past even when trawlers were sinking or were aground there were not many cases of the lifeboats getting away from the vessel. Since she had been used as a minor war vessel, we had found these boats and davits very hard and cumbersome to use in any other conditions but a flat calm sea, and there was always the danger there that the davits would cause trouble and fail with the weight of the boats. Sure enough they had done just that on the last patrol we did before going in for the refit.

The smallish seamen's and stokers' mess-deck had been rebuilt, and now covered the whole of what used to be the fish room area. There was now an alley-way which ran fore and aft all the way along the entire length, on each side of which was a large roomy mess for sleeping in and for recreational purposes. There were bunks for some forty or so men, and these were going to be needed, as our crew went up in numbers from about 16 in 1939, to 25 at the end of 1940, and then between 40 and 50 after this refit. Finally when I left her in July 1943, there were 67 officers and ratings of all kinds in the crew, so in just under four years another 41 men had been sent onboard to maintain and operate new equipment and also to fill the requirements for more deck, engine room and gun crews.

On the top of the casing, where the old twin Lewis had been between the two small boats, we now had a circular gun platform, with twin point fives installed on it, and other more useful guns were now in the wings of the bridge. We stored ship taking on ammunition for use on the various guns, tons of tinned food and all the other things necessary to feed our large crew. All the things that had been put into the warehouses on the dock side had to be checked back onboard and signed for. There was quite a lot of sorting out to do in the time before we left the dockyard and took up our new duties, for now we had become a rescue ship as well as an escort vessel, and things looked as though they were going to liven up from now on.

Under the mess-deck alley-way forward, there were several small store rooms, one of which was now packed out with sacks, each one containing a complete new kit of gear for each survivor that was picked up out of the water, underclothes, and a thick shirt or a Canadian lumber jacket, I was told these were a gift from the Canadian people and their Government. If this was so they were very welcome because on many occasions previously when survivors had been picked up, many of them had very few if any clothes on their backs, or if they had they would often be covered in fuel oil. These clothes then had to be cut away from them and thrown away, and the men had to rely on the generosity of the *Gem*'s crew, who all came forward unstintingly with bits and pieces of clothing to give to these unfortunate survivors. No matter what the nationality of the men picked up turned out to be, they were all given the same consideration; after all we were all fighting the same war, and the cameraderie between seamen of all nations had to be seen to be believed. In peace-time it was the same, but in war I don't think there was a more patriotic set of men than the merchant seamen. They gave of their all when at sea, while people onshore either did not understand what these men were going through day in and day out to bring the much wanted and needed commodities into the country, or they just did not care as long as they got their portion and a bit more besides. I'm sorry to have to say that but it is true.

Before I go on to tell of the next voyages that we made in the *Gem*, I would just like to put a word in here about a job of work that was rather unpleasant, but one that had to be done by someone, and I thought that as I was the coxswain, even though only acting, it should be one of my duties. Thus with one volunteer, Jack Sullivan, it was my job to see that any of the men that we picked up who were dead at the time, or who died later, were prepared for burial at sea. They were treated with respect and care as much as was possible, but with a great deal of haste in many cases, that I will admit, in order to get the job done quickly, if the weather was bad, or if other circumstances warranted it. A piece of stout canvas, needle and twine, and two fire bars were all that were needed to complete the task.

When all was finished, the body was placed on a plank of wood, and was then covered with a flag, a White Ensign or the Red Duster of the Merchant Navy; we then reported to the officer of the watch, who in turn would let the CO know, then either he or the first lieutenant would come down to the deck where most of our crew, and those of the dead man's shipmates who could do so, would gather round while the officer read out of the Holy Bible the usual service for burial at sea. When he had finished, the plank would be picked up and one end placed on the ship's rail; the other end would be raised until the body slid over the ship's side and into the sea, feet first to its eternal rest. The ship which had been stopped for the short time that this had taken, would then get on its way as quickly as possible, for while it lay stopped it made a good and easy target for any U-boat in the locality. There were the odd occasions when the senior officer of the escort would not give permission for the ship to be stopped for the purpose of a burial, for it might be too dangerous and not very prudent to do so.

These were sad occasions for everyone who remained behind to carry on the struggle, especially if one was a person with a sentimental nature. I must confess that I was like that, and often thought about the relatives of the ones who had been Discharged Dead, who they were, and how long it would be before they got to know that their husband, father or sweetheart would not be coming back to them. But I was not a man to dwell on these things for very long – you could not allow yourself to do so, or you could soon lose your nerve and crack up altogether.

During the January and February of 1942, ex-fishermen like myself onboard these anti-submarine trawlers, who had worked in those treacherous waters so far from home in the prewar years, scratching a living from them, heard with mixed feelings that convoys had started to sail to and from the North Russian Coast. At first we did not believe that this could happen, but then we spoke to men from other trawlers who had already done the trip. Apparently they had started in the August or September of 1941. Soon we were to get confirmation and know for certain, as we were destined to take part in them, but before this we were lucky enough to get another leave.

There are not many things that I can remember about any of the home leaves that I had. I suppose that I enjoyed them all and made the most of what time I had at home, like all service men and women did. It was a relief in our case to get away from the constant and never ending strain of being at sea for days and weeks on end, and from seeing good ships being lost and men dying terrible deaths, especially in the tankers and those carrying ammunition. Many of the latter were gone in a second with a mighty explosion and a brilliant flash of flame, with only a huge tower of smoke being left to show that a few seconds before a ten or twelve thousand ton merchant ship had been steaming along with thirty or forty human beings like us on board it. But even if there were no attacks on the convoy, the strain was always there for one was always keyed up waiting for something to happen. I guess that the people at home went through a similar sort of thing during the raids by the Luftwaffe. At least we had a chance to hit back, whereas they had to sit in their shelters and take all that came down from the heavens. I know that on my leaves if there was a raid on Hull, I felt helpless sitting in an Anderson Shelter in the garden, while other folk sat playing cards or just having an impromptu sing song. The citizens of Hull had a tough time of it as did many others in the country and spent more time in their air raid shelters than they did in their own beds.

The girl who was to become my wife eventually, even though we were not engaged at the time, was now a member of the Women's Royal Air Force and was stationed in Hull, helping to defend the city against attack with barrage balloons. She and her mates had to stay there on the balloon site once their charge was in the air come what may. It was hard work for the girls from what I could see of it, but they were a great crowd of lasses that she was with.

Unfortunately on this leave, my future wife and I had a few words with each other over something that neither of us can now remember and we parted not the best of friends. But during the next year or so I found that I could not forget her, and apparently she felt the same about me. In the meantime however there was still a war to be fought, and so it was back to the *Northern Gem* and whatever was in store for us.

The crew of the old *Gem* were a happy crowd of men. On odd occasions there would be a clash of tempers, but nothing serious, but I suppose this was to be expected due to the conditions under which we lived and worked. Little things seemed to get under the skin at times and cause a bit of friction, yet by and large although the discipline wasn't as strict as on a larger naval vessel, the men knuckled down and did their jobs as they should have been done. Local leave was very rarely abused and only a small number found themselves on the CO's defaulters' list.

In the early part of the war I can remember one thing that did get at the crew no end, and that was the destroyer escorts. They all did trojan work, and we were always pleased to know that we had one or two with us but as far as I am concerned I would not have swapped the *Gem* for any of them, especially the old lease lend ones from America. I know from some of the men off the newer built British destroyers, that even these were never dry, for the mess decks were continually awash with water with all sorts of gear and stores floating about. We on the *Gem* at least kept dry down below, apart from the inevitable sweat and condensation that dropped from the deck heads (or ceilings to landlubbers), and trickled down the bulkheads and ship's sides. There were the odd times when she would dig her head into a heavy sea and some of it would find its way down the companionways or the ventilators and flood everything, but by and large the trawlers were good sea ships. Being a lot lighter than they were in their peace-time occupation of fishing, they were inclined to ride over most of the seas; although they got thrown about tremendously, we suffered more from bruising by being in contact quite heavily with immovable objects than by getting wet.

To get back to this niggle about the destroyers. The trawlers, once they had taken up their allotted positions on these earlier convoys, were glued there in that place regardless of how long the voyage out and back took, yet to us the destroyers seemed forever to be getting relieved to go back into harbour for refuelling, for at that period of the war there was no tanker with the convoy for them to get their oil from; those came along later when there was more of the larger class of new escorts available, and the Battle of the Atlantic got more and more hectic, so that escorts could not be spared to steam back to Iceland or wherever for oil. The trawler men got more than a little frustrated at the thoughts of these crews being able to get at least one night's good sleep in relative comfort, and as well as the oil they took on board to replenish their tanks, we had visions of them being topped up with more fresh food of some kind, while we had to slog it out on the old four hours on and four hours off routine, feeding off the seemingly endless Red Lead, Sardines and Bangers, and the continual supply of Chinese Wedding Cake. We felt at times that we were not really accepted by the RN (Real Navy), only when it suited them.

We were only Reservists and Hostilities Only men, but by heavens we did a difficult job to the best of our ability, with what armament and speed we could muster, and as far as I am aware none of us ran away from danger at all. I think that the trawlers did a good job during the first couple of years of the war, when the Royal Navy was being pushed to their limit by their lack of numbers of escort ships. In the Norwegian Campaign they were Jacks of all Trades, being sent into the most inaccessible places in the fiords, harried by the German bombers, bombed and shot up while they were speeding along at their steady nine or ten knots full out, with the entire ship being shaken to pieces with the vibration of the engines and exploding bombs. About ten of them were sunk in the course of the campaign, one of them, the *Arab*, earning a VC for gallantry at Namsos, so we could not have been all that useless.

It may be interesting to some to know that the pay for this work that we were engaged upon, was the princely sum of eighteen shillings and nine pence a week, two shillings and five pence per day, plus six pence per day (Hard Layers, a term used I believe to denote that there was some discomfort in being one of the crew of a small ship in the service).

At last in the middle of 1942 we in the *Gem* found ourselves going north once more, this time to the Russian port of Archangel, not knowing that the convoy we were to escort was to become the most tragic and controversial of all the convoys during the whole of the Second World War.

The middle of June 1942 found us in company with three other A/S trawlers, the *Lord Austin*, *Lord Middleton* and the *Ayrshire*, the first two being ex-Hull trawlers, and the latter ex-Grimsby. All three I knew pretty well from pre-war days, having often fished alongside of them on the different grounds. We four minor warships left Reykjavik, the Icelandic capital, for Hvalfiord on the north-west corner of Iceland, supposedly to sail with convoy PQ17 early in June. This was not to be, for we had a long wait until there were enough destroyer escorts to accompany the convoy of merchant ships which were arriving almost daily to drop their anchors and wait for the day of sailing. It wasn't until the afternoon of the 27th June that we all left the shelter of Hvalfiord, and meanwhile we saw with amazement the fiord filling up with the ships of several nations. There were British, American and Russian merchant vessels of all sizes. Some of them were piled up with deck cargo lashed down and chained securely to the decks, and consisting of tanks, lorries, planes and huge wooden crates. The contents of these we could only guess at, and what they carried below decks in their holds must have been war equipment of all kinds to aid the Russians in their fight against the invading German armies. We could see by the way they sat in the water they were loaded to capacity, right up to their Plimsoll lines.

From where we four trawlers were anchored, we could see not only the mass of merchant ships, but also British and American warships at anchor in the deep blue and still icy waters of Hvalfiord. Even now in June it was cold from the snow and ice melting from the tops of the high mountain peaks surrounding the fiord. The view from the deck of our small ship was awe-inspiring. I had seen such sights before many times, but with so many ships in the anchorage it was even more beautiful. An aircraft carrier, for all its huge size, looked tiny with the backing of those high mountains, the lower regions of which were decorated here and there with colourful farmhouses, and the mauves, yellows and greens of the plant life.

Once the anchor was in the water, and the routine of squaring up of the ship was completed, some of the crew got out their fishing lines to try their luck at catching some fish to give us a change of diet. Soon the CO left the ship on one of the many duty boats that were chasing about all over the fiord, to attend a conference about the future convoy. As the days went past, the usual buzzes started to go around the *Gem*, gathered from the occupants of these small boats. We learned that this was the largest convoy yet to set sail for Russia. There were more rumours going the rounds of the mess decks, and the fact that so many ships were in the vicinity seemed to give credence to what we were being told. My heart goes out to all who sailed in those great lumbering merchant ships during the war years. It must have been terrible to have to plod along at times at the same speed as the slowest ship in the convoy, expecting to be mined, or bombed or torpedoed, sometimes even shelled by German raiders who managed to evade the naval and air patrols in the Denmark Straits. Yet, at the bottom of their hearts, they must have been saying, if they were anything like me, 'It can't happen to me'. But unfortunately it did to so many of those brave men whose ships went to the bottoms of the many oceans of the world, where they still lie rusting.

As we cast our eyes over this array of ships at anchor in the fiord on those days in June 1942, I suppose we wondered which of them would be the unlucky ones, the ones which would not make it to Archangel, and how we ourselves would fare on the trip, for it was being said that we, the convoy that is, was to be the cheese in the

(*Left*) The author on the depth charge rail of the *Northern Gem*. (*Right*) The *Admiral Hipper* taking on water from a Norwegian mountain spring in 1942 just prior to operation 'Rosselsprung', the proposed attack on Convoy PQ17. Photo sent to author by the ex-chief navigating PO. Fritz Spangenburg who was on bridge of *Admiral Hipper* during the attack on Convoy JW 51B on New Year's Eve 1942.

The German built HMT *Northern Gem* leaving Hvalfjordur in Iceland on June 27th 1942 to escort convoy PQ 17 to North Russia. Later the convoy was ordered to 'scatter' by the Admiralty in London – following the execution of this order 24 fine merchant ships were sunk with the loss of many lives. (*Photo. Imperial War Museum*).

(*Left*) From left to right: Not known, the author, L/S Tim Coleman, 1942. (*Right*) Sitting (with hands clasped) 2nd Engineer Jim Edmonds from Hull and standing beside him is Johny Wardle, 1942.
Front row, L to R: Gunner Bill Reed, Wireless Operator. Second row, L to R: Not known, Skipper George Loades, Skipper Lt. Mullander, First Lt. Jack Pooley. Standing, L to R: Ernie Thain, fifth from left, Bill Cody, Angus Graham QM on *Athenia* when sunk, Jimmy Budd (Officers Steward), not known, Ginger Innes, Jack Sullivan, not known, the author. At back: Charlie Keen, L/S Tim Coleman. 1942.

trap, the means of drawing the *Tirpitz*, *Lützow* and the *Admiral Hipper* from their anchorages, along with others of their tribe, and that the other and smaller convoy which sailed at the same time as PQ17, would make them think that an invasion of Norway was on the cards. We know now from the books written since the war, about PQ17, what the plan really was, but I am trying in this record of the *Northern Gem*'s war, to record what we on the lower deck felt about things that were going on around us at the time. The ordinary matelot was lucky if he was in a ship where the CO gave them a good insight into what was going on. I'm not certain which was best, to be told or not to be told.

On the afternoon of the 27th June, several things happened when the convoy cleared Hvalfiord and formed up, which in our position at the stern of the convoy we mostly did not see. For a convoy of thirty-five ships along with their escorts and accompanying tanker, and in this case three rescue ships, covers very many square miles of ocean, and what is going on at one side of such a huge and very complex conglomeration of ships, is not necessarily known at the other side. While one side was in clear sunny weather, apparently the other was in fog, and encountering ice which holed one vessel so badly that it had to turn back to Iceland. We in the *Gem* were in clear weather as far as I can remember with no knowledge of what was happening some ten or fifteen miles away, and so we just plodded on, a small part of Convoy PQ17, to whatever was in store for us in the tiring and frantic days ahead, which would bring memories of sights, sounds and fears that have stayed with me to this very day: the two or three air attacks that were beaten off with such ferocity by the escorts and the merchant ships, and then, when everything seemed to be going well for us and our morale was at its highest, the signal that came from the Admiralty which sent us off to all points of the compass, seeking a place of safety and in great fear for our lives.

I don't intend to even try to put down here the reasons that caused the Naval High Command to scatter this fine convoy of ships. All this has been gone into by far better brains than mine, and argued about by those more knowledgeable than I. With their hindsight maybe many of the twenty-four ships that were lost could have sailed on to reach their destination, but more important still, many more brave merchant seamen would still be alive and others might not have lost their minds and reason as they did. Here I am trying to state the feelings and thoughts of myself and others on the *Northern Gem* on this tragic convoy. I am certain that many of the men on the other ships taking part, whichever nation or service they belonged to, will have similar memories to mine, and that they will feel the same as I do, after all these years.

PQ17 was our first Russian convoy, and during the few days before sailing, a feeling of quiet apprehension and foreboding as to what would happen, circulated round the crew, I told myself, 'Well here goes, either we get there or we don't'; we had to take our chances along with the rest.

After coming out of Hvalfiord, leaving Akranes on the starboard side, and Reykjavik on the port, the convoy formed up, and we in the *Gem* took up our position on the starboard quarter. There seemed to be ships stretched out as far as the eye could see. The cavalcade carried on until we left 'Snowy Jokell', (Snaefells Jokull) a large extinct volcano on our starboard side, then Patriksfiord and Isafjiord, then once past there we turned on to a more north-westerly course which would take us further away from the north coast of Iceland until we reached the point somewhere off and to the north-east of the rocky island of Grimsey, where the destroyer escorts were to join up with us at a certain time. They had been waiting at Seydisfjiord for some of the latecomers who had been on a Malta convoy. What a comparison from the lovely sunny blue Med, to at that time the sunny but cold Arctic Ocean, and only God knew what.

By this time although we didn't know it, one of the ships, a fairly large merchantman, had turned back to Hvalfiord, having had the good or bad (whichever way you look at it) fortune, to run into some ice as she steamed merrily along, and put a hole in her hull. There were reports of fog around, but whilst I was on deck or at the wheel, I don't remember seeing any at all. With the convoy taking up so many square miles of sea space, this was not unusual. At times we did not hear for some time what was going on, on the opposite side at all. As the other escorts joined us, we breathed a sigh of relief at the knowledge that at some point just over the horizon were the big boys, the cruisers *Norfolk* and *London*, and the United States Navy with their *Tuscaloosa* and *Wichita* and battleship *Washington*. There was also the *Duke of York* and the aircraft carrier *Victorious*, from which I believe the photograph of the *Northern Gem* was taken. I remember passing her as she lay at anchor in Hvalfiord. I was at the wheel on the bridge at the time and I felt very proud just looking at her. This knowledge that they were at hand made our foreboding turn to a feeling of exhilaration, and with it that 'piece of cake, and easy' attitude, which, although we didn't know it at the time, would in a matter of a few days be knocked out of us by something that no one on this vast array of ships ever expected or had even thought about.

In our minds, I think that all of us were pretty certain that the enemy ships would not come out to fight when they had a report from their spotter planes about the armada moving across the Arctic Ocean, the outer covering force and the inner escort of destroyers and corvettes, two submarines, and two anti-aircraft ships, the *Pozerica* and the *Palomaris*, not forgetting of course the four armed trawlers, coal burning ex-fishing vessels. After all we were equipped with Asdic gear and depth charges to hunt the U-boats, and they were hunted and some were sunk by trawlers manned by men of the RNR and ex-fishermen like myself, along with some men and youths who in some circumstances had never seen the sea before being called up.

Of course we did expect the usual U-boat attacks, but the weather as far as we in the *Gem* were concerned was great, with the sea almost as flat as a mill pond. At that time of the year it was daylight for the whole twenty-four hours; we knew that we could be seen for miles and miles. The smoke from the merchant ships and coal burning trawlers was going straight up into the air, until it reached a certain height, and then it spread out horizontally helped by the winds in the upper atmosphere to form clouds in an otherwise lovely blue summer sky.

A few hours after sailing from Hvalfiord, the ships had got themselves into their allotted positions; the crews had settled down once they had taken in the inspiring sight around their vessel, to the usual watch-on watch-off routine. When off watch, they would play cards and dominoes which were the favourite off watch pastimes, as well as reading and sleeping of course. All the usual duties had been carried out, all the guns had been cleaned and checked over and over again, the depth charge throwers and rails, the lifeboats, rafts and the gear in them had been checked and checked again, to ensure that they could be dropped into the water should the need arise with, we hoped, very little effort. The old four-inch quick firing gun that was positioned on a platform over the whale-back, was pulled through, and cleaned, traversed and elevated up and down, to make sure that the movements were loose and free, the dust and crystallized salt was removed from the telescopic sights, which were then polished up to perfection. Yes, we were fit, and as ready as we would ever be.

Being the coxswain, I had no regular watch as I had to be ready for any emergency, and in the event of an attack my place of action was on the steering bridge, at the wheel. One of my favourite spots, when things were calm and quiet, was on the point five gun platform over the galley, just abaft amidships. There I kept a few tins of tomato juice (purchased in Reykjavik) to keep them cold. To me they were a luxury that I enjoyed very much when we were not able to get a pot of tea or Kye. I was up there on one of my voluntary vigils, when I saw my first German spotter plane, the nose to sea bloodhound, as I christened him. He went round and around the convoy, and looked as if he were set to escort us all the way to the White Sea. Some days later on 2nd July, I was up on the gun platform when I saw six or eight planes come up over the horizon, right astern of our position on the starboard quarter. Action stations were sounded, and I just had time before running to the bridge to see that they were biplanes, of a similar appearance to the Swordfish, but these had floats below them instead of wheels, and they were carrying torpedoes.

Thinking back, it seems to me that they had no intentions of coming in too close to the convoy, or that was my impression. I was on my way to the bridge and had just got to the foot of the bridge ladder, when I heard someone shout at the top of his voice, 'Torpedo on starboard quarter'. I stopped and looked around, and on sighting its track of air bubbles, I stood rooted to the spot, one foot on the ladder and the other frozen to the casing. I saw that it was approaching the ship's side at an angle of about fifteen degrees, and heading straight for the engine room under where I stood. My heart was thumping like mad, and I was scared almost to death, believe me. I heard the CO shout, 'Hard Aport', then 'Steady', and to my relief, saw the track of the torpedo was now travelling on a parallel course to that of the ship, and was gradually overtaking us. I heard the order given to bring her back on to her original course, and hypnotized I watched the track of bubbles from the torpedo sweep under the cut-away icebreaker bows of the *Gem*. I came back to life taking in deep breaths and gulps of that sweet and clean Arctic air, then continued on to relieve the man at the wheel, where both of us commented that it had been a close thing.

Whether this 'fish' had been dropped from one of the planes or from a sub, I don't really know, but I would assume that it had come from an aircraft. The *Gem* was doing about eleven knots at the time in order to close up with the convoy, as laid down in the orders during an attack on the convoy. What bit of wind there was that day was coming over the port bow causing the smoke coming from the funnel to lay along the surface of the water off our starboard quarter; this was helped by our speed through the water, so we came to the conclusion that one of the Heinkels had crept into our smoke, before dropping the torpedo. Still it missed us, or our skipper evaded it, and from our warning signal other ships on our port side were able to keep clear of it. We lived to fight another day, with the faithful nose-to-sea bloodhound still keeping his eye on the convoy.

If I remember correctly, it was about twenty-four hours later, that we got a second shock. We were at this time nearing an old haunt of mine from pre-war fishing days, Bear Island. We had received a warning of a further air attack, and as I was standing on the after gun platform, waiting for the alarm that would send me rushing to the bridge, we gazed in awe at the sight astern of what looked like a flock of birds coming into sight over the horizon. I started to count the planes 1-2-5-10-15-25. There I gave up and ran for the bridge. The alarm had not been sounded for everyone was on his way to action stations, or was there already, hearts beating sixty to the dozen, and the saliva was thick in our mouths; we were hoping that they would not come for a small ship like ours. Once I got on the bridge, I saw very little of what was going on around us, except for the area immediately ahead of the *Gem*. I saw the leading plane go flashing past the port side of the bridge, and another along the starboard side and across our bows, very close and making for the convoy. All of our guns were having a go. It appeared to me that tracer shells were hitting this last one from all sides; then I heard one of the look-outs shout from the top bridge that he had crashed onto the tanker, a Russian ship named the *Azerbijan*, and that she was on fire. Taking a quick glance in that direction I could see the smoke and flames billowing out from her bows.

One or two merchant ships seemed to be slowing down, and the two small rescue ships, the *Rathlin* and the *Zamelac* were manoeuvering around. One merchant ship that I had in sight just vanished as I was looking at her; one second she was there and the next all there was left was a huge pall of smoke, reaching up towards the blue sky. I had not the time to see if she was a tanker or not. The crew would not have known what hit them. It was an unbelievable thing to see happen, and quite unforgettable. Also in my memory of those few hectic minutes of the attack, is the sight of an American destroyer, steaming full out and being very, very aggressive towards these intruder German planes. She was turning in towards them and letting fly with all the guns she had, and I would not have been surprised to see her crew popping off with rifles and revolvers at anything that was airborne, I've found out since that she was the USS *Rowan*.

Personally, I did not go much on being cooped up in the bridge on the *Gem*, while all this was going on around at the time, so I felt the greatest sympathy for all engine room staff who could not see what was happening. At least I could hear the shouts from the men on the top bridge, and I did know a little bit of the local and close incidents. Yet I felt bad enough for all that, especially when I heard them shouting, 'Here's one', and 'Christ, look at that', and I could not dash out to see. Our chief engineer, Bill Maitland, a dour Scot from the granite city of Aberdeen, once told me when I asked him how he felt down there at the time, 'I'm all right all the time I can hear the thumps and bangs of the explosions; it's the silences that I cannot stand.'

One incident happened within a few hours of this attack. To us in our state of mind at the time it appeared rather funny, though I cannot imagine the pilot and his crew seeing our side of it. An old Walrus plane from one of the larger ships of the outer escort, wandered over the convoy, and ran slap bang into the enemy spotting plane, who immediately chased the Walrus around the convoy. The Walrus of course wasn't fast enough to get away, and after making several attempts to get back to his own ship only to be met by the spotter each time, thought that discretion was the better part of valour, and landed on the flat surface of the sea, to be taken in tow by one of the escorting corvettes.

On 4th July, American Independence Day 1942, one that a lot of our American friends will never forget, the sight of the outer escort of battleships and cruisers, along with their own destroyer escorts, closing in towards the convoy, the American ships amongst them having a great display of flags flying all over the place, had us all guessing for a time, but suddenly the penny dropped. Someone had realised what day it was. With the success the convoy had had in fighting off the attacks, and now the sight of all these large warships celebrating the day dear to the hearts of the people of the United States of America, my pride and the feeling of being safe in their hands came back to me, and I say once more that I am proud to have been there and to have witnessed this great display. That the feeling was destined to be so short-lived is irrelevant.

Even though the skies had kept fairly clear for us, there had been patches of fog in various parts of the convoy, and we soon got our share of it. Though it was not too clear at sea level, there seemed to be clouds of the stuff forming overhead, but we kept on moving along very nicely. So it was with great surprise that a single plane dropped through the clouds and sent a torpedo into one of the merchant ships, the crew being picked up by one of the rescue ships. Not long after this the convoy sustained a heavy attack from bombers flying above the clouds of fog. We could hear them in the air, but never caught sight of one of them. Yet again while this was going on, in came more torpedo-carrying planes to carry out a brave and damaging attack during which two or three more merchant ships were sunk. As suddenly as it began, so the attack finished, and all was quiet after the noise of the exploding bombs and the roar of the many guns of the convoy. Several of the planes were seen to be shot down by the members of our crew, and each time a cheer went up from those who had seen them go down.

By this time we were somewhere to the north of Bear Island, and this put us well within range of the enemy airfields in Norway which was not so very far away as the seagull flies, and as the clouds and fog began to thin out, we began to think that we would be getting many more of these heavy attacks. Here we were wrong, for suddenly we saw flag hoists going up on all the destroyers and the big ships, and Aldis lamps flashing in all directions. As the outer escort closed in towards us, we sensed that something out of the ordinary was going on. It was. A few minutes later the word was passed around that the convoy was to scatter; apparently the German Navy had dared to come out from their bases in Norway after all.* Word had come from the Admiralty in London, and it was to be every ship for themselves as far as the small escorts and merchant ships were concerned.

To say that all of us on the *Gem* were stunned would be putting it mildly. I can remember the words that I said at the time, 'What are we splitting up for, we're better off as we are, on our own we have no chance at all'. The more we thought and talked about it, the more horrified we became. I was only twenty-two, and like many others of my age, was still young enough to want to live and come through this war, but now I felt that my time had come. It was probably only because I had a responsible position that I was able to keep my worst thoughts to myself.

More than two thirds of our crew had never been to sea before they joined up. One of them acted up badly, constantly saying to everyone

---

* In fact they had not. The Admiralty faced with conflicting intelligence reports, made the wrong deduction, and sent the 'scatter' signal.

'We'll never get there, we'll never make it', and 'We'll never get home again', until in the galley an hour or so later, I literally had to shake him by the shoulders to get him to stop saying what most of us were thinking; by saying it out loud, he was making everyone feel much worse. Standing on the bridge a bit later on, my own thoughts sorted themselves out, and I thought, 'Well, we are a small ship on a very large ocean, and with a bit of luck we should take some finding.' The sea was my life, and I had loved every minute of it, but this was different, and I wondered if my Mother knew what we were going through now, as she had done in 1940.

The departure of the outer big escort vessels and their attendant destroyer force, who were joined by the close escort destroyers, hell bent on getting at the German ships for a right royal battle, meant the convoy now no longer existed. The merchant ships, the rescue vessels, and the remaining small escort corvettes and trawlers, along with the two ack-ack ships, 'scattered' to all points of the compass. Ships were making off at their top speed in all directions, and many had already vanished from our sight over the horizon by the time we on the *Gem* realised how serious the situation was. But here and there we could still see the odd plume of smoke from one or other of these ships, its crew no doubt praying as we were for a safe landfall. The deadly game of hide and seek was on for us once more in deadly earnest, the ships piling on the revs, and each man with his own thoughts and a prayer of God Save Us.

As our speeds through the water were about the same, at the most about eleven knots, the *Lord Austin*, *Lord Middleton*, and our own ship *Northern Gem*, decided to stay in each other's company for mutual protection, and in line ahead we made to the north to find the edge of the ice. Since the *Gem* was German-built it has crossed my mind on more than one occasion since then as to whether a U-boat skipper, (and one must have sighted us at some time during the next four days), from our shape and our silhouette, the ice-breaker bows, and the cruiser stern, typical of their own fishing vessels, might have mistaken us for one of their own units, or did he think that we were not worth one of his torpedoes, or that we might eventually lead them to bigger game?

Our two lifeboats were now slung out over the port and starboard rail respectively, ready for a quick getaway in the case of an emergency. Owing to the calm sea, there was very little rolling movement in the ship, and the boats could be lowered almost level with the ship's rail. Into each one we put extra food, clothing, and blankets, water, a couple of gallon jars of navy rum, rifles and quite a lot of ammunition for those and some revolvers, last but not least we threw in one or two tins of 'Tickler's', (Tobacco), fag papers and packets of cigarettes. All of these items were made secure, along with the mast, sails and oars, in case there were any accidents, in the event of us having to make a quick getaway. We had seen too many upturned boats over the last couple of years which had lost all their equipment, and we were determined that this would not happen to our boats. The life rafts of which we had three were also made ready. Two of these were on small wooden platforms level with the top of the galley, and over the deck, as they were laid flat on these platforms, the lashings holding them were released so that if the ship were hit and went too quickly for us to get the boats away, they at least would eventually come to the surface, to give those who had survived something to get into if they could. The third raft was a different proposition, as it was secured almost upright on end to the starboard rigging of the foremast, by quick release grips. But with a ship the size of the *Gem*, the chances of anyone being able to get at these grips to release it would depend on how quickly the ship was going under. Of course there was always the problem that a torpedo hit would leave nothing at all, but that was one of those horrible thoughts that one tried hard to bury at the back of one's mind. However, we made all the arrangements that we could to escape as quickly as would be possible under all but the worst disaster. Now we had to think of ourselves, as well as the survivors of other ships that we might have to pick up, and to save time we made certain that the rescue nets were hung over the sides of the vessel, ready for this act of mercy should it arise.

Each man put on extra clothing, for the further north we went, the colder it was getting. Even though the sea was calm, there was the odd shower of snow now and again; there were a few fog banks about for the three trawlers to dodge into, the temperature of the sea being well below freezing point even though it was summer in the northern hemisphere. A swim of much more than two minutes and one would lapse into a deep sleep of unconsciousness, and inevitable death. Apart from the clothing, we all made certain that we had our bicycle inner tubes on, the navy issue life belts, our steel helmets at the ready; also we had our pockets full of personal things that we did not want to leave behind. One man even packed a small pusser's suitcase. This gives an idea of the feeling that was touching every one of the crew. Old Frampton, the second engineer, who had been called back to the service after being pensioned off, and now found himself in a ship that was hardly pusser's Navy, as he had known it for most of his early life, now had his pension book and all of his other private papers, hung around his neck in a well-used oilskin bag, and underneath the few bits of clothing that those below could stand to wear in the oily heat below.

The usual ship's joker, Jack Sullivan, when not on the Asdic set, was helping everyone along with his wit and joviality. Never seeming to be down in the dumps, he would always come up with something to make us laugh when we were feeling low. On our way to the ice barrier, we saw on odd occasions a ship in the distance either on fire, or lying abandoned after being attacked, but due to our slow speed and small amount of armament, we could do little to help. How we regretted it, we really did. After all, the three skippers of our small flotilla had about a hundred and sixty men in their care, and had their lives to consider, as well as their ship's. Selfish, probably some would say, but those who did not go through this awful experience have no idea just what the feeling of self-preservation was at the time, nor how awful we ourselves felt, knowing that somewhere out there were probably men in rafts or boats, maybe wounded, but definitely in serious trouble as the temperatures were freezing during the night, even though the sun never sets in those latitudes at that time of the year. Our hearts went out to those men but we were in no position to give them more. When I took a spell at the wheel with Leading Seaman Tim Coleman, as we carried on at top speed to the north, the showers of snow came down with more frequency, and we could see far away in the final spells between these showers, a thin layer of fog low down on the horizon. I told Tim that I could smell the ice, and that it wasn't so very far away now.

An hour or so later we were in the ice, thin pancake stuff at first, and then as we pressed further on into it, we got amongst the smaller floes, and then the larger and more dangerous lumps. The skippers had to ease down on the speed of the ships, for safety's sake, and for hours on end which seemed endless Tim Coleman and myself stayed in the wheel-house, taking turns at steering the *Gem* along, following the open water and leads through the much larger and more dangerous lumps of ice. Soon there was plenty of ice between us and the open sea, and we felt that here at least, we were reasonably secure and safe, from torpedo attacks, both by U-boat and torpedo-carrying aircraft, should they find us. What we would do if the enemy bombers found us was another matter, as there was no room to manoeuvre amongst the ice, as there was always the chance of being holed, or even losing blades off the propeller, which would make us or one of the other trawlers a lame duck. So we were having to take extreme care when coming upon the much larger floes and small bergs that were in our path, and we listened intently to shouts from the top bridge and the men on the forecastle head, who were keeping a good look-out from both places.

Our CO, Lieutenant Mullender, now let it be known that we were making all haste for Novaya Zembla, hoping that no German ships had arrived there before us. If they had, and it was thought that escape by sea was impossible, then the three trawlers would be run ashore on one of these God-forsaken islands. We would then salvage what we could from them and try to make our way overland and the sea ice, until we found a settlement, or until we reached the Russian mainland. Not a very charming or happy prospect to look forward to, but at least it would be a great deal better than freezing to death in open boats, if the enemy gave us the chance to get away in them. Others were now already going through that ordeal much to our regret. I don't know just how long it took us, but it seemed an eternity, before we saw on the horizon, two humps of land rising out of the sea ahead of us, the two islands of Novaya Zembla.

We made our way carefully out of the ice and into the open sea once again, all hands now standing at some vantage point around the ship keeping a good look-out. By this time Tim and I were having trouble with our eyes, through the constant staring at the ice for so long. Until getting clear of the ice we had not needed to use the compass to steer by, but now in the open sea we found that the only way we could see the compass points was by almost closing our eyes in concentration, otherwise we felt as though we were looking through frosted glass. Distant sight did not seem to be affected, and later we both found that our eyesight was back to normal. The order for full ahead was given, and the three trawlers were soon going full out and making for the gap between the two islands, the Matochkin Straits. We had at least made a landfall. The only problem was what was waiting for us in the straits? Some of our side, or some of theirs? We kept our fingers crossed very firmly indeed.

When we got closer to the shore, we turned beam on to the land and the speed of the ships was reduced to allow us to creep up to the entrance to the straits. This was a vital period. All eyes, something like three hundred or so of them, were hypnotized by the sight of the strait opening up like a page of a picture book. From behind the port side promontory appeared the bows of a ship, and as the angle of our approach opened up the straits more of the vessel came into view. In those first few minutes we thought that the enemy had got there before us, and were waiting ready to blast us out of the water, but to our intense relief, an Aldis lamp flashed in English. We saw that it was a corvette, and the three of us made our way past the *Poppy*, for that was her name, to make for a spot to drop the anchor and come to rest if only for a short time.

Once in the strait, with the anchor down, we had time to take a proper look around, and saw the *La Malouine, Pozerica, Palomares* and one of the rescue ships, the *Zamalek*. There were also three Fleet sweepers, *Halcyon, Salamander* and the *Britomart*. Five merchant ships had also found their way in to uneasy safety of the strait, *Samuel Chase, Ocean Freedom, El Capitan*, the *Hoosier* and the *Benjamin Harrison*. Later there was another welcome arrival, the corvette *Lotus*. Her decks were crammed with survivors; she had gone back after hearing reports on the RT of ships being bombed and torpedoed, and had picked up about a hundred men from the sea, and certain death. What pluck and courage the crew of the *Lotus* had shown, with complete disregard for their own safety. If only the *Gem* had been able to give us a few more knots, we might have been able to do the same, but of course we did not have those few extra knots under our belt. We had to be satisfied with being one of the lucky ones who had got this far. It had not seemed possible some twenty to thirty hours previously, but then neither had the order for the convoy to scatter. Now here we were at anchor in the Matochkin Strait, between two almost barren islands, with what may well have been the only ships remaining out of that magnificent array of fine ships, Convoy PQ17. It was unbelievable.

There were, perched on one side of the strait, what appeared to be a few wooden shacks, which we were told were a Russian settlement, and we did occasionally see one or two people moving about, and I seem to remember at one time some kind of a boat coming alongside from the shore. We were also told that the strait was alive with fish, but even if we had felt like putting out the fishing lines, I do not think that we would have caught any as there was a very strong flow of water rushing past the ships, suggesting a very strong tide. However none of the crew had any interest in fishing, for there were much more important things to do first. There was not much else to see of the land, the coast appeared to be very rocky, and there was not much vegetation to be seen. The two islands were pretty much the same in appearance; from the shore line the ground climbed steadily upwards, until it came to the top of the two large 'mountain' tops, which we had seen when we were coming out of the ice. I remembered that there were some great plaice fishing grounds around here and the Sem Islands not so far away, but this was actually the first time that I had seen these islands in the daylight. Usually these fishing grounds were worked by trawlers of many countries, but mostly in the winter months. During the summer and when it was daylight the trawlers were mostly working the Bear Island and Spitzbergen grounds, when the ice receded back towards the North Pole.

While we lay there wondering what was in store for us next, we talked of the land we could see, and of what it would be like if we had to try making our way over it, had we been forced to run our ships onto the shore. I for one would have been sorry to have had to leave the *Gem* on that barren shoreline, for she had been my home for almost three years. Some people may think me stupid when I say that I loved every inch of her, and the affection I had for her is still with me to this day, I often 'walk' around her in my thoughts, and can remember how sad I was when I learned that she had been broken up for scrap in the early fifties.

The officers from each vessel in the group of surviving ones that were anchored in this barren but welcome place, which was giving us at least the chance to get a small amount of respite, went over to the ack-ack ship *Palomares* for a conference about what the next move was going to be. Some sort of plan of action had to be arrived at, because we all realised that we could not stay in this haven of dubious relief for very much longer, without being found by the German bombers. In here there would be no room for manoeuvre, and we should become sitting targets. Not only that but the longer we stayed, there was always the chance that U-boats would be gathering for the slaughter outside the Strait. The outcome of this conference, the CO told us when he came back aboard, was that first the three trawlers had to coal ship, for supplies were running low; it must have been fifteen or sixteen days since we had last coaled at Londonderry, and I don't recall taking any on board during our stay in Iceland at all. Each trawler went alongside the *Ocean Freedom*, and took on a specified amount of the precious stuff; the whole of the crew got stuck in to the job, and we soon had our quota down below in the coal bunkers. The CO also told us that the conference onboard the *Palomares* had ended with a unanimous decision to form a small convoy of the ships already in the strait, along with any others who came in before we sailed, and try to make our way along the coast of Novaya Zembla, and into the White Sea, where it was hoped we should be able to expect some air cover from the Russian Air Force, and possibly some help from their Navy.

When all was ready, anchors were hove up, and each ship made its way out of the Matochkin Straits, and back into the open sea once again. The six merchant ships which included the rescue ship *Zamalek*, soon formed themselves into a small and compact convoy, and the escorts took up their allotted positions around it. There was a cold wet fog covering the area, and the visibility was not too good, though we welcomed it at the time as being heaven sent. Our position in the screen this time was on the port quarter of the convoy, so we were between it and the land. We found ourselves alongside the *Ocean Freedom*, but there was no freedom in this bloody ocean. As we steamed along the fog got thicker, and we edged nearer to the *Freedom*; at times all that we could see of her out of the bridge window, despite our close proximity, was the white foaming water rushing past a dark patch of her hull; her upper structure could not be seen at all. The ships in the middle of the group were streaming fog buoys at the end of a cable, so that the next in line could follow at a safe distance, but in this lot there must have been some very near collisions at various times. My job at the wheel was to keep as near as I could without actually hitting the *Freedom*, and with Tim Coleman keeping a wary eye open alongside me, it wasn't a hard job.

After steaming along in these conditions for a considerable period, during which Tim and myself spelled each other at the wheel and on lookout, we broke out of the fog into brilliant sunshine and clear blue skies. It was like walking along a blacked out street at home and opening the door of the house to walk into a brightly lit room. On looking around, apart from the *Ocean Freedom* and ourselves, there were no other ships to be seen at all. The others had vanished. At some time in the past hour or so we had got separated in the fog. That old feeling came back, once more we felt fear, and this time something else which I find hard to describe. Only people who have been in, and experienced that sort of situation can know what I am trying to explain. It was a horrible lonely feeling of being watched akin probably to being locked in a haunted house at the dead of night all on your own.

There were ahead of us to port and starboard banks of fog lying low in the water, but which of these the other ships were in was anyone's guess. After a hurried conversation over the loud hailers, the two skippers decided to make for the fog bank on the port bow. It seemed to be the nearest and would also keep us closer to the land, so we steamed for it, still close alongside each other. It turned out to be a real pea-souper, and once again we huddled close up to the side of the big merchant vessel, just close enough for us to be able to see the dark bulk of her hull at the water line. Both ships went on in this way for some time, until suddenly on the water under the fog there was ice, masses of it, too close to avoid. I was at the wheel, and, as we both saw it, Tim reached out for the handle of the bridge telegraph, anticipating the order to go full astern even as he made the move. There was no order for an alteration of course, and in the bridge Tim and I stood there, bracing ourselves for the inevitable crunch, for there was no time to do anything else.

The old *Gem* hit it stem on, and with the forward momentum of the ship, the ice-cracker bows started to lift up into the air, and right on to the thick layer of ice. The order came down the voice pipe to stop engines. She had gone onto the ice almost up to the foremast, and stayed in that position for a few seconds, then broke through and was afloat once more along the whole of her length, shivering from the shock of the impact, and the way she had launched herself back into the sea.

The voice pipe from the top bridge came back to life again, with the CO shouting down it, 'Coxs'n, go forward and see if she is taking any water in, and check for any signs of damage'.

Leaving Tim in the wheelhouse, I ran down the ladder and onto the deck, and forward to the fore-peak hatch. Lifting it up after knocking away the wedges holding the tarpaulin cover on, I peered down expecting to hear water gushing in from a hole, caused by the first explosive meeting between the ship's bows and the solid layer of ice, but I could hear no more than the sound of the lumps of ice, hitting the ship's side with the motion of the swell. Going down the ladder into the fore-peak with a couple of the seamen, I left them to have a look around, while I made my way into the cable locker, where the anchor chain is stowed when it comes inboard as the anchor is hauled in. I could see no signs of any damage by the light of the torch that we always kept handy down there, nor was there any water, except for the usual amount that was down there at any given time. So breathing a sigh of relief, I made my way back onto the deck, from where I shouted up to the CO on the top bridge that she was dry, and that everything was OK. She was snuff dry. The old girl had brought us through again. What a fine ship she was; they had certainly built her well in Bremerhaven. Thanks Jerry, I thought to myself.

While I was inspecting the fore-peak, some conversation had been going on via the loud hailer, with the *Ocean Freedom*. Apparently she had not been as fortunate as the *Gem*. With her square cut stem and her huge dead weight of cargo, plus the speed at which we both had been going through the water, she had not been able to ride up on to the ice as we had done. She had gone right into it and had finished up with a fair-sized hole in her bows. This, although it was not too bad, was serious enough for her to have to cut her speed down by a knot or two. Eventually we both went astern to get clear of the ice, and with the *Gem* again taking up station on her port side, the *Ocean Freedom*, now having to keep down the flood of water which was entering through the hole in her bow, set off in the general direction which would we hoped take us to the entrance of the White Sea. The fog was still thick, but skirting the edge of the ice which we could still see faintly, and keeping a weather eye on the spot ahead where the fog met the sea, we both plodded along at a reduced speed.

As had happened before, we shortly burst out of the fog into the blue skies and sunshine, and there a few miles ahead of us were the rest of our small convoy. They were under air attack. We could see the black specks of the aircraft and the flashes of sun glinting on perspex noses and cockpit covers as they wheeled about over the ships, and in the water alongside them we could see huge fountains of water rising into the air from the bursting bombs. Later we were to find that the *Hoosier*, and the *El Capitan* had been sunk, and that all the other vessels had suffered from near misses. The *Gem* and *Freedom* now went along at the best possible speed to rejoin the other ships. The sky over them looked as though it was now clear of aircraft, and we hoped that the planes had gone for good. But they did not give up so easily. When we got to within a couple of miles of the convoy or what was left of it, we saw coming up over the horizon some six or eight aircraft, and we noticed with not a little apprehension that this time they were making for us and the *Ocean Freedom*. In no time at all they were on us, and bombs were falling all over the place. The *Ocean Freedom* vanished from our sight two or three times, and we thought that she had gone, but each time she came out of the deluge of foam and spray caused by the near miss explosions of the bombs. We wondered how long the luck would last. Answering an enquiry from our CO, her Captain shouted across that she had suffered some

Three of the crew after coaling ship at Matochkin Straits, July 1942.

En route to Russia before scattering of Convoy PQ 17, July 1942.

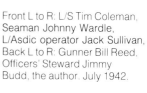

Front L to R: L/S Tim Coleman, Seaman Johnny Wardle, L/Asdic operator Jack Sullivan, Back L to R: Gunner Bill Reed, Officers' Steward Jimmy Budd, the author. July 1942.

On the way to Russia 1942.

(*Right*) The author catching forty winks on deck after a long spell at the wheel whilst navigating through ice floes July 1942.

'On the run' – HMT *Lord Middleton* steaming around ice pack after Convoy PQ 17 scattered July 1942.

damage but nothing that they could not handle. Almost as quickly as it had started, the attack finished. The silence after the noise of the bomb explosions and the chattering of the guns was startling. Now there was just the noise of the sea rushing past the *Gem*'s hull as we made all speed to get back into the company of the other vessels. Finally we made it, and away on the horizon ahead of us we could see land. It must have been around midnight because the big red orb of the sun just touched the horizon for a few minutes and then started its climb back into the heavens to start off another day. It was 11th July 1942.

During the next few hours before we reached the White Sea there were a couple of half-hearted attacks by the Luftwaffe, but none of the now much smaller convoy suffered any further damage. We were met by two British fleet sweepers, and a couple of Russian ships which helped to escort us out of the Barents Sea, and into the confines of the White Sea proper. We were almost at our destination, though not quite for we now had to wait for the Russian pilots to come on board to take us up the River Dvina, and up to our moorings at Archangel, or wherever they decided to put us.

CHAPTER FIVE

Maimska – North Russia

As soon as the pilot came onboard, we proceeded down the River Dvina between muddy looking banks, small sandy bays overlooked by forests of pine trees. The air was impregnated by the smell and aroma of the scent from these forests. Huge tree trunks floated past the *Gem*, hitting us on the hull at times and sending a dull clanging sound throughout the ship. We were to see many of these tree trunks during our stay in Russia, some made into large rafts, being towed or sometimes rowed along the river with families living on them. There were other things we saw too, but these will come later; first let us reach Maimska, for this was where we should stay for an unknown length of time, owing to certain circumstances which at the time we did not know of.

We finally put our ropes ashore on a wooden jetty. Maimska, or what we could see of it from the top navigating bridge of the *Gem*, seemed to consist of nothing but pit props, piles and piles of them. In fact Maimska was an island built on wooden piles, and the buildings on it were made of pine logs. There were lots of shabbily dressed women and girls, and seemingly hordes of young children around. Watching these poor unfortunate people and the guards who stood over them, was to become a regular thing in the weeks to come. Moored at the same wooden jetty were two of the other trawlers, the *Lord Austin* and the *Lord Middleton*, with whom we had kept company since the scatter signal. Of the other one, the *Ayrshire*, we had seen or heard nothing since the convoy broke up. The fleet sweepers, the *Halcyon*, the *Britomart* and the *Salamander*, and also the *Leda*, were tied up to the same jetty ahead of us; so was the A/A ship *Pozerica*, with the writer and journalist Godfrey Winn onboard. He had come along on the voyage to see what life on the ocean wave was really like and subsequently wrote a book about Convoy PQ17, though limited at the time as to what he could write about it.

Once we had moored up securely and exhausted our conversation with the lads from the other ships, the next thing was to catch up on some sleep. I know that I felt absolutely shattered, and I am certain that everyone on the other ships must have felt the same. What bit of sleep I had been able to get for at least five or six days and nights had been odd snatches lying on the deck or on the top of the engine room casing where it was warm, and near to the bridge ladder and the ship's wheel-house where my action station was. My eyes were in bad shape, but did eventually get back to normal. Following our much needed rest, it was time to take stock of what food and ammunition we had left; we had certainly got rid of a great quantity of small arms ammunition, but provided that we did not have to go through the same sort of gauntlet on the homeward run, we should not be too badly off. We had enough food for two or three weeks, so with what we could get from ashore, (we thought), we would be all right for that. While all this checking and cleaning was going on, it gradually dawned on us that we had made it; talking together on the deck, we found that we all shared the same sense of relief, which I suppose is only to be expected after such a harrowing journey as we had just completed. We were the lucky ones who had a ship to finish the journey on. There was also a feeling of remorse for those fine ships and men, who had not reached safety as we had. The full impact of what had really happened out there in the Barents Sea, came to us gradually, as we talked to the crews of the larger escort ships alongside the jetty at Maimska. We believed at that time that out of the thirty-five merchant vessels that had left Hvalfiord in Iceland on 27th June, only the four that had arrived with us via Novaya Zembla had survived. But this was later amended to eleven surviving ships. What a tragedy it had been, though many more years were to pass by before the full and true story was published for all to see. This including those of us who had taken part, for, as I have mentioned previously, we only knew to a certain extent what was happening in our immediate vicinity, and everything else was hearsay.

Routine returned, and an armed quartermaster was on the deck at all times of the day and night, while on the jetty Russian soldiers both male and female paced up and down, watching both their own people who were working in the area, and of course the movements that we made as we moved from ship to ship for a natter. Sometimes we got Russian children coming right up to the ship's side, begging for *Patuskas*, (potatoes), *Paani*, (bread), *Chocolad* and cigarettes. Food was very scarce as we soon found out. While the Russian guards had their backs turned, many scraps of food and other edibles that were left over from meals, were bartered for badges or crudely made pen knives for souvenirs to take home. Many things could be had for a slice of corned beef or chocolate as we could see from the top bridge when some seaman or other went ashore and made for the wood piles where the young women and girls worked. It was a box office attraction in the weeks that were to pass, watching the antics that were supposedly going on unnoticed by anyone but those who were taking part in these clandestine nuptials.

To get to the village of Maimska, one had to pass through a rather long wooden hut. There was a door at each end, and at each of these doors stood a Russian soldier, at times female, all armed to the teeth with sub-machine guns, or rifles with bayonets attached, and on some occasions they had both. Each time you went into the village, and when you came back to the ship, these soldiers stopped you at each end of the hut. Sometimes they came up to the ready as you were approaching. You would have thought that once would have been enough to be challenged, but it wasn't. On going ashore for the first time, each of us was warned that if we heard anyone shout at all, even if it was not directed at us personally, we were to stop and stand quite still until we knew what it was about. At that particular time the Russians were not taking to us very kindly at all, considering what we had gone through on the way over. We were given to understand that they did not believe that all the convoys of ships promised were leaving Britain and ports in America, and that so many were being lost on the way in the process.

The atmosphere was very strained, and could be frightening at times. On more than one occasion, while I was waiting for the ferry to take me to Archangel, about eleven miles away, I was disturbed by the fact that I was surrounded by a score or more ordinary Russian civilians who were asking me in rather excited Russo-English, questions which at first I could not understand. Ultimately I gathered that they wanted to know when the Prime Minister Mr Winston Churchill was to start the Second Front, and when the British and the Americans were going to start fighting in the war. I made out that I did not know what they were saying, '*Niet capiesh*', *Niet capiesh*'. I kept repeating that over and over again until I was able to board the ferry, where I felt a bit safer.

After a couple of weeks, I had to make this trip to Archangel almost every day, to forage for food for the crew. We were down to drinking tea with no milk or sugar, hard ship's biscuits, and Purser's Peas. On top of this we had left a few tins each of tomatoes, beans and soya link sausages. There was flour on board but no yeast to make bread with, and pretty soon we were on a diet of hard peas, ship's biscuits, and black tea without milk and sugar. This was to last us until we were given passengers to bring home, when we were allocated a few cases of mixed tinned stuffs, but this did not last the trip home, as you will see later.

I never had any success with either the Russian or British authorities in Archangel, with regard to food, even though I went on many occasions during our stay there to try and get some. Anything would have done. As it was, eventually we had to get one of the boats into the water and pull up and down the River Dvina, to see what we could beg off the merchant ships which were anchored at various intervals along the river, or tied up alongside some jetty or other. Luckily we managed to get some liquid yeast off an American vessel; you can't realise how smashing it was to taste once again freshly baked bread, and to be able to dip it into the old and the last of the red lead.

Word had been going round for days that there were not enough ships to make up a convoy to take back to the UK, and that we should have to wait until the next one made the hazardous journey from there, and was unloaded ready for the return. What we did not know until some time later was that sailings to the Russian ports from the UK, had been suspended for the time being, due to the losses on the outward voyage of PQ17. So then we began to feel as though we were going to be left here in Maimska for the winter, for if we did not get out before the sea froze over, we should be frozen in, and we were not looking forward to that at all. But like all the other ships' crews, we knew that we should just have to grin and put up with it, as some of the fleet sweepers had done during the previous winter months, when they had been based in the White Sea area, carrying out sweeps to keep the approaches clear.

One day we heard a buzz that three destroyers had made a short but quick trip along the Norwegian Coast, from England, and had brought over some new gun barrels for the A/A ships, *Pozerica* and *Palamaris*, who had worn out the rifling on their old ones on the way over. They had also brought with them some more ammunition, a bit of food, and more welcome still, the buzz had it, some medical supplies for the sick and wounded. The Russians were desperately short of medicines, and our wounded were having a bad time of it. So much for the efforts that we had all put in to get war supplies over to them; this was the thanks that these unfortunate men were receiving. That the *Martin, Marne* and the *Middleton*, had in fact made the quick dash over, was made evident to us by the delivery onboard of no less than eleven full bags of mail. We could not believe our eyes, as we had not had any mail from home for two months. The longest time we had gone previously had been about three or four weeks without news of our families, so this was a field day for us. Never before had we had such an accumulation of letters and parcels dropped on the foredeck.

During the first month we were laid alongside at Maimska, two Russian civilians dropped a sackful of vegetables on our deck, and as we had not tasted fresh veg for some considerable time, we were to say the least looking forward to a good dinner the next day. But alas, almost before we had time to move the sack to the galley for the cook, they were back, this time with two armed soldiers. They regretted, they said in broken English, that they had left it on the wrong ship. It was for one of the fleet sweepers. There was nothing that we could do in that case but watch them take it away as our mouths watered with the thoughts of what we almost nearly had. We realised later that we had been slow, and that we should have had a few of them stowed away. There and then we decided that if such a thing should happen again, we should definitely make certain that we at least got a taste, but there never was a next time.

A great morale booster for us while we lay alongside, came after a get-together of the officers from the fleet sweepers, and the three trawlers to help to try and get rid of the boredom that was creeping gradually over us all, both officers and men alike. They came up with the idea of holding intership sports of various kinds; in some of the sports the trawlers were classed as one ship, the men from all three who wished to take part putting their names down for any type of sport which took their fancy, and were then chosen for a team to represent us all. This made for great rivalry, and despite the weather, we enjoyed some good sport and fun, either by taking part, or by just watching and cheering the teams on to do their best aided by some ribald comments.

The *Northern Gem*'s own newspaper, the *Sunday Buzz*, Vol I. No I, for Sunday 2nd August 1942, gives this story and the following list of results:-

> *Sports. . .* Despite inclement weather, we have enjoyed some good sport during the past week, in which the trawlers have by no means disgraced themselves. For the benefit of future historians the results are summarised below. We hope that these events are only the forerunners of a series of contests, thoughtfully provided to relieve the monotony of our sojourn.

Whaler Pulling	Shooting	Whaler-cum-Canoe Race
(1) *Halycon*	(1) *Halcyon*	(1) *Halcyon*
(2) Trawlers	(2) *Britomart*	(2) *Leda*
(3) *Britomart*	(3) *Leda*	(3) Trawlers
(4) *Leda*	(4) *Northern Gem*	(4) *Salamander*
	(5) *Lord Middleton*	(5) *Britomart*

Sailing (1) *Britomart* (2) *Leda* (3) Trawlers (4) *Halcyon* (5) *Salama'r*

Tug of War At the time of going to press this event had not been held.

Around about the last week in July, the trawler *Ayrshire* arrived, bringing with her three merchant ships. We had thought her lost but she had gone due north into the ice, escorting the three ships of her small convoy. They had used up all their white paint and many bed sheets, making themselves look as much like the ice that they buried themselves in as possible, in order not to be seen by the enemy bombers, and had eventually made their way to Novaya Zembla, where they were picked up and escorted in to the White Sea to an anchorage and safety. *Ayrshire* was later moored some distance away from the rest of the trawlers, and one evening, two boats set out on a social call to her. One of these was from the *Lord Middleton*, and the other from the *Gem*. Both were manned by officers and men from these ships, and apparently they all had a good night's entertainment on the *Ayrshire*. They were rather late returning, and were caught in a sudden squall which sprang up from nowhere, as often happened. Efforts were made to lower the sails before the full force of the wind struck them, but only one boat succeeded in doing so, and then only after a struggle. The other boat was overturned and its crew were thrown into the icy fresh waters of the River Dvina. The rescue operations were hampered by the fact that a strong tide was running, and due to low cloud and heavy rain so late that night, complete darkness reigned, but by dint of good seamanship, and by some skilful manoeuvering by the crew of the other boat, all the men were picked up out of the water, and no one seemed any the worse for their involuntary ducking. When the storm abated shortly afterwards, almost as quickly as it had started the other boat was salvaged, and returned to the *Lord Middleton*.

Other ships in our vicinity that took part in the sports were, as I remember, the corvettes *Lotus*, *La Malouine*, and *Dianella*, and also the rescue ship *Rathlin*. They all enjoyed the fun, and of course the opportunity to keep themselves busy and their minds off what could be in store for us in the future. During our stay in North Russia,

which began on 11th July 1942, we saw many different things, some
of which have stayed in my memory more than others. One of the
most vivid of them was the air raids, of which there were many. The
German bombers dropped mostly incendiaries, many tons of them,
into the pine forests around Archangel in an effort to set them ablaze.
These fire bombs hung like huge chandeliers in the frosty night air,
and seemed to fall very slowly, eventually disappearing from sight
amongst the trees for a few seconds, then flaring up into huge fires
which could be seen many miles away, the glare reflecting up into the
sky and illuminating the tall columns of smoke that reached up to the
dark ceiling of the sky.

I think though that most scary of all, though most exhilarating
during these raids, were the antics of the Russian fighter planes,
which would take off from some aerodrome a short distance away,
and streak past where our ships lay, with all of their navigation lights
on, then would zoom straight up through the barrage of flak which
was being sent up to greet the German raiders. After the first one or
two raids we got used to them and refrained from shooting as they
thundered past, but I am sure that some of them must have been shot
down or at least damaged by the firing of their own countrymen,
though I never saw this happen. But it was something to see, believe
me, watching these planes dashing past our ships, and through all
the anti-aircraft barrage that was being put up.

Then there was the day that I and several others of our crew stood
on the *Gem*'s bridge and watched a man shot down in cold blood; his
crime was making off with some food stolen from the community
soup kitchen. Set back on the jetty was a large wooden hut, and in the
first few days of our stay in Maimska we noticed that around noon a
long queue of the poorly dressed workers gathered outside this hut.
The way they were treated made us think that they must be some
kind of political prisoners, or slave workers. Each one of them carried
a container of some kind, either a tin, a jar or a pan, inside of a bag
made of netting; it gradually dawned on us that the hut was a food
kitchen, and that these unfortunate people were queueing for what
looked like a broth or a soup.

On this particular day when we were watching, a man ran out of
the hut and along the wooden jetty as fast as his legs would carry
him; one of the guards on the jetty shouted for him to stop, but the
man either failed to hear the shouts, or was too afraid to stop, and the
guard who was carrying a sub-machine gun as most of them did,
immediately opened fire with a short burst which hit the running

figure squarely in the back. This was swift and animal-like justice, and it sickened me; those poor devils were starving, and killing in that way for such a small crime as that of trying to alleviate one's hunger made my blood run cold. It also made us more aware of the repeated warnings we received from our officers when we went ashore, to stop dead when we heard a shout, and to stand still until we knew what it was all about.

A happier memory of those now far-off days is that of watching a group or platoon of both male and female soldiers, marching along a muddy track in perfect formation, with their arms moving in unison, with their guns slung over their shoulders. They were singing in their deep and loud voices one of their rousing marching songs. It was one that at the time made us feel proud to watch them, and to know that here was a people fighting for their country and its very existence, and yet they could still sing like that. They had, as far as we knew, done nothing to help us or even to make us welcome during our stay, but I still could not bring myself to run down the ordinary Russian people after seeing things like that.

On our weird trip through the ice towards Novaya Zembla, we had seen the amazing sight of ships steaming along upside down in the sky. On one occasion as we got closer to the islands, there, hovering above the horizon, was the replica of a complete town; even the factory chimneys could be seen smoking quite clearly, with towers and spires and domes of churches reflected in the sky along with some tall buildings. We guessed that it was Archangel being shown up as a mirage, yet although the reflected image showed what looked to be a fine-looking town, the real thing was nothing like it at all. On the many times that I went into it, I felt as if I was in some old wild west town, with wooden pavements for walking on, and the roads in a terrible state especially when it rained. The houses and the shops, as well as some local government buildings, appeared to be very dilapidated. Above all it is the smell that lingers in my memory, the scent from the pine forests, mingled with the smell of rotten sewerage amongst other things; it smelt more like a scented cesspit than anything else. It's a wonder that the whole population of the town did not die from some disease or other, I was always glad to get back to the *Gem* as the air smelt somewhat sweeter there, even though the scent of the pine forests was still noticeable to some extent.

On reflection, I suppose that we looked for faults at the time because of the reception we received when we arrived there, and I can only think now that we might have been biased by the things we saw, and the fact that we never got any help in the way of food etc. during the whole of our stay there. But after all we were in a country at war with our common enemy, and they were it seemed giving one hundred per cent action on their land fronts, so this could be why everyone not engaged in that fighting was in such a bad way for food and clothing, and why nothing was being done to keep towns and villages clean and in good repair. Now we were waiting to see if we had to go through the same ordeal on our homeward journey, but if we made it at least we should be in a more civilized country.

CHAPTER SIX

The Road Back With QP14

At long last, during the first week in September, the buzz went round that a convoy had left the UK, and was well on the way to Russia; we were told that soon we might be on our way home. As though to confirm this, the trawlers were told to proceed to Ekanomia to take on coal. We went alongside the quay there, with its cranes and mounds of coal, and were amazed to see clambering on board, a gang of women coal heavers in all sorts of dress, armed to the teeth with shovels. All we had to do was to take off the bunker lids, stand back and leave them to it to do the work. It was a revelation to see them get stuck in to it, and in no time at all the job was finished. The driver operating the crane which was dropping the coal on the deck was a shapely blonde girl, very attractive in spite of the coal dust that covered her. She received more than her share of wolf whistles from some of our lads, and some of the comments that had been going back and forth were very ribald indeed.

As soon as the last of the coal was onboard, and the gang of women had left the ship, we moved further along the quay to let one of the other trawlers into the berth to take on her quota. We set to and as the engine room staff greased the bunker lids, and screwed them tightly down for the return journey, the rest of the deck crew set about the job of getting rid of all the coal dust that had settled everywhere, both above and below decks; it is always surprising where one finds this dust after coaling ship, and it was a good job done when the filthy stuff had been washed away. Meanwhile I took delivery of a small but welcome quantity of some cartons of tinned food of the usual kind, but it was very acceptable for we could now have a good meal for once before we went back on to a rationed diet once more, for even now we did not know how long it would be before we sighted good old England's shores, or even if we would be included in the escort for the convoy; it all depended on whether we could keep up with them if it was a fast convoy. Another valuable commodity that we took onboard was some cigarettes, real ones in packets. It was a change to have a good smoke instead of drying tea leaves and rolling them in toilet paper – they were horrible but at least they had been smokable, and we had been getting used to them.

One thing we had not been short of was rum; many of the ships had become so toward the end of our stay, but they were mostly the ones who had picked up survivors on the way in.

Saturday the 12th of September came, and with it about a dozen Merchant Navy survivors for the passage home; three or four of them were Americans who were not very happy about the size of the vessel they had been assigned to for the passage, but they soon settled down and after giving a little trouble they knuckled to and gave a great deal of help down in the stoke-hold. It was from these survivors that we heard how they and some of the wounded and frost-bitten men had been treated; they had suffered a rough time compared to what we'd had to put up with. They had been herded into wooden huts with only sacking at the windows to keep out the bitterly cold Arctic winds and the nightly frosts. They slept on bug-ridden straw mattresses, if they were lucky that is; others had to sleep on bare boards and even the cold frozen earth. On most days they had to make do with one meal a day of what was laughingly called by their providers, vegetable stew. As for the wounded, they told us that the Russian hospital was filthy, and that there had been no anaesthetic available for the amputation of frost-bitten limbs, and very few medicines of any kind. It must have been hell for them. Those who had been able to move were shared out between all the ships that were to make up this convoy, and they were more pleased than we were, if that was possible, to be on the way home at last, and like us were prepared to take any risk to get away from North Russia. They vowed that never again would they sign on a vessel bound for that area of war, but I have no doubt that many of them did just that, and in my opinion all who sailed in merchant ships during the war years were very brave men doing a dangerous but necessary job of work.

One of the American seamen whom we took onboard was sent to us straight from a mental hospital, where he had been kept since he was put ashore in Russia. The poor chap had lost his reason during the latter part of his trip out. As soon as he stepped on to the deck of the *Northern Gem*, he made several attempts to throw himself over the side and had to be physically restrained from doing so each time. Eventually with the help of some of the crew, I managed to get him into a bunk in the foreward mess-deck, but from then on he would take nothing to eat or drink, saying that we were trying to poison him. It was tragic to see a man like this; his nerve had completely gone. Nothing we did would pacify him, and it became evident to me that we could not keep him onboard.

I went to the ward-room and spoke to Mr Pooley, our first lieutenant, and asked him to come and see the man for himself, explaining as I did so my reasons for coming to this decision. I told him that I did not think it was fair, either to the man himself, or to the rest of us on the *Gem* to keep him onboard as I should constantly have to keep either one or even two members of our crew to watch him at all times, and that if action stations were sounded this was not possible as every man had his own job to do, not only this but that the man would neither eat nor drink. This was all true and when he had seen the man, Mr Pooley went to the CO and explained the situation, the outcome of this was that several signals were sent, and when we had left the jetty in the early hours of the Sunday morning, a motor launch from the rescue ship *Zamalek* came alongside of the *Gem*, and the unfortunate man was taken to her for his passage home. He would be much better looked after there than with us, for she had qualified doctors onboard who could give him the treatment he so badly needed. What an awful thing it would have been if we had been ordered to keep him with us, only in some unguarded moment to have him succeed in throwing himself over the side.

On this Sunday morning, 13th September, (what a date to sail on) we had a convoy designated QP14. Wondering what was in store for us, we at last steamed out of the White Sea, and into the Barents Sea. It was going to be an unlucky day to sail for some of the vessels, and also for some of the men who sailed in them, before many days had passed. It was a fairly fast convoy, but the four trawlers were determined to keep up with it. Failure to do so would mean turning back, with the possibility of staying the winter frozen in in some backwater off the White Sea. So the necessary revs had to be kept up and the speed maintained. It would prove to be a fair struggle as the coal we had taken on at Ekanomia was nothing more than dust with a mixture of earth amongst it. We were fortunate in that some of the survivors we had taken onboard before we left were firemen, used to working in a ship's stoke-hold, and they volunteered to a man to help keep the fires burning and the steam pressure up. They did a good job too, for they did not fancy going back any more than we did.

Convoy QP14 was made up of fifteen ships, including the ones which had survived the outward bound PQ17. The rest were some that had been left there previously awaiting a return convoy. There were also the two rescue ships, *Zamalek*, and *Rathlin*, along with a fleet oil tanker the *Gray Ranger*, which we were to come up with later. The weather through which we steamed was typical for that time of the year, thick fog patches and heavy snow squalls, and it was bitterly cold again. Fortunately it wasn't blowing with it or we should have been frozen up in no time at all. There was an atmosphere of hope now in the *Gem* as the convoy formed into their positions, and the screen of destroyers, minesweepers, ack-ack ships, corvettes and the four trawlers formed up in a wide circle around the merchant ships, and settled down to the job of trying to get them all safely home. Course was set in the general direction of that lonely bit of rock sticking up out of the Arctic Ocean, Bear Island, known to the fishermen who worked around it in the days before the war as 'Bum Island'. It was a place to nestle up to when the fierce Arctic gales started to blow, and that could be often.

On fairly calm seas, but passing through the banks of fog, and squalls of snow, we progressed onwards with no scares, and on 18th September when we had passed somewhere in the region of the southern tip of Spitzbergen, we were pleased to have join us some aircraft from the escort carrier *Avenger*, which at the time was with the other convoy outward-bound for Russia. It was on this day that one of our officers, Skipper Tommy Buchan, was confined to his bunk with a very severe bout of influenza, and the CO Skipper Lt Mullender showed his trust in me by asking me if I would take over his watch. I said yes and felt mighty proud and confident in doing this; it would give me more experience of watch-keeping on my own, though I had naturally to keep in touch with the CO by means of the voice pipe from the bridge to his quarters, in the case of there being an emergency. And so it was that I came to be on the top bridge in charge of the watch from four a.m. until eight a.m. on the morning of 20th September.

It was a fine morning, an early morning breeze ruffling the surface of the sea, but there was hardly any swell. Visibility was very good, but there was an overcast sky which threatened more snow. The ship was on station astern of the starboard column of merchant vessels at a distance from them of about two-thirds of a mile. On our starboard bow was the Fleet sweeper HMS *Leda*, I had to keep my station on her at forty-five degrees on my bow and astern of the starboard column. Several times since I had come on to the bridge to take over from the previous watchkeeping officer, I had checked on our position. I did not want to be caught off station should the Skipper put his head out of his cabin, and it was getting on for half past five that morning when I lined up the *Leda* to take a bearing on her on the bridge compass. As I was going through the drill I noticed a huge cloud of smoke come out of her funnel, and the thought that she had just flashed up a boiler had hardly got into my head when I saw a column of flame shoot upwards and at the same time heard and felt the crump of an explosion. Sticking to my orders from the CO, I shouted down for full ahead and a course to take us towards the *Leda*, at the same time pressing the alarm on the bridge to sound general alert and shouting down to the CO what had happened. But he was by that time on his way up the bridge ladder, took over from me, and I made my way to the steering bridge.

Taking over the helm I kept on for the *Leda*, and as we got closer the CO shouted down that he was going right alongside her as she lay stopped in the quiet water, so that the crew could step on board without getting their feet wet. It would save the need for putting a boat over the side. When we reached within a hundred and fifty feet of her, and starting to ease round to go alongside, the crew started to abandon ship by jumping over into the sea on her port side, and we had to go full astern to stop, making certain that we did not run some of the faster swimmers under; one of the first to be picked up was a lieutenant, and he was followed by eighty or more of the crew. Fortunately they were not in the water very much more than two or three minutes before we got them onboard, so they were able to help themselves to a certain extent. Our CO told me later that one of the other ships came up in between the *Leda* and us, running down an officer and some ratings on a raft. As I did not see this happen I cannot say whether or not it was correct, but I know that we did not pick them all up, including her CO; I don't know yet what happened to him.

We had the rescue nets over the side for them to climb up as quickly as was possible, and as they did so a destroyer came up our starboard side and shouted through her loud hailer for our skipper to get back to the convoy, for we were not supposed to stop to pick up survivors on the run back. Our skipper told him to f . . k off, whereupon the destroyer's CO said he would report him when we arrived in port, though as far as I know nothing came of it. It was all go, just backing and filling with the engines on slow to save men who were in danger of drifting past ahead or astern of the *Northern Gem*. Having picked them all out of the water, we came hard to starboard and made our way back to our station, and astern the *Leda* turned on to her starboard side and slid under the cold waters of the Arctic ocean. I did not see her go for I was relieved at the helm by Tim Coleman, so that I could go down below and dish a tot out to all onboard. By the time I got down I found that we had three dead onboard, an SPO, a PO and an ordinary seaman, all having been injured in the torpedo explosion which I think hit her in the forward boiler room.

We had a total of eighty-one survivors onboard, including nine of the men getting a lift home on the *Leda* from the SS *Navarino*, and the SS *River Afton*, both sunk on the way out with PQ17, thus getting their second ducking in the water. We sorted them out and took their names down, and gave them bunks to sleep in. They all had to share with our lads, and I had three or four chiefs and petty officers sharing my cabin in the after quarters. They were great lads and appreciated the situation and what we did for them. One of them sharing my cabin, Basil Potts, an ERA, later sent me a leather-backed Bible, along with a letter asking me to thank the whole of the *Gem*'s crew, for all the help we had given to them, I have kept and treasured them to this very day. They had all been sad to see their old ship slip beneath the waves into the depths of the sea, taking with her those who had been killed or trapped when the torpedo hit her. There was nothing anyone could do to save those who were trapped as she was going too quickly, and all who could had to save themselves.

Almost twelve hours later, when we had just about caught up with the convoy, though it took some doing when they had got so far ahead during our rescue work, as we had only a knot or so to spare, we were coming up astern of the *Silver Sword* when we noticed first of all two great columns of water shoot up from her starboard side, and we immediately thought that a high level bombing attack was in progress. Then there was a third splash of water this time on her port side, I remember. Then we knew that it was a U-boat attack, and that the *Silver Sword* was doomed with three hits on her, and quite suddenly she started to sink. By the time we arrived on the spot all of her crew had been picked up, and there were just swirls on the surface of the water. Then a second or two later large sacking covered bales from her holds shot out of the water and into the air, before settling back to float quietly and serenely to some other destination than where it was originally bound. What was in them was anyone's guess, some suggested silver fox furs, and one or two of the crew tried unsuccessfully to snare one with a grapnel on a heaving line, and it's probably as well they didn't because we were doing somewhere in the region of eleven knots, and they would have been dragged over the side.

Shortly after this sinking, the *Avenger* and her destroyer escort left

e of crew en route to
sia July 1942.

e of *Northern Gem's* crew
coaling ship from the
chant vessel *Ocean*
dom in the Matochkin
ts, Novaya Zemlya July
2 – note strain and the
s of lack of sleep on the
s.

he jetty at Maimska
ust 1942 with Russian
dren who asked for
kolat' 'parny' (bread) and
rettes.

Matochkin Straits, Novaya
Zemlya with rescue ship
Zamelak in background.
August 1942.

Russia 1942.

Russian children with some
crew at Maimska, Russia,
props were used for fuel until
coal could be taken on board.
August 1942.

the convoy. It was the first and last time that I saw an aircraft carrier at work. From the distance she was from the *Gem*, the aircraft looked like beetles crawling along her deck, but it was very fascinating and reassuring to see them take off. About an hour or so after they had gone, the Tribal Class destroyer *Somali* was torpedoed. She did not sink straightaway, so was taken in tow, and was to keep afloat for some time before a severe gale blew up, and she went down, unfortunately with great loss of life and far away from our position, so we did not know much about it. I only know what I have read since so cannot comment too much of it.

The convoy was now moving forward at a reduced speed of about five or six knots, with the *Somali* being towed by another Tribal Class, the *Ashanti*. The darkness of the night closed down on us, and it proved to be a quiet night even though we now knew that the U-boats were in contact with us.

Tuesday September the 22nd came along and with it a fine morning with a calm sea and a slight swell, which caused the ships to roll a little, but nothing to give any discomfort even to the trawlers. All was quiet until just before the watch below was called out for their breakfasts at seven-thirty. Then in the short space of half an hour or so, three ships were hit by torpedoes. The first one was the *Ocean Voice*, the second the *Bellingham*, and the third the fleet oiler *Gray Ranger*. The latter two were hit within seconds of each other. The rumble of depth charges sounded and reverberated through the half-empty ships that were left sailing along; they were being dropped by the escorts over on the port side of the convoy, but it was a job to pick up an echo from a submarine in those cold waters with so many fresh water layers hidden away amongst the salt sea.

I saw the stricken ships heel over as they were hit by the exploding torpedoes, for we were fairly close to them. Skipper Mullender then ordered me to steer the *Northern Gem* between the *Gray Ranger* and the *Bellingham*, which was an American vessel. Once reaching the point between the two we went full astern to take the way off her, and then lay dead in the water, awaiting the crews of both vessels, who were by then climbing down into their life-boats. We took onboard twenty men from the *Bellingham*, six of them originally from the *Pan Atlantic* and two from the *Pankraft*, those eight taking passage on the *Bellingham* from Russia, after having lost their ships on the way out. We also took onboard twenty-two men, including the Captain H.D. Gausden, from the *Gray Ranger* which had joined us from the outward-bound PQ18. They came alongside in their motor launch, a fairly big one, and when it was emptied of all that would be useful to us, it was streamed astern of us, so that we could tow it along as a standbye escape boat, for we had more men onboard now than we had life-saving boats and rafts for, should anything happen to the *Gem*.

As we started to steam off to catch up with the convoy, the chief officer of the SS *Bellingham* told our skipper that there was another boat on the other side of his ship, so I was told to take the *Gem* in a wide sweeping turn around the stern of the American ship, where we found the rescue ship *Rathlin* or *Zamalek* already taking them aboard. *Gray Ranger*'s master said that he had some men missing, but we found that they also had been picked up by the rescue ship, as had those from the *Ocean Voice*, and as the three ships were now in their death throes, both the *Gem* and the rescue ship in company made all speed now to reach the remnants of the convoy.

Going round with the rum jar, and taking the names of the survivors I found that we had onboard now some two hundred or more men, taking our crew into account, four times more than we had bunks for. Although we were prepared to make the best of it, food was the main concern. What we had left was a mere mouthful for the complement we now had; our CO thought that he would have to do something about it, and sent off a few signals. In the meantime, Captain Gausden of the *Gray Ranger* was bewailing to our CO the loss of his ship, which was only natural, and because he had just remembered that he had left over five hundred English pounds in the safe in his cabin. Our skipper said in his broad Suffolk voice, 'Why the Hell didn't you say so when we picked you up? We could have gone back for it and shared it between us.' But it was too late now as she was at the bottom of the Arctic Ocean with all of the other fine ships that had gone that way. When things were happening as they had done, it was difficult to notice all that was going on. When so much concentration has to be used to pick up survivors, every one concerned has to work as quickly as possible, for in that sort of a situation, when U-boats were about and the ship is stopped in the water, there is always the danger that one of them has his sights on your vessel. A ship lying dead in the water is as far as the commander of a U-boat is concerned a legitimate target, and one that he would not let go, especially if he thought he had no chance of catching up with the convoy. I suppose it is akin to that old saying, 'A bird in the hand is worth two in the bush'. I had been relieved at the wheel once we had all the survivors aboard, and found that luck had been with us once again. The CO said, 'As you go down, Cox, take a look and see how the old boat is towing along; you never know when we might need it'. It made me think, I can tell you.

However, here we were now steaming as fast as we could go away from the barren islands of Spitzbergen, Bear Island and that other little one, Hope Island, which had at its southernmost end Cape Thor, alias the God of Thunder. We had heard plenty of him since the 27th June, though little did we know it but he had not finished with us yet, anyhow as far as the weather was concerned. We awaited now replies to the signals which the CO had sent regarding food and our survivors, and it wasn't long before I was called to the bridge again to take the wheel. When we had left the White Sea, it was touch and go as to whether we had enough food to see us through, water too was going to be a problem. We had picked up the men from the *Leda*, and they had now been biting into our rations for over two days. With over two hundred souls onboard things were getting a bit chaotic, and with all these extra mouths to feed, I had estimated that we should be lucky if we lasted two more days with the food we had, though the water situation was not too bad as yet.

Conditions in both the seamen's mess and the petty officers' mess were terrible, with all the bunks full and men either standing or lying on the decks, taking up every available bit of space. Moreover there were many of the merchant seamen who would not go down below, and just roamed about the upper deck, blocking the entrances to the various companionways, which would have obstructed our crew getting to their action stations if the need had arisen again, but fortunately it did not. While we were steaming, the dead American fireman who had been brought onboard from the SS *Bellingham* had, because of the situation we were in, been buried while the *Gem* was forging ahead, a thing we had not liked to do, but had to.

Now I was called to take the helm it seemed as though the answers to the signals had come through, for I was told that we were to go alongside one of the destroyers to pick up some food. Which one I don't remember; it could even have been the *Somali*. It probably was for she had to be lightened and many things were ditched over her side. However it was always a ticklish piece of work going alongside another vessel, as one had to keep an eye open for anything to happen. This time we went close enough for them almost to pass the cases of tinned stuff over, with the use of a heaving line. Soon that job was done, and it was time for us to close on the *Seagull*, onto which ship we transferred two naval officer survivors from the *Leda*, and thirty-one naval ratings along with three merchant navy seamen who were transferred to the SS *Rathlin*. So this made things a bit easier on the *Gem*. At first it seemed to us that most of the merchant seamen wanted to go, as they had not been too pleased about being picked up by a small trawler, but when they were given the chance to go, only three went, the remainder saying that they stood a better chance of getting home on a small ship. In the words of one man when asked if he wanted a transfer to the *Rathlin*, 'The chances of my being tin-fished on this "Coggy-boat" are far less than on one of yon big uns.'

Later in the day the weather started to freshen up, and by nightfall there was a very heavy sea running. The wind started to howl in the rigging, and soon we were engulfed by a fierce gale. The *Northern Gem* dipped and rolled and plunged into the heavy seas, and was being swept by spray and at times snow. She was a great sea ship but we felt this lot. Our passengers, though not used to the violent motion of a trawler, were adamant that they would rather be where they were, and not on a fleet sweeper, or a destroyer. At least they said quite convincingly that they were dry, which is more than they would have been on a bigger ship. According to them, by now the mess-decks would have been awash with all sorts of gear swilling about, everyone wet through, with no one getting any sleep at all, so I guess that in that respect, we trawlermen were fortunate for we could turn in and sleep, even if we had to wedge ourselves in our bunks, and not have to rely on whether we could sling hammocks or not.

This gale really stirred up the convoy, and it lasted for about two days and nights, before it abated to a more normal kind of blow. The merchant ships suffered badly as they were mostly in ballast, and must have been like empty tins on a weir according to what the merchant seamen passengers whom we still had onboard told us. The poor old *Somali* must have decided in the night that she had had enough of it. It was circulated around the *Gem* the next morning that she had broken in two, and had gone down taking many of those who had volunteered to stay with her in her hour of need down with her. We had not seen it happen, but we could imagine what it must have been like on such a wild and dark night, bitterly cold, and a freezing and raging sea. What rotten luck, after getting her so near to safety, and despite the fight to save her. We must have been very close to Iceland at the time she went. The following day the winds dropped away almost completely, and the sea gradually flattened itself out, with blue skies and the sun overhead. The few ships of the convoy and escort which were remaining, gathered themselves into an orderly convoy again, and made all speed towards Loch Ewe, where we finally dropped our anchors, in those glassy-looking waters on 26th September 1942. It was three months since we had left Hvalfiord with those thirty-five merchant ships.

The things we had missed? As Skipper B.F.G. Long wrote in the *Sunday Buzz*.

> Thinking back on the dim distant days when we were operating in home waters, it occurred to me to try to enumerate the homely pursuits and pastimes in which we were engaged. I leave it to the reader to guess who the cap fits in certain instances.
>
> Civvy suits-Church at Derry-Honkey tonks-Stage acts-Husband watching-Irene and Maisie-Locks of hair-Mail-Mixed guest nights-Moville eggs-Outsize waist lines-Pitmans Derby-Ration cards REPEAT Cards-Ray and Eileen-Rothesay Frolics-Sergeants Mess at Eglinton-Sheep hunting at Stornaway-Small boat pushing-Spider Kelly-Spragging-Stocking hoarding-Taxis for C.B. Officer-Trawler Dances-Wrens (Frolics with).

Russian Recreation by Skipper T. Buchan. From Sunday Buzz.

In this age of strife we find,
Some see places they don't mind,
But we cannot say how long,
Russian shores will be our home,
After an exciting trip,
We find ourselves confined to ship,
For, ashore we fail to find,
Satisfaction of any kind,
Then we put our heads together,
And, provided that we get the
      weather,
We'll start a sports and then
      you'll see,
That we will soon forget the sea,
Some as quite a change from labour,
Prefer to go and toss the caber,

Others think it would be fine,
To go and throw the heaving line,
Rowing, sailing, and relay races,
We all strive for leading places,
Soccer in such brilliant ? weather,
Quite a thrill to pass the leather,
Last of all we think of cricket,
With home made bat we seek a
      wicket,
After such a thrilling game,
'Just like home' we do proclaim,
In years to come when the fightings
      over,
When we are back on British clover,
And meet a shipmate, then we say,

    'CHOCOLAT', 'COMRAD', that was the day.

Arriving at Hull's Paragon Station on leave, I quickly made my way to the bus station. Boarding the bus, I went up onto the top deck to get a better view as it made its way through the city centre and along Porter Street, then right along Hessle Road, where I had been brought up, and where most of the fishing fraternity lived. I could see many piles of rubble and gaps in the rows of shops and houses that had not been there on my previous leave. Each time that I went home I saw more evidence of the air-raids that the people of Hull were having to contend with. On the news bulletins that we heard from the BBC on the radio, no towns were mentioned, it was just, 'A north east Coast town,' and these words made many servicemen and women look forward to the next letter from home to hear if their folk back there were all right. But air-raids or not, it was nice to be back home again.

All too soon the leave was over and it was time to go back to the *Gem* in Belfast. When you are having an enjoyable spell it is very surprising how quickly the time seems to pass by. After a quick look around the house and the garden to imprint them deeper into my mind, I left to catch the train and ferry, back to whatever was in store for us until our next leave.

Both during my years at sea pre-war and during the war, mostly on night watches, I often thought back when I had a moment or two to spare, about the folk back home. On a dark stormy night, I often got to wishing that I was back in my own bed at home, and that I had never started going to sea, but really I did enjoy the life, even every other job had its moments when you felt a bit under the weather. One of my greatest desires was to walk through a huge forest of trees when the wind started to howl through the rigging of whatever ship I was sailing on. I tried to imagine what it would be like in a gale of wind ashore, I should think that the sounds in a forest at the dead of night must be similar to the sounds of being at sea. The water rushing past the hull of the ship, like the wind shaking the branches of the trees, and though I often promised myself on those occasional mind-wandering nights at sea on watch, that I would carry out this desire, but I have not yet done so. Looking back on those years that I spent at sea, I realise that I would never have known the friendship, and that special camaraderie which is only to be found on a ship, where you all had to work as one and each man's life was in the hands of the other members of the crew. Since leaving that kind of life, I have found that it is a back-biting world working in shore jobs, and that the same sort of friendship that occurred at sea, both in peace-time and in the war years, is very hard to find.

Back on the *Gem*, as each member of the crew returned, news of their time spent at home was talked about, girl friends being the most predominant and interesting subject to most of them. Pub crawls and booze ups took second place, and soon through talking about what we had all done at home, it became hard to believe that you had been home at all. Routine was picked up again immediately, and it was not long before we found ourselves letting go the ropes which secured us to the quayside, and getting prepared for another trip. Then we were steaming out of the dock and up the Belfast Loch and into the wide Atlantic Ocean on yet another patrol, or to help to escort yet another convoy on its way to the New World and other places far away.

Some of the men on these outward-bound merchant ships would be on their way home to see their families and friends, and it was up to the escorts to see that not only the ships and the cargoes that they were carrying, but also the men in them got home safely. In between these voyages we managed to get a bit of time ashore in Belfast or Londonderry. We had made some good friends ashore in both places, servicemen and civilians, and we had a few good nights and parties to remember. Then one day at the beginning of December 1942, word was circulating around the ship that we were again going as an escort and rescue ship, on another convoy to Russia, this time to the Kola Inlet in Murmansk.

CHAPTER SEVEN

Convoy JW51B

Arriving back in Londonderry we found that our Skipper, Lieutenant Mullender was to be relieved for the trip to go on another course of submarine detecting. In his place we were to have another ex-fishing skipper, Lieutenant H.C. Aisthorpe RNR who hailed from Grimsby. All of us on the *Gem* had some misgivings about losing Skipper Mullender, even for one trip – it was the old thing about changing a winning team. We had come to know and like him very much indeed. To me he had been more than just a CO; he had been a friend and a confidant, but, much more than that, he had been an advisor and teacher. I had learnt a lot from him and would miss him. I felt that if he did not come back to the *Gem* after this trip at the school, I should definitely put in to go to Lowestoft to sit for my mate's certificate, I was in two minds in a way. At that particular time, I had been in the *Northern Gem* for just over three years; they had been active but happy years, and we had been blessed with more than our share of good luck. A new skipper might change all that, and yet if I were to leave her, my own luck would probably change. Chewing this over in my mind, I finally decided to leave things as they were for the time being, and see how it all turned out.

Rumours were circulating around the trawler crews at the base, that instead of convoys sailing to Russia, individual merchant ships would set off from the UK with a gap of twenty-four hours between each one, and that in between these would be a lone trawler. None of us had any liking for this idea at all, but of course we should have had no choice in the matter if this was to happen.

On 18th December we sailed from Belfast with the trawler *Vizelma* for company on the way to Loch Ewe to join the escort for Convoy JW51B, and five days before Xmas once more our anchors were heaved up and made secure for yet another trip, and another eventful one at that, to North Russia. This time we were hoping that we would arrive safely at the port of Murmansk. The two trawler skippers had in the meantime been ashore for the briefing. Merchant ships were already there when we arrived, but we could only see from the bridge of the *Gem* a couple of corvettes and a fleet sweeper at anchor, and as we waited for the return of Skipper Aisthorpe, we wondered if this was the complete escort for the convoy, and if the rumours that we had heard in Belfast were true. There was not much to do onboard, for much of the stowing away of ropes and other tackle had been done already.

We were to sail on 20th December, the following morning, for Murmansk, with fourteen merchant ships in the convoy, two corvettes, *Rhododendron* and the *Hyderabad*, the fleet sweeper *Bramble*, and the two trawlers *Vizelma* and ourselves, the *Northern Gem*. Other escorts would join us when we were passing Iceland. A short route was to be taken to Murmansk depending on weather conditions, and how far the ice had come south this winter, we should most likely be at sea for ten to twelve days.

The time to weigh anchor and sail out through the boom came, and we steamed out of the loch and into the Minch on the first leg of our two thousand mile journey. Once outside the boom, I watched from the wheelhouse as the deeply laden vessels made their way out and formed up into two columns in order to move more comfortably up the narrow Minch, between the Outer Hebrides and the West Coast of Scotland. This was to be the only peaceful and calm part of the trip as far as the weather was concerned had we but known it. Once out of the Minch, and well clear of the Butt of Lewis and Cape Wrath, the sky took on that look of approaching bad weather, the sea looked oily and sullen with the long Atlantic swells rolling in from the west and starting to break off at the tops, the white crests being whipped up by the cold icy winds coming from the Greenland ice-capped mountains, winds which were freshening up with each watch as they changed. Somewhere off the north-east coast of Iceland, the escort was reinforced by six destroyers; the sight and presence of these vessels made us feel less vulnerable. They were the *Onslow*, *Obedient*, *Oribi*, *Orwell*, *Obdurate*, and the *Achates*. In the not too distant future, the *Achates* and the *Northern Gem* would be involved in a life and death situation.

As the arrival of the destroyers lifted our hopes, so did the sure knowledge that at this time of the year inside the Arctic Circle, there would be no daylight as there was at the height of summer on the PQ17 episode. We knew that the enemy bombers would not be able to get at us as they had done then. I had been asked many times by those of the *Gem*'s crew, who had not come by this route before at this particular time of the year, just what it was like. I told them that daylight 'happened' around mid-day, that it was no more than just a twilight world for about an hour, and then once again darkness settled in for the remainder of the twenty-four hours. The weather could be fine, but more often than not, the area was being swept by gales of wind and blizzards that whipped the seas up into a frenzy, and that it was so cold that your breath froze on your beard, eyelashes and eyebrows.

Now as we got clear of Iceland, the wind was howling through the rigging, sounding a warning of much worse weather to come. The cold water of the Arctic Ocean was beginning to throw its weight about, and making itself felt, as malevolent as ever, reminding us of what it was capable of. The old *Gem* was plunging and rolling, as were the rest of the ships. The merchant ships that we could just see in the darkness from our position at the stern of the convoy were rolling heavily under the weight of all the deck cargo they were carrying. Keeping station in these conditions and the darkness that prevailed was very difficult, and at times could be downright dangerous, for no lights other than a very dim stern light could be shown from any of the vessels. It was possible to creep almost under the stern of the one ahead of you before you saw its dark heaving bulk, for now along with the gales of wind and wild seas, we were on the receiving end of snow and rain squalls, and visibility became worse by the hour.

It became difficult to tell whether it was midday, or midnight, and after a few days of four hours on watch and four hours off, when tiredness from being thrown about, and the staring out into the never-ending darkness began to tell, time was defined by meal-times. Even then some of the crew were not certain whether they were having breakfast or supper; all they were concerned about was that they were either going on watch after their meal, or coming off watch to get into some dry clothes and a warm bunk for an hour or so, even though it was being heaved about in so many directions at once.

Apart from the deterioration of the weather, and the difficulties of station keeping, which I mentioned earlier, the *Northern Gem* with the rest of the convoy had no other visible worries at all. Our Christmas Day had come and gone, with dinner consisting of corned beef sandwiches for those who felt like eating. Strong and sweet tea washed the meal down the throats of those who had, and it was the same ones who were downing their tots, and any others which they could get hold of, not only on Christmas Day, but on any other day that the weather was bad, and those days were prolific.

Inevitably, due to the full gale that was churning the sea into mountains and valleys of tormented water, some of the larger and heavily laden merchant ships were having to steer a course which would save them from taking too much punishment, and some became separated from the convoy. Our accompanying trawler, the *Vizelma*, keeping station on one or two of these ships, found herself to have been led away with them, and not until we arrived at Vaenga on the Murmansk coast, did we learn that the *Bramble*, a fleet sweeper, had been sent off to try and contact these vessels to shepherd them back to the fold. She was never seen again.

On the morning of the last day of December 1942, New Year's Eve, I had my breakfast as usual at 7.30 am, put on some warm clothing, and then made my way up to the point five gun platform to have a talk with the look-outs who were keeping their cold vigil up there. It was a miserable morning, bitterly cold, with thick black clouds sweeping across the dark early morning sky whichever direction I looked into. Snow squalls were sweeping over the ship, driven by the north-easterly gale, and visibility was very limited even between the squalls. The day before the lads had taken part in their first ice-cracking and shifting job. Wherever there was an accumulation of ice that they could reach with safety, I'd had them knocking it off with axes, hammers and even hatch battens. It was essential but backbreaking work, and despite the cold everyone got quite a sweat on. The thickest and worst of the ice was broken up and shovelled over the side, or into the scuppers so that the sea swilling over the deck would wash it away and into the sea. The starboard boat deck was covered with a thick layer of ice, almost like a skating rink, and after spending some time having to go at trying to clear it on my own, I considered that it was much too dangerous for anyone to tackle it. After having a look for himself, the first lieutenant agreed with me as he did not want any of the lads to slide over the side as it would be almost impossible to find them in that sea.

Standing on the gun platform that New Year's Eve morning, before I went the rounds of the ship to see if the ice had built up on the deck again during the night, I sat on one of the ammunition boxes taking stock of what I could see of the nearest vessels. I followed the bottom of the low scudding black clouds where they touched the sea, at a distance of what I judged to be some five to seven miles away on the starboard beam, around to the stern, then up across the port quarter, I saw suddenly some dark orange flashes. In that second or so my mind registered that it was lightning of some sort, but then, almost immediately, the alarm bells sounded, and I saw nothing else as I made my quick dash to the bridge to take over the wheel. On my way I felt that I had seen, rather than knowing that I had seen, reflected by those flashes, some kind of ship, which was just a black shape. Nothing had been mentioned of an attack of any sort, no warning of an enemy presence from our officers or any of the W/T ratings, so it came as a shock that the convoy was now under attack from enemy surface vessels.

Taking over the wheel, my view was now limited to the port, starboard and front bridge windows. I reported to the top bridge that I had taken over, and I could feel the vibration as the *Gem* picked up her speed from the order to ring the engine room for full ahead before I got up there. The CO shouted down for me to keep as close to the merchant ships ahead of us as I could. From this point on, although I knew that there was a battle raging around the convoy, I saw very little; I remember at one point seeing what I took to be a destroyer over on our port beam, dashing about with smoke pouring out of her funnel laying a smoke screen across the stern of the convoy. During the next hour or so I was given the order to alter course several times; the engine room had been ordered to make as much smoke as possible, which was an innovation for us for normally we made too much being a coal burner. I was told that the *Onslow*, the escort leader, had been hit and put out of action, and also the destroyer *Achates* which was the vessel I had seen laying smoke; I wondered now how long it would be before we ourselves copped a few heavy bricks. We must have made a grand sight belching out thick black smoke. It was usually the other way on convoys, trawlers as well as some of the merchant ships were the bad boys, and were often told to cut down on the fog, especially on fine days, when the smoke could be seen for many miles, and was easy to spot by any patrolling U-boat. This was a different kettle of fish; the smoke was needed to hide the merchant ships at any cost to ourselves.

For some time we helped to cover the convoy of ships with our smoke, and then I was told that Tim Coleman was coming up to the bridge to take the wheel, and that I had to go on to the deck to get the heavy towing cable out of the forehold, and prepare it in readiness to take the destroyer *Achates* in tow; she had been badly damaged and had requested our help. I went down on being relieved by Tim, and found Mr Pooley the first lieutenant, already at the fore hatch with a gang of the lads, and working as quickly as possible we had everything we required up on deck in readiness, laying out the cable or towing wire, flaking it up and down the whole length of the port side. No sooner had we completed this job, than we were told that the *Achates* was in a bad way, and was in no condition to be towed, and that we were going to stand by her. Rescue nets were put over the port side, and heaving lines were got ready; those of our crew who were not doing essential work were positioning themselves along the full length of the port side, as we came up on the starboard side of the stricken *Achates*.

She certainly seemed in a bad way, from what I could see of her as both ships were being lifted on the top of the heavy broken swell. She looked well down by the stern, and had a great list over to port. Within minutes of our arrival, I saw her going further and further over, until she lay completely on her port side. I could see the figures of men, some with red lights on their life jackets and some even smoking, clambering through the rails and on to her starboard side which had now become her deck. As she went further over until she was floating completely bottom up, the men slid down her side and into the water, her keel now pointing to the heavens. Then as the men in the water started swimming towards the *Gem*, we stood on our deck and listened in amazement as we heard their voices giving out with a rendering of 'Roll out the barrel'. Here they were in dire peril, not only from drowning, but freezing to death if we could not get them out of the water within a few minutes, singing at the tops of their voices. Those who had survived the action and the struggle to keep their ship the *Achates* afloat, were now fighting for their own lives, to save themselves in those cold and freezing waters of the stormy Arctic Ocean. Their agony was our agony, and the few minutes, until the gallant *Achates* slid beneath the surface of the disturbed seas, taking with her the dead and the badly wounded who could not be moved for ever, seemed more like hours, until we had got safely onboard all that was possible of those who were still alive.

Along with several others of our crew I took a spell for a few minutes over the side on the rescue nets. We entwined our legs in the nets to leave our arms and hands free, making sure that we should not be pulled away by the suction of the seas rolling under the ship's hull, or by the weight of the men in the water, as we grabbed them and hauled them up high enough for others of our crew to pull them over the ship's rail and onto the deck, from where they were taken below as quickly as possible into the warmth of the seamen's messdeck. It was freezing as we were rolled incessantly and completely under the water, and we could only stand it for three or four minutes at a time; we were relieved by others of the crew who

took our places on the nets, while we stamped up and down the deck
to bring some life back into our limbs. Then we picked up a heaving
line or anything like that to throw to those in the water. I myself at
this time took a line to the port quarter of the *Gem*, and managed to
catch one man and drag him back to the nets and safety. Running
back to the same place, I saw a young lad drifting passed the stern
with his arm outstretched to catch a line; as I threw it to him it
dropped over his shoulders, but he seemed to have lost all the feeling
in his body due to the cold. I screamed at him to hold on, but he could
do nothing to help save himself, so I tried to throw several loops of
the line around his arm, but in those last few seconds, I distinctly
heard him crying out for his mother. 'Mother' was the last word I
heard as he disappeared below the surface. I know that I was crying
myself with helplessness and frustration as I saw him go.

Just at that precise moment, there was a terrific underwater
explosion, and the *Northern Gem* was lifted bodily out of the water.
The surface of the sea shivered for a few moments then burst into a
boiling cauldron of confused froth. When it returned to its former
state, there was no one left alive in the water, there were probably six
or eight bodies floating past, still with their life-jackets, on which
glowed the red lights, but there was no sign of any life; they had
either been killed by the explosion, or had succumbed to the frightful
cold of the water. Our CO then thought it wise to go onto full speed to
catch up with the convoy as the German surface vessels as far as he
knew were still lurking in the area, and the *Gem* wasn't built to fight a
ship to ship battle of that sort.

Everyone was now clear of the deck for with going full ahead the
ship was being swept with heavy seas, and it was not safe to linger
about. I had run down to my cabin and changed quickly into some
dry clothes, my others being frozen. When I had done so, I went
down to the forward mess deck, dodging the seas on deck as I went. I
had to take stock of how many survivors we had managed to pull
aboard. The total was eighty-one officers and ratings; some had been
wounded in the action, twelve seriously enough to warrant the
attention of a doctor, but unfortunately we did not carry one. One of
the wounded was a young sub-lieutenant named Barrett; this young
man never uttered a word all the time he was being stripped and
made comfortable in a bunk. There were no obvious or outward
signs of wounds or injuries on his body, but he was in a very serious
condition. I went round the mess with the old rum jar and gave every
one a liberal 'dose' of the stuff to help get the blood moving again.

Those survivors who were able helped themselves to towels, dried their bodies and rubbed their limbs briskly to bring back some life to them, then climbed into bunks, and were wrapped in warm blankets; I made certain that I missed no one with the rum jar. As the circulation gradually came back to the limbs of many of these men, some were screaming with pain, a pain which must have been excruciating. Our lads were doing their best to alleviate this by massage, followed by covering them with warm blankets or clothing brought up from the store of survivors' clothes, after some time the sounds of the men in pain gradually died away as they lapsed into various depths of sleep.

The wounded were a problem, for as I mentioned we had no doctor onboard, but we had amongst our crew an ordinary seaman named Eric Mayer. He was forty years old, and had been a bank clerk before joining the service. His wife was a State Registered nurse. He also had a friend who was a doctor, and of course Eric Mayer had picked up a bit of medical knowledge from these connections, so he was put in charge of the wounded. He soon realised that many of them required more skilled attention than he could give them, and with the few medical stores that we had onboard at the time, he could do no more than clean and disinfect their wounds and bandage them up to the best of his ability.

As I was going the rounds taking names, I came across Lieutenant Peyton Jones, the first lieutenant of the *Achates*; it was he who had taken command of her when the captain was killed on the bridge during the action. He was sat in the forward mess-deck, very concerned about his crew, though he realised that we were doing our best. I apologised for the fact that he had been taken to the seamen's mess, and conducted him to the wardroom to join the other three surviving officers where he was greeted warmly by them and our own officers who were present. They had all thought him to be lost with the ship, and the surprise and pleasure on their faces when I took him in was good to see after the happenings of the last few hours. Later, he and our skipper made plans to go alongside a destroyer at the first opportunity to get a doctor onboard to attend to the wounded. With the sub-lieutenant, in the forward mess-deck who was to die later, this made five officers and seventy-six CPOs, POs, and other naval ratings taken aboard out of the sea.

Some forty or so others, including the captain, had been killed in the action by the shelling, and apparently another thirty very badly wounded men who could not be moved, had been taken to the skipper's day room on the *Achates*. These unfortunate men had, with two brave men who had volunteered to stay with them to the end, gone down with the ship, together with those who succumbed to the freezing waters of the Arctic Ocean, and those last few who had been killed by the explosion which had occurred. I think about one hundred men had been lost, but I don't think that we could have done any more than we had done at the time. We had worked as quickly as was humanly possible under the circumstances, and as far as we knew the enemy vessels were still in the vicinity, and could have found us at any time.

When the explosion blasted the surface of the sea into, first of all, a flat shivering expanse of water, then into a boiling white foam, we all apparently had thought the same thing as the *Northern Gem* was lifted bodily out of the water – that we had been hit by either shells or a torpedo on the opposite side to where we were pulling the men onto the deck, our starboard side, yet no one panicked. It must have been either the boilers of the *Achates* blowing up, or her depth charges, but whatever it was, the explosion had given us all a fright. Much of our crockery had been broken, and some of the cabin clocks had been blown off the bulkheads, but more than that it had killed off all the men who may still have been alive in the water, and had robbed us of the chance of saving them.

While taking the names of the survivors, one of them told me that the sub-lieutenant, had been on the bridge when the salvo of shells hit the *Achates*, one of which had exploded on the bridge, killing most of the men up there and in the wheel-house. What a shambles it had been. The cries of the survivors were dying down now, and although they were still in a state of shock, they were beginning to find that the *Gem*'s mess deck was a warm, dry, and friendly spot to be in, even though it was heaving up and down like a tormented and demented thing.

Going up on to the deck was like going into another world, a world of total darkness, a shrieking and howling wind going through the rigging like a tortured and mad being, snow blizzards helped to make it look like another planet, and feel like Hell. During all this there was a scare on the *Gem*'s bridge, when in darkness another destroyer was seen going across our stern. At first it was thought to be an enemy vessel, but fortunately for us it turned out to be the *Obedient*, another of that gallant band of destroyers that had fought off the attack made by the German surface forces. We were still steaming at full speed, making every effort to catch up with the convoy, the Skipper only guessing at the course to steer to pick it up once again, for it could have altered direction to any point of the compass to keep away from the enemy.

Seeing the *Obedient* going across our stern, signals were passed with a shaded Aldis, and the Skipper learnt that he was on the right track; a short time later we caught up with the convoy. At one point we passed the *Onslow* fairly close and in the dim light of the Arctic day, saw what a fight she must have had; men were on the for'sle head apparently trying to get a collision mat over the bows, all around the bridge and funnel we could see signs of damage, and we wished her a silent good luck. Now amongst friends again we got ourselves tucked in astern of the ships of the convoy, to stay there for the rest of the night, greeting the New Year of 1943 as we did so.

When the northern skies had turned a shade lighter, getting on for mid-day on 1st January 1943, orders were given for the *Gem* to approach and close the destroyer *Obdurate* to take on her surgeon. A boat could not be launched, the weather being still very bad and sea conditions still atrocious. Even though we were fortunate in that the wind had dropped away a little, the fierceness of it had gone at this time. In any case our port boat had been swept away during the gales earlier on, I went up to the wheel-house to take over the wheel on the run up to the *Obdurate*, getting the feel of it in those heavy swells and choppy seas, ready for when we finally went alongside the destroyer, but at the last moment Skipper Aisthorpe entered the wheel-house and said, 'Right Cox, I'll take her. See if you can get the starboard boat inboard, if possible, but don't take any chances. We don't want to lose anybody'. I got some of the hands who were standing watching, but try as we might with axes, hammers and shovels, we could not even clear a part of the small boat deck without using both hands to hold on with. So I reluctantly told the men to stand down from that dangerous job, and to get some fenders ready for going alongside the *Obdurate*.

This also was a hazardous thing to ask them to do, for as a ship the size of a trawler rolls with the swell, the rail tends to dip under the water and the midships deck becomes flooded. One has to keep a weather eye open for the heavy ones and be prepared to jump for the engine room casing and safety. But they stood by their task very willingly, knowing that the presence of the surgeon was sorely needed onboard for the treatment of the badly wounded men. With the *Obdurate* going slowly ahead into the wind, with just enough way on her to keep her as steady as possible in the turbulent seas, the

Northern Gem, with Skipper Aisthorpe at the wheel, crept up to the port quarter of the destroyer, *Gem*'s starboard bow coming within heaving line distance of her and creeping closer every second. We could pick out in the grey watery daylight on her deck a small group of men standing on the quarterdeck. Amongst these was the surgeon, Maurice Hood, who had a line around his waist, waiting to risk his life. A reception committee of two of our officers and several men waited to catch him as he jumped, and to release the line quickly so that the two ships did not stay too close for too long.

As our starboard fore-deck came abreast of the *Obdurate*'s quarterdeck Skipper Aisthorpe slowly edged the *Gem* in towards her, waiting for the correct moment to bring her alongside as close as possible, without too much risk of a hard collision which might damage both vessels, and of course to give Surgeon Hood a closer and steadier platform form to leap on to. Suddenly, as he thought the moment had arrived, a quiet moment between the heavy squalls, we watched with apprehension as our bow swung in towards the destroyer. Then with only a few feet separating the two vessels, Skipper Aisthorpe put the wheel over to port to straighten her up; her previous course and momentum, added to the helm being put hard aport, with the engines full ahead, caused her to keep sliding steadily to starboard, just enough to close the last few feet of the gap. The two ships touched momentarily. As they did so, Surgeon Hood bravely jumped some seven or eight feet on to the deck of the *Northern Gem*, and into the arms of the reception committee.

The hearts of everyone watching were in their mouths for the few seconds that he was airborne, in case the *Gem* swung away from under him. This was the most dangerous part of the operation as far as he was concerned, and we were happy to see him land safely. The damage caused by the touching of the two ships was only very slight. It was a satisfactory operation, successfully completed by all concerned, and we now had a surgeon aboard.

Surgeon Hood was taken below with his bag of instruments, to prepare himself for the job of work he had come to do. And this was to prove no mean feat on his part due to the conditions in which he was to work in. The forward mess-deck became the operating theatre, and the mess-deck table the operating table; this had to be held firmly in place by several other members of their crew, so that it would not be thrown on to the deck by the crazy gyrating movements of the ship. How the doctor managed to carry out these operations and to keep his hand steady to cut away the damaged flesh, I shall never know, but he did. Lieutenant Peyton Jones of the old *Achates* administered the anaesthetic. Both he and the surgeon had to be held in their positions at the table, and many of the *Achates* survivors volunteered for this.

After our last search around the area in which the *Achates* sank, while I was going round with the rum jar and the stripping of the survivors was going on, I came to one man who was standing up against the mess-deck table, in a state of shock and kept looking down at his right shoulder. Two of our crew were about to take off his jersey, and as they eased it over his head, the whole fleshy part of his shoulder came away with his clothing. I shouted to Eric Mayer to come over and have a look at it. He separated the piece of flesh from the clothing, did something to it and the wound that it had come from, then bandaged them both together again. He was doing a responsible job and making good work of it considering that he had no qualifications, and when the surgeon did start to do his operations with Eric as assistant, he complimented Eric for what he had done.

There was also a young seaman that I found sitting in the galley, he was keeping himself warm by the galley fire. When I gave him his tot of rum, during our conversation, he said the back of his head was hurting him, and asked me if I would have a look at it for him. I did so and could see a piece of metal at the back of his left ear, it was sticking up out of the bone, with no sign of blood; the metal was a good quarter of an inch thick, and was protruding about half an inch from the skin. When Surgeon Hood saw it eventually, he said that he would not attempt to take it out as he had no way of knowing the length or the shape of the metal, which was a piece of shrapnel. When it was taken out at Murmansk, it was a jagged piece almost as long as a cigarette packet; this young man had been very lucky indeed to survive this.

The young Sub-Lieutenant Barrett was examined in his bunk by the doctor, who said that although there was no visible signs of injuries or wounds, he had apparently taken the full blast of an explosion in his stomach, possibly from the shell that had hit the bridge. There was nothing that could be done for him, and we were told to give him anything that he asked for, as he was dying. All he did ask for was a drink of water; he never complained and passed away sometime during the night. He was buried the next morning, the service being read by Lieutenant Peyton Jones, while the *Gem* lay hove to in the now worsening weather. He included in his service those of their crew who had gone down with the *Achates*, and now lay many miles astern of us, somewhere in the vast spaces of the Barents Sea, amongst the many who had gone before them on other convoys taking aid to our Russian allies.

Taking stock of the convoy now that we were back with it, we knew that the trawler *Vizelma* and two merchant ships along with the fleet sweeper *Bramble* were adrift since losing the convoy the night before the attack by the German force. The *Onslow* which we had seen as we closed the convoy had by this time left the convoy, and was trying to make Murmansk on her own but a lot of her crew had been killed and wounded. We were to lay close to her later when we arrived at Vaenga, and we saw more plainly how much she had suffered. Her CO, Captain Sherbrooke, who was severely wounded and had lost an eye in the battle, was later to be awarded the Victoria Cross, for the successful defence of the convoy, whose attackers had been the *Admiral Hipper*, the *Lützow*, and several large destroyers, one of which was sunk by our covering cruiser force *Jamaica* and *Sheffield*. *Onslow* looked a shambles when we saw her at Vaenga; there was a great gaping hole in her starboard bow, and the crew had put the collision mat over it, to stop the flow of water that was threatening to sink her; the mat had frozen to her hull on her trip back to port. Her bridge was a tangled mess of ruptured steel, and the funnel like a colander with holes that had been made by the jagged pieces of shrapnel.

The wireless room had been ravaged by splinters, and those on watch there at the time had been killed at their posts. Once again the *Northern Gem* had been most fortunate; this time in the midst of an attack by enemy ships, the heavy cruiser *Admiral Hipper*, and the pocket battleship *Lützow* along with six large destroyers, one of which, the *Friedrich Eckholdt*, was lost. They were all out of our league and we shuddered to think what our fate would have been if we had come face to face with any one of the enemy.

The weather on the way in to Vaenga continued to be at its vilest, with storm force winds which caused havoc with the heavily laden merchant ships, but all of them survived. Blizzards which swept continuously over the convoy and the escorts, made station keeping a hazardous job due to almost nil visibility, but we all arrived at the Kola Inlet safely with no more incidents. All the survivors of *Achates* were put ashore here from the *Gem*. From what we saw of the port from the ship during the short period of daylight, it seemed to be a place that none of us would relish staying in for any length of time – not that I went ashore very often, once to see the young lad out of the galley, and to see how the other wounded were getting on. I had a walk around the area out of curiosity more than anything else but I would not like to compare it with Maimska or Archangel from our previous run to North Russia. I know that once again, when we arrived at Vaenga and made fast to a merchant ship alongside of the jetty, I was almost out on my feet, having been at the wheel for a considerable period. And I remember quite well, as though it were only yesterday, that I rolled into my bunk just as I was, sea boots, duffle coat and life jacket still on. I can remember Tim Coleman shaking me and calling me, telling me that he had been down several times before and could not wake me up. On the last occasion I had apparently swung my legs over the side of my bunk, without waking up.

When he did finally get through to me, he told me that the *Northern Gem* was on fire and that I had to get on deck as quickly as possible. Still with my eyes full of sleep and hardly open, and to be honest, with hardly a bit of interest, I pulled on my gloves and put on my helmet, asking him what the 'whooshing' sound was that I could hear; he replied that the noise was incendiary bombs, dropping in the water alongside, and also into the almost empty merchant ship which we were tied up to. Then I became wide awake and ran onto the deck with him. Great fiery chandeliers were failing and coming to rest in many places around about. Apparently several had fallen on the *Gem* but had been shovelled over the side; only one had been difficult to get rid of and it had almost burnt through the engine room casing before it had been dealt with.

Just after this we moved alongside of the *Onslow*. I must have been completely exhausted at the time I turned in, as never before nor after was I like that. Normally I was a very light sleeper and woke up before I was called, sensing that something was going on or that I was about to be called. This was a condition that I had got used to in pre-war fishing days. Previously when we had picked up men from ships which had been sunk, one or two had mentioned that they had called one of their mates who had been asleep in his bunk after the 'Abandon Ship' had been given, and that person had not awakened; it was something that I could not readily believe, but I now found this to be only too true. The *Gem* had been on fire and I had slept through it.

What if she had gone down? The date would have been the 3rd January 1943, the day we arrived at the Kola Inlet, and were secured to Vaenga Pier.

The following day, the *Onslow* moved away from her berth inside the *Northern Gem*, at Vaenga Pier. She was proceeding to a place called Rosta, for a quick repair job before going home with the next available convoy. As to the weather at the time, the thermometers were showing minus zero degrees, everything was frozen up, and snow was in abundance. The Russians were not a very friendly people on the whole, considering what all the men in the numerous convoys had been through to bring them their much needed supplies, and as far as we were concerned, we could not get on our way home quickly enough. The Germans had one or two airfields, not so very far from the Kola Inlet in flying time, and we did not want to stay too long within reach of them.

The *Northern Gem* pulled away from *Onslow*'s side, to allow her to slip out to make her way to Rosta. Most of our crew were on deck, and I was at the wheel with most of the bridge windows down. There was no daylight yet and to keep most of the windows up and closed meant that they would be soon steamed up from the heaters and would make it difficult to see where we were going. As *Onslow* began to move out slowly, the sound of a trumpet was heard, and soon all other sounds from the dockside cranes, and the winches on any merchant ships which were being unloaded were silent, and everyone within the sound of the lone trumpet, stood still. It was being played on our forecastle, by one of our officers, Skipper Tommy Buchan, and I'll bet that he never played to a more receptive and appreciative audience than he did on that morning.

At first everyone stood in complete silence, looking around in the faint light, to see where the sound was coming from as it was so unexpected, then, first one group, then another, joined in singing, until all round men were giving out at the tops of their voices, a rendering of that lovely old song 'Auld Lang Syne'. There must have been many salty old sailors, both Royal Navy and Merchant Navy, who were close to tears as the *Onslow* and her gallant crew moved away, and past the *Gem*. It was a very moving and never to be forgotten scene, believe me, and one which all who were present at the time will remember for ever.

We stayed at Vaenga for just over three weeks. There were many air raids by the Germans, and Murmansk was a ghost town of shattered buildings, with burnt timbers sticking up in the air, the smell of burning mingling with the smell of death, a sweet sickening smell which clung to your clothing. Yet it was here in Murmansk that I tried out skiing. I was looking at some skis outside a hut and an elderly Russian came out and motioned me to put them on. There was a gentle slope, running away from the hut, so I thought, Why not? After two attempts during which I was on the floor in the snow more often than I was on my feet, I passed the skis back to him, thanked him, and gave him a new packet of twenty Senior Service cigarettes.

The *Vizelma*, our 'chummy' trawler, had got in with her two merchant vessels, so although the convoy had lost none of the stragglers, or any of the merchant ships come to that, we had lost two of the escorts the *Achates*, and the *Bramble*, which we learned had been sunk somewhere in the Barents Sea. There were no survivors. Theirs had been a lonely struggle against both the elements and the attacking force.

So with the two trawlers from the previous convoy JW51A, which had left Loch Ewe on 15th December 1942, and had arrived in the Kola Inlet on Xmas Day, there were now four trawlers to coal and take on provisions. These were the *Lady Madeleine* and the *Northern Wave*, (the latter being a sister ship to our own which had been on the Norwegian Campaign with us), the *Vizelma* and the *Northern Gem*. On 29th January 1943, a convoy of eleven merchant ships left Murmansk, escorted by a larger force consisting of seven destroyers, including the *Onslow*, two fleet sweepers, three corvettes and the four trawlers. With the Kola Inlet astern of us and fading away in the right direction, and the weather not too bad, we had a fairly quiet trip back. Only one merchant ship was sunk by a U-boat. This time we were not in the position to be of help; this job went to the *Lady Madeleine* and the *Northern Wave*, and not one man was lost.

We arrived at Loch Ewe on 8th February 1943, ten days out from Murmansk, a pretty quick trip by the shortest route possible. The four trawlers diverted to Belfast, from where some of us got leave. When I got my turn, and arrived in my home town of Hull, I saw the *Onslow* again, this time in the hands of the ship repairers. As I stood on the Monument Bridge, where once the statue of William Wilberforce looked out over the docks, my mind went back to the Barents Sea, on that cold, dark and wild New Year's Eve day, with its snow squalls being driven by storm force winds, and to the events of that day, when Captain Sherbrooke of the *Onslow* won the Victoria Cross. Now here that same ship lay, in my home town, having her wounds attended to. I watched with pride and I wondered if the men working on her decks at that moment, knew what she had been through, and did they feel as I did about her? What a difference to that other convoy, PQ17, when so many men lost their lives for nothing more than pitting their courage and their determination against such great odds. JW51B had been a great victory, and had helped to boost the morale of those of us who had been on both convoys. On PQ17 we had finished up as a disorganised shambles, feeling disgusted, dismayed, discouraged, and utterly shocked at the way things had gone. But after JW51B we thought, 'That's a smack in the eye for you, Jerry', and 'Who's doing the shouting now?' If the backing and trust of those in command at the Admiralty, had been given to those in command of the escorts on convoy PQ17, in July 1942, there would have been another successful convoy of ships for Russia. There would have been losses of course, but not on the same scale as those that did happen, though I realize that in saying those words, that I am being wise after the event. I only hope that the men of the merchant navies who were left to their fates, have seen fit to forgive us after all these years. It was not the fault of the ordinary sailors that they were abandoned, nor those of the officers in command of the escort ships. All of us would have seen it through, come hell or high water, make no mistake about that.

CHAPTER EIGHT

Leaving the *Gem* for the Last Time

This leave from the *Northern Gem* after our return from Russia, was to prove my last from her. Arriving back in Belfast, we found that the minor repair jobs onboard had been completed, and we now got down to the work of getting stores onboard, cleaning the ship up and getting her ready for sea again. We had the usual shore leave, the odd pub crawl, met old friends, made new ones. Then we sailed out of Belfast once more, helping to escort the convoys of ships out to Iceland, or on the first leg of their journey to the various destinations around the world to which they were bound. If we sailed out into the vast and open spaces of the Atlantic, we would still stay with the ships until we reached the halfway boundary, then switch over to another lot of ships that were on their way back to England and home.

Our job then would be to shepherd this new flock of ours, laden down as they were with food and war materials, both below and above decks some looking for all the world like huge piles of timber, with mast bridge and funnel stuck on the top, in the general direction of the Western Approaches, and say to ourselves, 'Well, that's that bit over, thank God, Now we are on the homeward trek.'

Some of these convoys turned out to be rougher than others. On one nothing untoward would happen, and then the next one would turn out to be a running battle with the U-boats. There were occasions when one or other of these U-boats got into the centre of the convoy, and created havoc amongst the merchant ships before the escorts found and attacked them. Rumours were rife on these occasions: such and such a corvette had clobbered a U-boat on the surface, and that her skipper had been so incensed that he did not stop to pick up any survivors, but just kept running them down until none were left. Now this may or may not have been true, but I do know the feeling after having seen some of your own countrymen, going down with their ships with no chance to be picked up, others, smothered in fuel oil, and choking and coughing their hearts up, their lungs burning away inside their bodies. Then there were those who froze to death before your eyes, just out of reach, and all you could say was, 'Christ almighty, I can't get to him'. Why such things were allowed to happen I don't suppose that I shall ever know.

What was to prove to be the last trip that I would do on the old *Northern Gem*, began on either 21st or 22nd of April 1943, when we sailed from Londonderry to join up with a convoy bound across the Atlantic, consisting of forty-two vessels, and was, from the way we waddled through the water when we had taken up our position on the starboard quarter, a slow convoy of about six or seven knots. After about a week or so during which the weather had been very bad with strong to gale force winds and heavy seas, causing the merchant ships quite a problem as a lot of them were in ballast, and they were being flung about like empty cans, by the long and turbulent heaving seas of the North Atlantic, we of the escort vessels were beginning to get weary from trying to keep the forty-two ships within the convoy confines.

The *Northern Gem*, although pirouetting about like a cork, was nevertheless weathering the storms well. She took nothing in the way of heavy water onboard, but was continuously being swept by spray and spume, which travelling at the speed of bullets, rat-tat-tatted on the bridge windows, making the look-outs on the top bridge, which was open to everything that the weather could throw at it, duck down below the canvas screens fastened to the rails forming the outer limits of the navigation bridge. In weather like this one was nearly always wet through, no amount of oilskins or protective clothing was adequate enough to keep one dry. Fortunately in the majority of trawlers, the engine room staff would always allow you to hang your wet and soaking gear to dry on a line stretched above the engines.

So now on a northerly course to pass to the west of Iceland, ONS5 wallowed its way along through the heavy seas, the escorts pulling out all the stops trying to keep the convoy together, not wanting to let the ships wander off to split up into small groups. This was no small task in the prevailing weather, and for the four trawlers whose top speed in fine conditions was ten or eleven knots, it was a problem to catch up with the convoy again, once they had been dispatched to round up the stragglers. Once alongside a straggler, to tell him to wind the elastic up a bit, the few words of reply that were not being blown away by the wind, were nothing short of blasphemy, but more often than not they gave us something to laugh about, even though it was a serious game we were playing.

Once we had passed Iceland, and turned on to a more westerly course towards Newfoundland, the wind and seas eased down considerably, and soon we had a smooth calm sea with a long rolling swell, common to the deeper water of the North Atlantic. This was U-boat weather, and soon we suffered the first casualty, the American freighter *McKeesport*, which was hit by a torpedo around about breakfast time on 29th April. As we were the nearest trawler to her, we were sent back to pick up the survivors from her. Her crew never got their feet wet as they came alongside the *Gem* in one of the ship's lifeboats and climbed comfortably onto our deck. The only exceptions were two dead men whom they had towed from the stricken *McKeesport*, who were given a burial held in front of all their shipmates, the service being read from a well thumbed Bible.

This was the stage of the war when I first began to realise that the strain was beginning to get at me. I had been almost four years in the *Northern Gem*, and much of that time had been continuous sea-time, I really did not know how much longer I would be able to stick it out, but I would not give in voluntarily, as to me that would have been cowardly. So I decided to say nothing for the time being and to stick it out until I could face it no longer. As coxswain I felt it my duty not to show fear in front of the crew, even though I felt it as much as they did at times. It was that thought which kept me going, for I like to think that they looked to me for courage and support, but the strain was terrific.

The larger escorts were now beginning to run short of fuel; at first it had been the bad weather which had stopped them refuelling, but now that the seas had flattened out a little and the wind had gone, the threat of enemy action put them off, for it was too dangerous for the escorts to hang on to the end of a fuel line from a tanker for too long.

We had so many survivors onboard, that Mullender had to get permission from the escort commander (I believe) to leave the convoy and head for Newfoundland on our own, as we were down to a state of severe rationing, both of food and water. Due to the speed of the convoy if we had stayed with it, we should have had neither food nor water to last the remainder of the trip. There were about two hundred and fifty merchant seamen spread out all over the ship by the time we got permission to leave. I have a blank spot about parts of this voyage, probably caused by the state of my nerves, the constant attacks on the convoy, the lying stopped while picking up men from the water during the attacks. All this coupled with the worry of sleeping, feeding, and fending for all onboard, caused me to lose track of the majority of events which were going on around me.

Leaving the convoy was a relief in one sense, but it only increased the worry for Mullender. I think that we were all a little reluctant to leave, and yet at the same time perfectly glad to do so, if one can understand that kind of muddle-headed reasoning. When we left, Skipper Mullender decided that it would be better if we made for the ice, as we had done the previous year, on the PQ17 debacle, knowing that if we reached it without being attacked, there would be a better chance of surviving to reach St John's. The ice, this early summer of 1943, was much further south than was normal for this time of year, and although there were a few thick patches of fog here and there which to some extent we were pleased to see, there were also patches of clear blue sunny skies, and the little bit of wind which was helping the movement of the ice south, was enough to burn the skin if you were not careful. Three of our stokers, fed up with the very crowded conditions of the mess deck, decided to sleep out in the open on top of the engine room casing, and later found themselves in some trouble with severe wind and sun burn. They went in front of the CO for not being able to carry out their duties, and were very fortunate to get off with a caution from Mullender, who said he thought that they were suffering enough from the burns and from letting their mates down through their stupidity, but he warned them not to come in front of him again with a similar thing.

We were not short of look-outs for most of the men we had picked up came along and volunteered for something or other, either below deck in the bunkers or stoke-hold or engine room, or on the deck as extra lookouts or watch keepers. But there were still the few, as we had found on other occasions, who would go below for no one, not even to eat or sleep, for the thought of what would happen if the *Northern Gem* were to be torpedoed was never very far from anyone's mind. With close on three hundred men onboard, most of us realised that being on deck would not help much in the event anyway. If she had got one under the forward mess deck where the magazine was situated, we'd not have known a thing, and if hit in the engine room she would have gone like one of those iron ore carriers which we had seen vanish before our eyes.

Then of course there was the ice. Small floes were not so bad for our ice-cracker bows were a big help there. It was the very big bergs that worried us; they were like great cliffs or shaped similar to cathedrals, and if we had run into one of those stem on then that would have been the end.

Not many days later, looming up out of the fog, we saw the dark bulk of the land, and quite suddenly we were in brilliant sunshine again, and there ahead we saw the two great headlands, denoting the entrance to the natural harbour of St John's Newfoundland. As we approached, the coastguard station on the top of one of the high cliffs which stick up so solidly out of the sea, started flashing to us wanting to know who we were and where we were from. The sea between us and the headlands was as smooth and as shiny as a sheet of glass, and as we steamed into the hive of activity that was St John's Harbour, I looked out of the bridge windows to see that both our port and starboard rails were packed with men all staring, in wonder of the fact that we had got there at all. We could see some of the other escorts of our group, and I wondered what had happened to the convoy after we left.

It was the last time I saw any action with the *Gem* and her crew, for it was to be my last trip in her, and also Skipper Mullender's.

I steered the *Gem* in between the headlands, and up to the quayside of St John's. The worry and the strain of the last week or so gradually gave way to a feeling of excitement, born first from the relief of tension, secondly from the knowledge that at last we had arrived safely, and thirdly, that we had never before been right across the 'pond', the Atlantic. True we had seen the coast and the mountains of that icy land called Greenland, whilst searching for survivors in the Denmark Straits some time before, but this was the first time that we had actually gone into a harbour on the other side of the pond, and put our mooring ropes ashore.

Our first task now, once the survivors had been taken ashore, was to get back to a normal routine, with all hands taking part in a general clean up of the ship, getting her shipshape and Bristol fashion once again, and did she need it! The accumulation of oil on the decks took some removing, especially in the messdecks where oily clothing had been cut off some of the survivors as they had been taken below. Most of this discarded clothing had been gathered up and put into the sacks dumped on to the jetty for disposal by burning; any other discarded clothing which could be used again, was placed in other bags ready to be sent ashore to a laundry for washing, and when they were returned clean, they would be put below with the rest of the remaining survivors kits in the store, ready to use again.

Previously, it had cost the crew of the *Gem* money from their own pockets, in order to replace their own gear from the 'slops' ashore, which they had given to the survivors that we had picked up. We did not begrudge doing this at all, far from it, but there had been times when we, or some of us, had nothing left to change into at all. This gave us the idea of washing any clothing left behind ourselves, for the future use of men pulled from the sea, and even when we started to get these 'survivors' kits' onboard the idea stuck, and helped us no end. All the men who had been picked up on this last trip and had needed a change of clothing, had been given a survivor's bag. By and large it was mostly the engineers and firemen who had been below and had not had time to dash to their cabins for some warm clothing who needed it the most. It also was these poor devils who were the casualties or the missing when a ship was hit by torpedoes and sunk.

After the chores were finished and the survivors whisked away, shore leave was given to all except a minimum of men who were to keep a watch on board in the event of the ship having to be moved to a different part of the harbour. Those who went ashore did so, or so they said, with the idea of finding something to take home to their girl friends, wives or mothers. Then there were those who did not get past the first bar or club, some went to the cinema, others had their own ideas of what shore leave consisted of, though this did not appeal to as many as rumour has it. With our signalman Charlie Keen, I and one or two more of the communications branch had a run ashore to do a bit of shopping and to have a look around the place. As far as I can remember from the short time that we were there, it reminded me of a frontier town of the kind that you saw on the films in those days, as I suppose it was really. We then went back to the *Gem*, dumped our parcels and got changed into some old clothes, then walked around the harbour towards the outlet to the sea. Once there we climbed to the top of one of the headlands, the sort of exercise we required after being cooped up on the ship. The view from the top was well worth the climb. Looking out to seaward we could see for miles and miles out over the calm sunlit waters of the Atlantic, and we sat and talked about how lucky we were to have made it so far, and wondered how many poor devils were still trying to reach this peaceful haven. On the way to the top of this headland, we had passed several pools of water which were crystal clear; someone suggested a swim and I think that we were all in agreement, until some one came forward with the idea that we touch the water first. When we did we realised that these were pools of melted ice and snow. I'm sure they would have given us a heart attack if we had dived in first. Charlie Keen and I were taken back in our thoughts to Norway where we had been prisoners of the Germans in May 1940;

there was a similarity in the terrain and certainly in the coldness of the ice pools. Charlie and I joined the *Northern Gem* together in September 39, and he was to remain with her until she herself was demobbed in 1945.

The ships in the harbour looked like toy boats moving across a pond and not the huge merchant vessels which they really were. If we had not known where the *Northern Gem* lay we would never have been able to pick her out at all. She appeared so tiny that we all voiced the same opinion, that you would not think a ship of that size could cross the Atlantic. Yet she had done so, as had many others, some much smaller than her. On our walk around the town, we noticed that most of the buildings were constructed of wood, and that they were painted in many colours, the whole town being surrounded by large trees. It was indeed showing a resemblance to the scenery in North Russia.

Soon we were on the move again, this time to join a convoy which had left Halifax in Nova Scotia a day or so earlier. We were to be one of the escorts to help it reach the confines of the Western Approaches safely, our own destination Liverpool. In spite of our forecasts of another great convoy battle with many ships sunk and a host of survivors to pick up, surprisingly we had a comparatively quiet journey home. None of us realised it at the time, but there were apparently very few U-boats remaining in the North Atlantic, for their losses had been so great over the months of May and June, that they had been withdrawn to other areas, by their Commander in Chief Admiral Dönitz. From that time on the battleground of the Atlantic, remained fairly quiet to what it had been over the previous years. But quiet or not, this was to be the last time I would cross the Atlantic towards the New World. My time in the *Northern Gem* was coming to an end the closer we got to England.

After a quiet voyage during which time we all lived like fighting cocks, (veal, ham, beef, and pork, you name it we had it to eat – in fact believe it or not, it was a pleasant change to get baked beans on a piece of fried bread) we arrived at the approaches to the Irish Sea, where we were despatched from the convoy to proceed to Liverpool. Skipper Mullender sent for me to tell me that when we got alongside, his relief would be waiting, and that he would be going ashore straightaway, this time for good, and we all said our farewells. Mine in particular, for he had been a good friend to me. His parting words to me were, 'You won't be long after me, Cox. Look me up when you get back to Lowestoft.'

We put to sea again for reasons which I cannot remember now, but we returned the next day to Liverpool, putting into one of the docks this time. It was not long before Mr Pooley came down to see me, to tell me that my relief would be onboard the next day.

Strangely enough my relief was another Hull man, an ex-fisherman like myself. I had known him slightly, as I gathered all my personal belongings together, I found one or two things which I thought would be more useful on the *Gem* than if I took them with me, my Arctic clothing for instance, I should not want them while I sat for my mate's certificate in Lowestoft.

After my last walk around the *Gem*, I said goodbye to those of the officers and men that I had known for so long, hoisted my case and kit-bag onto the quayside, and made my way to the railway station, taking a last look back before I got behind the cargo sheds on the dock side, and out of sight of the ship that had been my home for so long. I had brought her into harbour and into the dock for the last time without a pilot, or any orders or interference from any of the officers, and she had become like an extension of my right arm, if anyone can understand what I mean. On odd occasions I had stood four hours on and four hours off watch for one or other of the officers when they had been under the weather through illness. And apart from the small part of her that I keep in my heart, plus the key and brass identity disc of the oilskin locker which I still have to this day, my best and most cherished memento is a letter written by Mullender some years later in which he told me, 'You are the best coxswain that I had all the time I was in the service'. I cherish this letter for that, and because I believe him to be the best skipper that I went to sea with, I would have gone anywhere with him, for he understood men and was very fair in his dealings with his crew on the occasions that he had to deal out punishment for their misdemeanours. Very rarely did he lose his temper or vent his spleen on anyone, be it officer or rating. I don't want to appear big-headed when I say this, but the *Northern Gem* was a damn good ship, and she had a good and contented crew, because of the mutual respect between officers and men. Not many vessels were so lucky.

Back into peacetime dress – *Northern Gem* entering Grimsby docks after returning from a fishing voyage to the Arctic circle 1949-50.

Taken during an Atlantic convoy on a quiet day. 1943.

The author – photographed by RN Commander whilst taking panoramic views of Maddaloni harbour and anchorage from *Sidi Ifni's* motor launch. 1944.

The armed trawler *Northern Gem* refitting at Liverpool after the author had left her. (*Photo Imperial War Museum*).

CHAPTER NINE

The African Coastal Flotilla

After the fall of France, a clandestine boating organisation was set up under DDOD (1) at the Admiralty with the object of organising operations on occupied Europe. Agents had to be taken to and from occupied countries both for sabotage and for secret intelligence purposes. It operated from Gibraltar until the Allied Landings in North Africa in November 1942 and then moved its HQ to Algiers and became the African Coastal Flotilla. They continued their former functions, and as the Allies progressed through Italy coordinated their activities, picking up escaped prisoners of war and carrying out sabotage operations.

Arriving at Lowestoft I was given some digs, and was luckily sent home on two weeks' leave a day or so later. I was in a way disappointed for when I mentioned that I had been relieved from the *Northern Gem* to come back to Europe to sit for my mate's ticket, I was told that these classes had stopped.

Reaching home again I should have felt great, but somehow this time I felt like a lost sheep, for something had gone out of my life. I was a bit apprehensive as to what would happen to me once I got back to Lowestoft now.

It was while I was at home on this leave that my mother said to me very casually one day that she had seen Gladys, and that she had been to tea at our house. I had been thinking a lot about her on and off for the last couple of months, wondering if she had got herself a new boyfriend, and when I talked about her to mother, she said, 'Why don't you go and see her? She is only on the barrage balloon site, at the top of Pickering Road, only five minutes or so walk from our house. But I just could not bring myself to go there. I found out later that it would not have done me any good if I had as she had been moved to another balloon site on the other side of Hull the week before, and anyway by this time my leave was just about up. There seemed to be none of my old friends around in Hull, and I got fed up with going to see relatives, I did not know what to talk to them about. I think that it was the worst leave that I had been home on for that reason. I was happy to be home with my parents, of course, but I still felt that there was something missing, and it was in that sort of mood that I went off to the station to start my journey back to Lowestoft.

I passed for leading hand while I was there, and did quite a bit of square bashing and guard duty, and at sometime in August I heard that the Navy were looking for men to volunteer for a naval battalion, being set up ready for the second front. I thought to myself, 'That's not for you, Sid; if you're going to hand in your chips you're going to do it at sea, and not in the mud of some foreign land, fighting like your Dad did in the first war.'

So as soon as I heard that, I made for the drafting office and asked what the chances were of getting back onto an anti-submarine trawler. I was told that there was no chance whatsoever at that time. After giving the situation some thought, I promptly put my name down as a volunteer for the Special Service, thinking in terms of landing craft, or something like them. I wasn't really worried what it was as long as I was back on a ship, and at sea again. I wanted to get away from the Nest and out of reach of the possibility of being sent to the naval battalion. My main hope was that I would be sent to the Coastal Forces, but now that I had volunteered, I would have to wait and see now just what would come of it and where I would finish up.

As I gave my name in for Special Service, I got the impression that they could not get my name down quickly enough. They nearly snatched my hand off when I passed them my pay-book. I was relieved of any classes that I was on, and any guard duties immediately, and within three days I was on my way home on embarkation leave, prior to my being sent somewhere overseas. Two days before I volunteered I had written to Gladys, and the day before I went home on my embarkation leave I had a reply. I had asked her if she was going out with anyone else, and if not, would she care to see us both back together again, and would she meet me when I got home again whenever that would be. Now that I knew that I was going home on leave the next day, I answered her letter, in which she told me that she would like to go out with me again, and that there was no one else. This time I asked her if she would like to get engaged, and that I would see her at the balloon site at the top of Pickering Road when I got home for her answer.

I had no need to go to the balloon site, however, for when I arrived home she was there waiting for me. When we managed to be on our own, she told me that she would like to become engaged to me, and that she had been waiting and hoping for news of this kind from me ever since we had drifted apart some two to three years previously. I had not known that she felt like this about me, and deep down I must have felt the same way about her though in the early part of the war I was obsessed by a fear of my getting too close to someone, with marriage in mind, only to have to go away and not return. I hated to think that I would leave some girl in this way. Now I thought differently. I realized that she was the only girl I wanted, and getting engaged would give me more incentive to look after myself. We were both over the moon, and head over heels in love with each other. Our parents were delighted at the news and said that they always knew that it would happen this way. No time was lost now in shopping for an engagement ring, even though it was just a plain one. We had a quiet engagement, but one with much happiness. All we could talk about now was how long the war would last, where was I being sent to and how long I would be away from home. Even though the war with Germany at that time looked as if it would not last much longer, there were still the Japanese to contend with, and deep down in my heart, I was hoping that I would not be sent out there.

Of course we talked of marriage with the innocence of most young couples, but when we did it was always of 'When I got home', and not 'if I got home'. We went to cinema shows, but mostly for walks around the area, and on many of them we would see, if it was about seven pm, the bombers forming up over the river, ready to start off for a raid, their wings reflecting the sunlight. They used to go round in circles until they were all airborne, and then make for the coast in the direction of Norfolk. I felt sorry for them as I could imagine how they were feeling. Each night when I got her back to the balloon site for ten o'clock, the WAAF sergeant used to say to us, 'It's all clear. Duty Officer has done his rounds, off you go and be back at midnight'. We owed a lot to all the girls on the Railway Site as it was known, because of their help in covering for Gladys on several occasions when she should have been on duty. They knew that I was going abroad somewhere, as Gladys had told them that I was on embarkation leave, so it was thanks to all the girls and their Sergeant that we really enjoyed my leave, and were able to spend more time together than we really should have had.

This leave seemed to fly past quicker than any other one that I'd had, and all good things must come to an end. It had been marred by one sad happening; my younger sister, Mavis, then about fifteen, was taken into the hospital for an operation for appendicitis, but I was able to go and see her at any time.

On my last evening at home we found ourselves at the back of St

Nicholas Church at the top of Pickering Road, and it was there at the back of this church, where we hoped some day to be married, that we embraced and spoke so much of our love for each other, and of our hopes for the future. That was the last time we saw each other for almost two more years.

I set off from home feeling very much down in the dumps. More than ever I was wishing now that this war would soon be over, and that our lives would soon return to normal, I had been nineteen and a half when the war had started and I had been called up as a reservist, and here I was almost twenty-three and a half years old already. At that time in 1943, the end looked as far away as ever. The Germans had been pushed out of North Africa, but the struggle for Italy was on. I had this feeling that I should finish up somewhere in the Far East, and I dreaded the thought of it. Back at the Sparrows Nest, I reported to the drafting office, and was told to go to my digs for the rest of the day, but to report back first thing in the morning.

The next morning with my shoes polished brightly I arrived on the dot at the desk in the drafting office, eager now to hear what the fates or the drafting officer had in store for me. There were seven of us present in the office and while we were waiting, we got talking and realised that we were all Special Service volunteers. The drafting officer came out and called out my name, Leading Seaman Kerslake, and it was then we were told that the seven of us were to be one boat's crew with myself as leading hand in charge of them. My first job was to see that we all received our inoculations and injections that morning. In the afternoon we were to pick up our tropical kit from the stores after which we could go back to our digs, reporting back to the drafting office in the morning to be told of our destination.

None of us fainted during our visit to the sick bay, I'm pleased to say, but I think that they all suffered as I did for the rest of the day from a stiff arm, and as we all marched off to the stores to be kitted out, we must have looked like a squad of windmills going along as we swung our arms around in circles to stir up the circulation to dissipate the stuff they had pumped into us. Next morning I was told that as yet they had no orders for me and my crew, and that as long as we presented ourselves at the office at the same time each morning, they were not bothered what we got up to for the rest of the day. This went on for several days, during which time we got to know a little of each other, then finally on 23rd October 1943, we got our marching orders.

The following day, we left the Nest, our destination being Algiers on the coast of North Africa. The first leg was to London, and then on to Swansea where we were, during the hours of darkness, ferried out to an American Liberty Ship. Once we arrived at Algiers, according to my orders, I with my crew would take over a petrol-driven motor boat, which had been a prewar pleasure boat and her name was believe it or not, the *Wild Bill*. What I had to do when I took her over, I had no idea as no one in the drafting office at HMS *Europa* could tell me anything more, except that she (or was it a he with that name?) belonged to the African Coastal Flotilla. Whatever that outfit was once again no one knew.

Getting aboard the Liberty ship just after midnight, we were taken to our quarters, a space in number two hold, just forward of the bridge, but below decks. It was quite compact, with about twenty steel-meshed bunks, which folded up against the ship's side when not in use. In the middle of the deck was a mess table long enough for twenty men to sit around in comfort, but on this trip only the seven of us occupied the mess. The meals which we received en route to Algiers were very good indeed; much better and with more variety than we had been used to on our own ships. For breakfast, just to mention one meal of each day, we could have as many eggs as we could eat, fried, boiled, poached or scrambled, or whatever the way the cook had decided to do them on that particular morning. The other meals were just as good and by the time we arrived at our destination, Algiers, I had put on quite a bit of weight, something I had not done for some time.

The only thing that worried me on the voyage, was the fact that we had been told that below us in the hold, was a cargo of TNT and aviation fuel in drums. Whether this was true or not it caused us some anxious moments, especially just after we had got through the Straits of Gibraltar during the night, and the convoy was attacked by aircraft just before dawn and while it was still dark.

What the number of the convoy was I never found out, but when the daylight came on our first morning at sea, I was on the deck and had seen the sun come up over the horizon. I had a good look around to port and starboard, and came to the conclusion that we were in the company of at least thirty or so more merchant vessels, that we were the fourth ship in the column and the column was the second from the port side, and there seemed to be quite a good escort around the convoy, which bucked me up no end. As we had nothing to do at all, I had a walk around the deck, noting where things of interest to me were positioned, such as liferafts and boats, also gun positions; then I went below to my bunk to catch up on some sleep, and hopefully to put some under my belt for future use. Only small things these, but one never knew when they would come in handy.

The sea was calm, and what bit of swell there was caused the vessel to roll slightly, quite a different motion to that of a trawler. Also the sea gradually got bluer than I had ever seen it before, and the bow waves made by the other ships in the convoy, cleaving their way through the calm waters, seemed to be much whiter and a lot frothier than those I'd seen in northern waters.

All went well and there were no attacks by U-boats on the convoy, and one evening just before it got dark, we could just see the vague outline of some land which we were told were the approaches to the Mediterranean, and so we passed between Spain and the coast of North Africa, through the Straits while we were asleep. But early the following morning while it was still dark and we were still asleep, we were awakened by the clanging of the alarm bells. We shot up on to the deck, and just as quickly threw ourselves onto the deck, and behind the shelter of the ship's rail. The Yanks were shouting to us at the top of their voices, 'Get down you, goddam Limeys, there's a f---- air-raid on'. Air-raid! It seemed as if all the ships in the convoy were firing at one another. From where I sat on the deck I looked up and could see lines of tracer, brilliant in the early morning cold air, passing between our ship's bridge and the foremast and just above the ship's rail. It was too bloody dangerous to attempt to stand up. Even the gunners on the platforms on both the port and starboard sides of the foredeck were shooting the rigging to pieces on their own ship, and how they missed hitting the bridge at times I shall never know. I'll bet that those on duty up there on that bridge must have been in fear of their lives. I've never seen anything like it before or since.

We never throughout the attack either saw or heard any aircraft, but all of a sudden we felt rather than heard, an explosion, and looking from our position on the deck, we saw a ship about four columns away on our starboard side with what appeared to be a small fire on her foredeck. Within seconds the whole hull of the vessel seemed to glow a dark red, though there were no flames; then from a dark red it changed to a bright red glow, just as suddenly the whole ship exploded and disintegrated in front of our eyes. Everyone dropped down flat below the ship's rail, for in the excitement we had all got to our feet without having noticed it. Now I shouted for those nearby to get under cover for it literally rained red hot chunks of iron and steel. When it had finished, all of us looked out to where the ship had been, feeling for the crew, and thinking what a sudden end it had been to their lives. But we were wrong as it happened, for not one life had been lost. All the crew had got away quickly in the lifeboats, and even though they had only managed to get some two or three hundred yards away from the stricken ship when she blew up, the blast had gone straight up into the air, and left the boats and the men untouched. It is surprising the way explosions and the blast from them behave; the same thing never seems to happen twice over. According to the report we had from some of the American crew of the ship we were on, the ship that exploded had been hit by a delayed action bomb, hence the escape of her crew.

All the time the attack was going on, we seemed to be in more danger from the gunfire of the other ships in the columns on either side of us, and we could hear the thwack as something hit the ship every so often, as well as seeing the tracer shells whipping just over the decks. It was a very hairy do, but no one was hurt on board. Apart from the rigging there were holes in the funnel and the superstructure made by the projectiles from other ships. Soon the attack was over, and for the remainder of the voyage there were no more scares. The last day at sea was quite a hot one, and I lapped up the sun as though there was going to be no tomorrow. My skin was beginning to turn a nice browny shade, I have always been fortunate that way. I never have seemed to burn and look like freshly cooked lobster as other people do.

We entered the harbour of Algiers, and the anchor was dropped, and I was told to have my party ready to leave the ship. A signal had been sent to the base onshore to let them know that we were onboard, and shortly afterwards a motor launch came up alongside, and we were told that it had come to collect us. We lowered our bags into it and then went down the long rope ladder hung down the ship's side and stepped into the boat ourselves, when we were all seated the coxswain let go and we headed in for the International Quay. Amongst the ships which we passed on the way in to the quay was a very smart steam yacht, painted in battleship grey, at anchor in the harbour, but no name could be seen to tell who she was.

On arriving at the quayside we found a fifteen hundredweight truck waiting for us; we were told to throw our gear into it and then climb aboard ourselves. Not long afterwards we found ourselves reversing the procedure as we had arrived at the gates of HMS

Hannibal, the naval shore base at Algiers. I reported to the office of the Master at Arms, told him who I was and passed over the papers that I had with me, these gave him the reason for us being there. He in turn told me that apart from the message from the American ship telling of the arrival of naval ratings from the UK, he had no further knowledge of us and why we should be there. They knew of no motor launch named the *Wild Bill*, and had no idea what the African Coastal Flotilla was, or where it could be. All I could say was 'What do we do now then, Sir'. I was told that they would make some enquiries, and until they found something out for us, we should be taken on to the strength of the base for the time being; nothing more could be done now except to wait and pray.

For a week we did nothing but play cards, sleep and play cards again, and then I was told that the *Wild Bill*, the boat we had come out here to take over, was still back in England somewhere. My thoughts about this can hardly be printed here. Of the African Coastal Flotilla, it was such a secret outfit, that they themselves did not know where they were, and consequently could not tell anyone. At least that's what the situation seemed to be. However investigations as to their whereabouts were still going on, and they would tell me as soon as they found out. In the meantime, we were turned into a street patrol, given white gaiters and belts and an arm band telling all sundry that we were in effect naval police. We had a roster for duties, and instructed each night as to what we were to do. This included, among other things, patrolling certain areas of the town out of bounds to the forces in Algiers, where some of the worst brothels were situated. Occasionally we had to enter one of the brothels which Allied troops were allowed to patronize, to make certain that things inside were quiet and normal. Never having been in one of those places in my life before I certainly had my eyes opened, seeing the soldiers, sailors and airmen of all nationalities watching the various non-virtuous ladies walking about, until they were eventually paired off with one or other of the waiting steaming troops. After all this time only one name sticks in my mind, the most popular (I believe), known as the 'Black Cat'.

Like the other members of my party, I did not mind the patrols that we took part in during the daylight hours, but at night I confess I felt like the others a little bit scared, more so after we were told of the finding of the naked bodies of the Wren and a chief petty officer. They had been mutilated beyond belief in the most obscene way. The description of their injuries made me feel sick, and took my mind back to a night in Belfast, when I had been in the *Northern Gem*, when two Wrens were found stripped naked, and bound to a lamp post. They had been tarred and feathered, but at least they were still alive and had not been molested in any other way. On another night patrol in Algiers which I can remember, we were called to a very large ship which was berthed at the International Quay; there was a great fight going on, both on the gangway and just inside the ship. This time we had been on standby. We were in the guardroom when the order came that this disturbance was taking place, and we were all rushed to the vessel in a fifteen hundredweight truck. In overall charge was a chief gunner, and in no time at all the commotion was all over. Some of the combatants lay in the bottom of the truck; they had all of them too much to drink, one or two had bloody heads due to not taking notice of the batons the sailors of the patrol were waving around their heads at the time, and they were all taken to the guardroom at the barracks for the night to cool off. The town of Algiers was no place to roam about in at night especially on one's own. It was best to go about in groups for safety, although it was a town full of servicemen of all nations at the time, hell bent on enjoying themselves in the best possible way that they could think of.

Three weeks passed by, two of them patrolling the town; it had been something out of the ordinary for us to do, and at least it kept us occupied. One morning during the fourth week of our stay at the barracks, I was called in to the Regulating Office, and with a smile on his face, the officer told me:

'At last we have found the headquarters of the African Coastal Flotilla for you and your crew.'

Within a couple of hours I was reporting to the First Lieutenant of the *Sid Ifni*, which turned out to be the steam yacht painted battleship grey, that we had passed in the harbour when we first arrived. The first lieutenant was a Scotsman from a small fishing port on the east coast of Scotland, and in civilian life in the days before the war, he had been a teacher. As there was nowhere else to send us at the moment we were to be kept on as the crew of the *Sidi Ifni*. Until we went onboard of her, the whole complement consisted of a captain RNR, the first lieutenant RNR, an engineer commander RNR, a radio operator, a cook, two stokers, and two seamen. Work such as cleaning the ship and any other ordinary chores was done by local North African people brought onboard each morning for that purpose, then taken ashore at night – all this on a ship engaged on a highly secret job.

As I was a leading seaman and once again the senior deck rating on board, I found myself as acting coxswain, the motor mechanic that I had brought with me went below in charge of the two stokers, the cook went to assist 'Taps', the resident cook, and the four seamen of my crew joined the other two, giving me six men to work with on deck. The local help was dispensed with, and the *Sidi Ifni* became a self-contained unit once more. It wasn't long before I found that I was more or less in charge of the running of the ship, for the officers had their hands full for most of the twenty-four hours in any day. There seemed to be a constant stream of visitors coming onboard at all times, who had to be met by a quartermaster armed with a revolver in a holster. Each visitor who came up the side ladder was asked to sign the book kept for that purpose; whether the signatures were their real ones or not I don't know, and never enquired. Some of them came at the dead of night, and were whisked down below out of sight. As far as I am aware, the only people who knew who the visitors were, were the captain and the first lieutenant.

Only once did the first lieutenant mention the people who came aboard to me; he said that there were men and women of many countries coming onboard, even Germans and Italians. They were instructed not to talk to anyone, and by the same rule none of the crew must talk to them or ask them questions. When we had first come onboard, there was a fifteen foot motor launch, covered over and secured to the deck, the visitors being brought to the *Sidi Ifni*, by a boat loaned from some place onshore, but the very next day, the ship's own launch was put into service, and from then on it became my responsibility to pick up these people, and then drop them back onshore, I was instructed what I was to do, where to pick them up and where to drop them again. Before so long I found out and it was confirmed by the first lieutenant, that the *Sidi Ifni* was a transit vessel for spies and other clandestine operations, but during the whole of my time on her I never once held a conversation with any visitor.

Sidi Ifni was, as I have said before, a smart-looking steam yacht, and was also a cargo-carrying yacht; she had a large hold forward which contained many canoes and folding boats as well as rubber and wooden pram dinghies. There was also a work bench for repairing these craft in the hold. Forward of this was the seamen's mess deck, reached from the deck by a steep ladder. The wardroom which was amidships and at deck level was something to see; the windows were shaped like the windows in a church, pointed at the top; the floor and the walls inside were entirely tiled, like a mosque and the woodwork was beautiful polished mahogany complete with lovely carvings. The table and chairs each had carvings on the legs, and leading down to a central passageway below was one of the most lovely flights of stairs that I have ever seen, fully carpeted, and with carved hand rails.

In my berth I had all the furniture I required, an ordinary single bed, wardrobe chest of drawers and a nice desk, and carpets on the floor. There was a huge porthole in the ship's hull, which when open let in a flow of fresh air. The cabin was complete in every way, including rather large rats which used to scurry around at night chased by my cat Ginger who invited himself onboard one night and followed me from the launch and down to my cabin where he stayed up to my leaving the ship.

I gathered that the *Sidi Ifni* was originally a North African ship, and then became Spanish owned. Following this she had apparently got into the hands of the Germans who had used her as a kind of supply ship to U-boats, carrying reliefs for any of the crews who were sick or injured; she was suspected of being a floating brothel, and looking at the way she was fitted out she would have made a good one I'm sure.

She was a vessel of around a thousand gross tonnes, built in the year of 1892, and taken into the government service on 20th February 1943 as a prize ship. She was used as an accommodation ship until May 1945 for Special Operations including the landing of agents on the enemy-held coasts of the Mediterranean, using boats such as the one that I had come over to take on, the *Wild Bill*, and fishing boats, (feluccas), and later on converted PT Boats, (American-built Short Boats).

I think it was about or getting on for the end of November 1943 when I was first told that there was a move in the offing. I got orders from the first lieutenant to put the ship in order for going to sea. Where we were moving to no one would say for certain; first it was said to be Sardinia, later this was altered to Bastia in Corsica. It was known that both of these islands were now in Allied hands, and it was also known to us that there was a forward base for our feluccas at Bastia, set up by some of the working ACF lads. The engineer Mr Barnes came to me and asked if I would get one of my lads to go down in the fore hold and dig out the paraffin navigation lights, and get them cleaned up and in working order. This was done.

Then the CO and the first lieutenant called me into the wardroom and asked me to join in with them in discussing the arming of the *Sidi*

Ifni against air attack during our sea voyage. The CO, by the way, had a Polar Medal for he had been with Shackleton earlier in his life. He said at this discussion that we should be lucky to get five knots out of her, and that she would be a so and so to steer if there was any sea running. After some thought and talk, it was decided to bring up six Lewis guns from the armoury below decks, and three would be spaced out down each side of the ship. As there were no fittings or proper stands to fit them to, I was asked to try and lash them loosely to the ship's rail, so that they were slack enough to be able to move the guns around, but tight enough to stop them from falling out of the lashings and into the sea, if it became necessary for us to shoot them off. Whoever manned them in the case of an attack would either have to be on their knees or lie flat on the deck, on their backs. There would be no cover for anyone at all on the decks. All the working parts of the steering gear were oiled and greased, loosened and tightened, and mucked about with generally. There was not much else to do on the deck, and Mr Barnes was getting his clockwork in order, and so to all intents and purposes, we were about ready to put to sea. We kept our fingers crossed ready for when we sailed, praying that the weather would stay fine and that it would be a quiet trip, wherever it was we were bound for. And if we were attacked we had plenty of weapons such as rifles, stripped Lewis guns, and revolvers. Even that helped to cheer us up.

CHAPTER TEN

MGB177

About 17th December 1943, the ropes were cast off from the quay at Algiers, and we now knew that we were going all being well, to the island of Maddalena, situated in the Straits of Bonifacio, between the larger islands of Sardinia and Corsica. This would bring us nearer to the beaches of the south of France and the coast of Italy, and we should be much closer to our brood of fishing boats. This was the most important thing of all, for in the past some of them had been forced to stay at sea off the enemy coasts for up to two weeks.

Our CO had been correct in his assumption that we should get no more than five knots out of her, and, as he said, she was a bitch to handle. It took two of us all our time to get the wheel round and I am certain that there was something wrong with her rudder, but steering on a mean course we would eventually get there. We had an escort of two MTBs, and I'll bet they were cursing their luck at being saddled with us at our slow speed, for they kept showing off with a quick burst of speed which took them right around the old *Sidi Ifni*.

We had two small frights on the passage. On the first occasion a plane was seen approaching from away over the starboard bow, but it never came very close to us. When it was still some way off, we saw it circle twice, and then it sped off in the direction it had come from. The second fright came when we saw ahead of us in the distance two bow waves from fast moving vessels which appeared to be making straight for us. One of our escorting MTBs, set off to intercept the strangers, and shortly they swept past us on a reciprocal course to our own. Our own MGB flashed a message saying that they were two MGBs, Motor Gun Boats, making their way back to North Africa.

Eventually we arrived safely and with no more scares, off the island of Caprera. We dropped the anchor, and the CO ordered the motor launch to be dropped into the water, our two escorts having by this time left us to our own devices and sped off for Bastia in Corsica, the new Coastal Force Base. When the boat was in the water, and the CO, the motor mechanic and myself settled in it with the motor already running, he explained that he wanted to go right round the island, and into any of the inlets there, to see if any of them would take the *Sidi Ifni*, and to see if there was enough depth of water. He told me that if he could find such a place, his idea was to get the ship in a position where he would be able to drop the anchor outside the inlet, then go astern on it until he was able to get mooring ropes ashore from each quarter to make her as secure as possible, and she would be away from prying eyes. Though we went the full circle around Caprera, there was no place with the necessary depth of water to take the *Sidi Ifni* so we returned to the ship.

The CO clambered back on board while the mechanic and I stayed on the launch to assist in getting the mooring ropes ashore on to the jetty at Maddalena, quite close to the submarine pens, and away from the main part of the small town. She was made fast securely to the jetty, the gangway was lowered onto it, and as far as I know, there she stayed until the beginning of 1945. Before I left her to become the coxswain of *MGB177*, I had about six or seven months enjoying one long holiday, the best one of my life. Apart from directing a bit of work each morning, the rest of the days were spent swimming in the clear waters, sunbathing, and sight-seeing. I even had a local leave, deciding to go to Bastia to our base to see one or two of the lads, and what Corsica looked like. I left to go on this leave with the first lieutenant; one of our feluccas ran us over to the fishing village of Bonifacio, where we stayed the night in some café that Jimmy had been to in better times; as he knew the people who owned it we were made very welcome, and were given a grand supper of whitebait and French fries.

It wasn't long after our arrival at Maddalena in the *Sidi Ifni*, that we received our first visitors, who just appeared late one evening and were whisked down below out of sight by the first lieutenant. Just as quickly, during the hours of darkness, they went onboard a small fishing boat and so they were just shadows of men and women to all of our crew, except for our three officers. For all that we knew that they were doing some dangerous work, as were those of our flotilla who were taking them to their dropping zone, and picking them up again. This I suppose is what I might have been doing if the *Wild Bill* had turned up. I would be lying if I said that I would sooner be doing that, instead of being on the best holiday of a lifetime, though it wasn't to last for so very long.

Within about a couple of months we had about six or eight feluccas or fishing boats lying on the opposite side of the jetty – this was about the time that the African Coastal Flotilla was changing over to the converted American PT boats. They now became our charges and it was my job to see that all the rigging and deck work on them was kept up to scratch. Down below was the engineer's pigeon. In between this work I had to take the motor launch up to the small naval depot in the centre of Maddalena, to pick up mail and stores or whatever they had for us. Mail came in quantity about every month or five weeks, but it was better than none at all. Food was more of a problem than it had been on the *Northern Gem*. There was very little of it to be had from the base, but we were able to get eggs and sometimes the odd scraggy chicken from people ashore, either to buy or on a barter system. Some of the locals we got to know pretty well, and occasionally some of us were invited up to their homes for a meal now and again, and we took up either sweets or chocolate for the children if there were any, and tobacco or cigarettes for the men. They too were friendly people. One man whose house I visited told me that he had been a pilot in the Italian air force, and showed me papers to prove it. He said that he had bombed Malta several times but that he had been very afraid of the Spitfires there. They were all glad that their war was over.

Later some of these men, including the ex-pilot, came to do the bit of cleaning up for us onboard. With having to do the maintenance work on the feluccas, keeping a quarter-master on the gangway throughout the twenty-four hours of each day, along with other jobs that crept up at times, my six seamen were in danger of becoming overwhelmed. There were often merchant ships coming in with stores and personnel for the base, and it became my job to bring them all ashore, or run out with signals. There was one night in particular that I have not forgotten. A large merchant vessel came in and dropped her anchor, and as usual I got my orders to go out to see what was to do. It was the usual job. The ship had twenty-four naval personnel to put ashore, including one officer and six Wrens, along with their kit, which would mean four runs or possibly five, as with the motor mechanic and myself the launch would only carry another eight persons along with their kit even in fine weather. This particular night the captain came out of the wardroom as I made my way to the launch, to tell me that there was a local gale expected and not to take any chances at all if I thought it was becoming at all dangerous.

I was head to wind going out to the vessel and although the launch bounced about for a time and threw a bit of spray over us, I did not consider it to be too bad at the time. We got there with no trouble and I shouted up that I would take the Wrens and two sailors with their kit ashore on this first run. We took the kit first to pack in the bottom of the launch, then the personnel, and set off making a dog leg of a course, with the wind and sea first on our starboard quarter then on the port quarter. This took us to the entrance to the submarine pens and alongside the feluccas, where we put them ashore.

The CO had watched the whole of the time and as we tied up he came down and asked if I was going again. I said that I would give it another go even though I realised the wind and sea were getting stronger all the time. I let go and took the same way out as before head to wind, but more slowly and arrived alongside the vessel OK. The officer in charge shouted over the ship's rail that he was giving the orders this time, and that he was sending all of the kit down first. I shouted that I would take six men and their kit only, as the weather was getting worse, but he was insistent and started dropping the kit bags. I shouted that's the lot, but he started to send men down although I had a launchful of gear. I told them to get back, and shouted to the officer that I was returning to the jetty.

This time was definitely worse. The wind had got stronger and the seas a bit steeper even though we were in a land-locked harbour, I took the same dog leg back to the submarine pens, and she dipped her quarters in very low on a couple of occasions. We made it however and tied up again alongside of the feluccas again, and I went up to see the CO and gave him a run down on what had happened, telling him that it was too bad to go back again. When the wind and sea got up like it was doing now, within half an hour it could, and often did, change from a flat calm into a raging cauldron, then back again in the same space of time, making you wonder what had happened. It was at these times that our hands were kept busy, making sure the feluccas did not break adrift or damage themselves. On one occasion during one of these blows, a tanker which was moored to a buoy, was blown on to the shore along with the buoy and the ton or so of concrete which should have held them both in place.

Happier things happened during my stay at Maddalena – there were several occasions on which we got mixed up with the locals on the island of Caprera, in their mixed bathing sessions, nude ones at that. There was a gorgeous white sandy beach there which ran out under the clear water which was only shoulder high. This was the first time that I knew that Italian girls did such a thing, as I had always been led to believe that they were such devout Catholics, and I think I was a bit shocked to find this happening, but I must say that I did not let the knowledge stop me joining in with them.

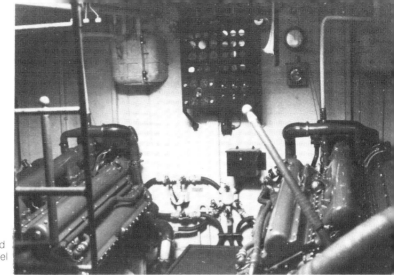

of the three engines of
3 177. Each engine used
gallon of high octane fuel
minute at speed.

rican PT boats at Bizerta,
dron 22.

rican PT boat Squadron
f Monte Carlo 1944.

(*Top*) PT Squadron 22 some of whom gave us cover during the 'no moon period' landings on the South coast of France. (*Left*) At front, Chester 'Nobby' Hall the best man at author's wedding July 1945. (*Right*) Author and motor mechanic of MGB 177 at Ischia in May 1945 after end of war in Europe. Two airmen had been calibrating the compass of MGB 177 ready for the trip home. (*Below*) May 1982 with the 'Oval' in the background, the author on a return visit to the 'Sparrows nest' Lowestoft. Former HMS *Europa* – now headquarters of the Royal Naval Patrol Service Association and their museum.

There were occasions when I was allowed to take one of the feluccas away for the weekend, from the Friday afternoon until Sunday night or even Monday morning if there was nothing special on, and in any case we were in touch by radio in case we were wanted back urgently. We put a bit of food aboard in the way of sandwiches, there was water and a small stove on which we could make tea, taking any members of the crew who wanted to come. Sometimes the first lieutenant or the engineer commander would come with us. We could go to one or other of the small fishing villages around the coast of Sardinia, looking around them and going for walks in various places, buying fruit just picked out of the fields, the huge red melons that were so delicious to eat if one was hot and sweaty. If the sea was calm and the sun hot on the way back, we would stop the boat and go over the side for a swim in the deep blue water which looked as if there was no bottom to it.

I think that one of the worst things that happened while I was on the *Sidi Ifni* at Maddalena, started on the day that one of our new PT boats came alongside of us to put onboard a rating, who was on a very serious charge for what must have been a very bad offence. I don't think that any of us with the exception of the officers, knew what it was. He was a Scot. For about a week we had no trouble from him. I had one or two conversations with him as he was under open arrest, and seemed to be quite all right as far as I could see, until one particular night, not long after we had all finished tea, around about six or seven o'clock, one of the seamen came down to my cabin. He came to warn me that this Scot had been round asking for money, and that as he had not had any success in the forecastle, he had gone into some sort of rage, and shouted that he was going to look for the coxswain as he would be sure to give him some but that if he didn't he would 'duff' him up.

Of course this put the wind up me, and I got the motor mechanic who was in the next cabin to mine to come in, explaining the reason why. Shortly after there was a knock at the door, and in walked the Scot. He had a quick look round the room and saw the motor mechanic, who was a fairly large well built lad. Whether this made the difference or not I don't know, but he was very quiet and just asked me if I had any cash that I could lend him. I said that I was sorry I hadn't, as we only got paid once a fortnight and that I was broke. He just thanked me and went away. Both the motor mechanic and myself thought that if I had been on my own in the cabin he would have attacked me, but he had kept a tight hold of himself. A few minutes later, there was a commotion on the ladder from the deck, and one of the seamen shouted that the quarter-master had been attacked and knocked to the deck, and his revolver had been stolen, the Scot being the culprit. I ran up onto the deck telling the seaman to call all hands, had a look at the quarter-master, then went to tell the First Lieutenant and the CO.

As it got dark, the new quarter-master spotted someone in the water between us and the town, swimming towards the ship, so he raised the alarm. Every one was on deck watching his progress for it was the Scot. He must have been a powerful young man to have swum the distance that he had done, because I eventually found him fully clothed. He swam round the stern of the *Sidi Ifni* and into the pens where the feluccas were, and clambered aboard one. The first lieutenant shouted to him to give himself up, and was told to go and f--- himself, whereupon we all took cover thinking that he was going to start shooting. It was now that the first lieutenant told me that the man was waiting transit to Leghorn to go before a court martial for reasons that he was not allowed to divulge, and that we had to get him back before he made more trouble for himself. I had a little talk with myself plucking up a bit of courage, then I stood up, walked down the gangway and slowly across the jetty to the cluster of fishing boats.

Stepping on to the first one, I shouted loudly, 'Jock, don't shoot. It's the coxswain, Sid'. There was no answer so I had a wary look all around me. I decided to go to the outside boat of the trot, thinking that if I was in his place, and had climbed on to that one, I would have stayed there, and that if he had not wanted to be caught, he would not have come back here. He could not have got away in one of the fishing boats as they were all immobilised for that reason, so climbing from one to the other, and shouting to him all the time, I finally reached the outer one; going to the side of the boat furthest away from the jetty, I came face to face with him; he was sitting on the ship's rail. I asked if he was all right; he seemed calm though he was still breathing heavily from his long swim and he replied that he was. I then asked him for his revolver, and he told me that it had gone from his trouser belt while he was swimming back. He stood up and I thought here it comes, but he just said, 'Come on, coxswain, let's go,' and we both went back to the jetty and walked up to the gangway to the deck of the *Sidi Ifni*, with no trouble at all. I was shaking like a leaf, more through relief than anything else. The CO gave me a glass of whisky and a 'Well done'. The next day a PT Boat came alongside and took him away, I never heard any more of him from that day to this.

It was here in Maddalena that I was handed my Russian Decoration, the Order of the Patriotic War 2nd Class. I hadn't known a thing about it until it was presented to me on the quayside during a little ceremony by the captain. When I left the ship, I gave it to Engineer Commander Barnes, who was kind enough to take it home with him and deliver it to my parents. Eventually I got a letter from my parents asking why I had not told them previously about being awarded with it, but I could only tell them that I had not known myself.

By this time we heard on the radio that the Allied troops were moving steadily up from the toe of Italy, and had as far as I can remember got somewhere near to Florence. One morning we were surprised to see a multitude of various ships moving through the Straits of Bonifacio, landing craft of various kinds, destroyers and several larger vessels; although we did not know it at the time, there had been a landing somewhere along the South Coast of France, and these were reinforcements. At intervals a few days later, landing craft ran into the submarine pens near us and offloaded the remains of aircraft that had crashed on landing, and it was amusing to see the crews of the MTBs, submarines, and some of our own lads, going over these wrecks for anything which they thought was useful, guns being the favourite target.

My last job in Maddalena for the captain of the *Sidi Ifni* was to chart the depths of the three or four submarine pens. To do this, I measured out their length and breadth, marking out the edges of the stone jetties at equal distances around the inside edges of them with white paint. I then made a plan on graph paper, drawing lines from each mark on the paper; where the lines crossed was where I had to take the depth and record it on the paper. It was a long and meticulous job, what it was for remains a secret, but I should think that those soundings and measurements will be in the dust on the same shelf as the log and records of the *Sidi Ifni*.

To close this chapter, I would like to finish off with a rather amusing incident which occurred at Maddalena at the start of our stay there. A few of us were on the deck when we saw three landing craft coming in to the anchorage at speed. They made straight for a sandy beach not far from where we were tied up to the jetty, and ran their bows onto the beach, dropping their ramps as they did so. Out poured lots of American soldiers who charged up the beach screaming and with rifles at the ready, as though they would have to fight their way onshore. Later on when we got to know them, we found that they were an American construction battalion and they had not been told that the island was in Allied hands. They had been sent in to set up an American base there, and had been very surprised to see a Limey ship there, but had gone through the motions just in case.

They soon got to work and in no time at all had built living quarters, mess halls, and a cinema, which we were allowed to visit now and again. I remember seeing a world première there of the Joan of Arc film. We got to know some of them very well and we were able to go into their PX, which was the same as our NAAFI, and get many things which we had not seen for some time. Clothing, believe it or not, was a thing we could not get at our naval base at Maddalena, but we managed to get fitted out with some American Army gear, and found out with the help of some of the Yanks that we could get into their mess hall for a good meal, joining the queue and going the rounds. Of course it cost us a tot or two of rum in return but it was well worth it as they were a great bunch of lads.

However my good times came to a close, when I was informed by the first lieutenant of the *Sidi Ifni*, that a flotilla PT boat was arriving the next morning, and they required a new coxswain, as I was the only one available, I had to go. I had passed for POPS while I was there, and was also rated up, so I was at last a PO Coxswain, instead of just acting as I had been since August 1940.

MGB*177* came alongside the *Sidi Ifni* in October 1944, and as I had never sailed on one of these boats before, I was given a run down on what my duties would be by her First Lieutenant Skipper Thomas RNR. Her commanding officer was a Lieutenant Brian Smith, either an Australian or a New Zealand citizen, I don't remember which. In no time at all I was being whisked away out of the confines of Maddalena and out of sight of the *Sidi Ifni* at some twenty-five or thirty knots, and I never saw either of them again.

This was an entirely new life, tearing about over the ocean at (to me) fantastic speeds compared with what I had been used to in the old coal-burning trawlers. Our first port of call was Leghorn in Italy, which had been won from the Germans in some hard-fighting only a week or two previously. Signs of the heavy fighting were evident as we approached the port. On the way over I found out that the *177* was staying on that side of Italy, but that the other boats of the flotilla

MGBs *178, 179, 180* and *191*, were going round to the Adriatic. They had all been working from Bastia in Corsica, and I had got to know a few of the lads on them when I took the week's leave there sometime before. One of them, Chester (Nobby) Hall, was to be my best man at my wedding the following year.

With the landings in the south of France, the Germans were being pushed back; both there and in Italy the coastline for the type of operations which had been carried out by these boats was gradually shrinking, making dropping or picking-up points difficult to find. So it was thought by higher authority, that only one boat would be needed on this side, to continue in this area, and that boat would be of course the *177*.

To enter Leghorn, we went in between two outer moles at the entrance before turning to port. On doing so we found ahead of us a row of sunken merchant ships, put down by the Germans as blockships with the idea of making things as difficult as possible for the Allies to use the harbour quickly. At some period shortly after the fall of the port, a huge hole had been blown in the row of ships so as to allow small vessels to make their way through and into the port proper, where there were two docks. One of these was quite a large one, and as we entered it through the lock gates, the whole area looked a shambles, warehouses around the dock were just heaps of rubble and the water seemed to be littered with the wrecks of vessels of various sizes including an Italian destroyer. Later we were told that most of this had been done by bombers of the American air forces, though much of it must also have been wrecked by the German engineers before they pulled out.

Turning again to port, we passed through a narrow entrance and into a smaller dock, which turned out to be a base for the Coastal Force units operating along these coasts. Here is where we made our base for a time, eventually spreading our time between here in Leghorn, and a small seaside resort between Nice and Cannes on the French Riviera named Golfe Juan, which was an American PT Base. Here in this small inner dock we laid claim to one of the ruined warehouses, and the two motor mechanics we had on board got together and knocked up quite a useful oven out of old bricks and steel ammunition boxes, and we were able now to eat hot dinners instead of sandwiches and tins of self-heating soups. We were also able to bake some bread – it's surprising what one can do when it becomes really necessary. These PT boats only had two hot plates to cook on, but when at sea it wasn't always convenient to use them due to the fairly quick movements of the boats in any inclement weather. There were odd occasions when we were out on a trip, when the skipper would take us alongside at some place, we would make a heap of some sand, soak it with 100 octane fuel, and set fire to it; this was handy for cooking a meal of bacon and eggs on, which was quite tasty too.

My bunk was right aft in what was termed the tiller flat, a small compartment where there was access to the rudder heads and steering cables. I shared this small place with the chief motor mechanic. He had the port bunk, while I squeezed into the starboard one. I mean squeezed in literally for when we did get laid down flat in the bunk, we each had about a six inch gap above our bodies, over which were the 100 octane aviation fuel tanks, the three hungry engines each used a gallon of this fuel per minute when doing forty or so knots – some difference to the old *Northern Gem*.

During our stay at Leghorn, we took it in turn along with the boats of the Coastal Forces to be duty boat, which meant that if there was any suspicion of the enemy trying to get into the harbour with their frogmen to plant mines or cause damage, we had to proceed to the harbour entrance, and patrol up and down clear of the two moles, dropping 5lb charges at intervals to scare any would-be saboteurs off. There were times when we went on patrol with the coastal force units on one of their sweeps up the coast towards La Spezia and Genoa. On our own particular job, we could only work when it was the 'No Moon' period on four or five nights of the month, as it had to be a black night to land on the enemy coast. The weather in this neck of the woods at the end of 1944 and the beginning of 1945 was atrocious, with gale force winds and heavy snow, bitterly cold and not the sort of weather to be gallivanting about in in those sorts of boats.

In the middle of January '45, some movement of enemy ships had been reported off Spezia, and we were sent off to investigate with an American PT boat, *313*, and a British MTB, *378*. Leaving Leghorn late at night, and proceeding at very high speed, we soon arrived at the designated area where the traffic was reported to be. It was not long before we spotted a convoy of flak lighters moving along the coast, but being at the wheel I saw little of the action which took place. The flak lighters were illuminated for us by star shells fired from shore batteries of the army, entrenched somewhere in the front line below Spezia, and working with us. It made it fairly easy for our three boats to take the enemy convoy by some degree of surprise; we sped in from different directions on a pre-arranged plan and as we went along the formation of F-Lighters we fired at them with all our guns. They must have left Spezia to make their way up to Genoa; as we got to within six or seven hundred yards of them the noise was deafening, tracer bullets flying all over the place. The other two boats were letting fly with their torpedoes; we did not carry any, and although I personally never saw any explosions on any of the enemy vessels, it was reported later that one F-lighter had been sunk for sure, another one possibly so, and three more damaged.

It was an exhilarating action, fast moving and quite a change to be on the delivering side, as opposed to all those Atlantic and Russian convoys, in which our charges had been the recipients. This action though was to be our first and last, though we did take part in several non-productive patrols. I'm not certain whether I was pleased or sorry about this at the time.

The last week in March '45, saw the whole of our crew with the exception of the two officers, setting off for a week's leave at the 54th Rest Camp at Florence. We had been given another alternative, Rome, but we chose Florence because it was the easier and the nearer of the two to get to. Rome was a day's drive either way and we did not fancy that. What looked like being a good week's rest and holiday came to an end after just three days for we were ordered back to the *177* immediately, a truck having been sent to pick us up. An urgent job had come up, two in fact; the first one was a de-lousing job since we had brought bugs back with us from the camp, and we sat naked in front of the fire in our ruined warehouse, searching the seams of all our clothes, and cracking or burning the things as we found them.

This other job which had come up was one of great secrecy. We had to team up with an Italian Mas boat, and between us we had to make certain that three two-man torpedo chariots were deposited in the correct place at the correct time. This was for an assault on Genoa for there had been a report that the Germans were preparing to sink blockships across the entrance to Genoa and these Italians were going to attempt to sink these vessels before this happened by blowing them up alongside of the jetty where they lay. *177* had to tow one of these chariots, the Mas boat taking the two remaining ones. She was fitted with a drop down ramp sort of thing at the stern, which allowed the two chariots to float in and out of the boat quite easily.

My first part in this operation, was to splice an eye in the end of a towing wire supplied by the Mas boat, large enough to drop over the

Bofors gun and platform fixed on our stern; this was the most secure point on the boat able to take the strain of the towing of one of these things through the water. At the opposite end of the wire, I had to splice a thimble in, to take a shackle for securing the end to the nose of the chariot. There was apparently no time for a practice run, and it had to work first time. Everything had been arranged for a pick up in the dark that very night, and going off straightaway to do the job.

Instead of its being dark, it was a balmy night when we set off; the sea was like a bathing pool, the sky full of the brightest stars, and the moon was full, giving the scene as a travel brochure picture gives it these days. In our case the chariot on tow behaved most beautifully; the six Italian crewmen were great fellows, full of spirit, not at all like the ones we had seen on the newsreels earlier on. Their job was to come later, when we had reached the position for casting them off; we would not be told if they had been successful or not, for that side of the job did not concern us. As we reached the place where we had to slip our tow, we wished these six brave charioteers the best of luck as they set off, two men to each craft to take them into the harbour of Genoa, and hopefully sink the merchant ships, their targets, where they lay.

With a final wave they were off shouting *Viva Italia*, as the huge golden globe of the moon, shone over in the direction of where Genoa lay, and to us it looked as though a long path had been laid out on the sea for them to follow. I can remember this sight very well for it was the last we were to see or hear of them. Our job done, we set off back to Leghorn. The Mas boat was to hang about for a time in case of accidents, but if all went well, the three crews, once they had set their charges on the targets, were to sink the chariots, make their way onshore, lose themselves amongst their countrymen in Genoa, and await their liberation as the Allied Armies fought their way along.

A couple of days later we were back in practically the same spot, this time in broad daylight; we could see the houses and villas perched up on the sides of the cliffs facing the sea, the same cliffs which hid the town of Genoa from our sight. This day we were sitting on top of a minefield, plotting its outside limits; we presumed that it was for a forthcoming landing in the area to give the sweepers some idea where to go to work. The Germans must have been waiting to see what we were up to, for it was quiet for a good hour before anything started to happen. Then the shore batteries on the top of the cliffs and in the hills opened up at us; they got fairly close but not near enough to do us any damage. Each time they fired the CO would tell me to head straight for the gun flashes, as he was plotting their positions on the chart. We had an old naval 'Walrus' working with us, flying around spotting the mines at the edge of the field, dropping smoke floats to mark its position; he must have been able to see the mines pretty clearly from up there as the water was very calm, almost like glass. As he dropped the smoke float, so we would run up alongside of it, staying with it until the CO and the first lieutenant had got its position marked on the chart, then we would move off to the next one.

At one time while we were involved in this job, we were horrified for a second or two when we saw several planes coming towards us low down on the water, almost touching it as a matter of fact. They were approaching us from seaward, and we were pleased to hear the skipper say that they were rocket-firing Typhoons. They swept over us making straight for the gun flashes as they fired at us from the shore. We had, you might say, a grandstand view of the Royal Air Force at work, making one of the famous air strikes which I had heard of on the news, but had never seen before. We could see the track of the rockets as they were fired from the planes by the smoke trail that they left in the air, as the planes dived down onto their targets. Where the trail ended there was a great eruption of smoke and flames on the side of the cliffs in the vicinity of the gun batteries. It was a good show as far as we were concerned, and from then on until the job was finished, we had no more trouble.

We spent about three months or so at Golfe Juan attached to US Task Force 86, commanded by Lieutenant-Commander Dressling USN, and worked on occasions with Motor Torpedo Boat Squadron Ron 22. When we were in harbour we ate with them in their mess, and were at times overwhelmed by their kindness to us; nothing was a trouble to them, provided they had not to go out with us on our next job. And of course we could not help but rib them about this; they thought our work was too dangerous, and we derived a sort of pleasure from this, although they themselves had taken part in many attacks on enemy shipping in the Med over the past year or so, and we thought that their job was much more dangerous than ours.

One particular trip we did to Ligurie, on the Italian Riviera, was a bad affair, and must have been known to the Germans before we set out on the operation. As we lay in the small harbour of Golfe Juan alongside the floating pontoons, we were in full view of anyone who passed by. We took on explosives, coils of wire, arms and ammunition, along with some mysterious looking packages, which were left on deck but covered with a tarpaulin. And during the course of the day, I was walking about the town, testing a new two-way portable radio, to see what range we could get out of it and what the quality of its performance was, by keeping in touch with the *177*.

All the afternoon, everyone on the *177* had noticed an elderly man, well dressed and wearing what we took to be a black Homburg hat. He was accompanied by an attractive young girl in a flimsy summer dress and of course all eyes were on her really. They sat on the sea wall and she was literally showing herself off, no doubt for our benefit. They were still there towards evening when we took onboard four men, along with more equipment, and as those men went below, we noticed something happen which we thought nothing about until much later on; we saw the old man wave to someone in a car, which then came up to the sea wall, and with a final look towards *177*, both he and the girl got in the car and away it went.

As it got dark, we set off for our rendezvous at Riva Ligurie, with one of Squadron 22 PT boats for company. We sped along the coast of Southern France at a great rate of knots, past Monte Carlo, which glowed with lights of various colours and looked like heaven to us.

Past there it was all darkness once more, like the world we had got used to over the last four years. Somewhere off to port we left behind the seaport of San Remo, still at the time in the hands of the Germans, and still heavily defended, and soon we came abreast of our target Ligurie. We turned to port losing speed gradually, to let us pick up the land and fix the exact position for our drop. The points for these drops were verified by silhouette drawings of the landscape as it would look with the dark night sky as a background, for no matter how dark the sky is where there are no lights, the land is always darker; therefore the contours of the land can be seen up against the lighter sky easily enough, providing there is no low cloud or mist covering the tops of the hills. On this night it was perfect for our mission, and conditions were ideal.

Leaving the American boat to patrol the outside of the bay with orders to keep a radar watch for possible intervention by E-boats or other enemy vessels, Lieutenant Smith took us into the bay between the two widely spread promontories, and just before the time arrived when signal lights would be flashed from the shore, he took the *177* in and eventually closed to within two hundred yards of the beach, stem on to it so as to make the smallest possible target to see and be picked up by anyone on the shore. From the boat it was quite easy to see the small waves breaking on the shore, and beyond the beach the coast road which ran parallel to the sea. At intervals along this road we could see what we took to be gun replacements, or block houses of some sort; we had to stay here at this spot, lying quietly with as little noise as possible, baffles on the exhausts, until we received the signal that all was clear from ashore. I was to take the four men and their gear in a pram dinghy when the time came, and a rubber dinghy with the rest of the equipment was to follow with all haste to get the job done and everyone out of the area as soon as we could. I was at the wheel already dressed for the trip in my old blue serge petty officer's uniform, with a dark jersey underneath and a revolver strapped to my waist. In my pockets was an escape kit, and a substantial amount of French and Italian money, which I should have to use if by some unforeseen circumstance, I was left on shore. In this event, the orders were to get up into the hills, the best place being, I had been told, about half way up where it had been found the local people were more sympathetic and prone to help.

The time arrived when the signals were overdue, and the two officers went below into the pilot house to check their figures and to make certain that they were on the correct position for the pick up. They told me to keep a good look out and to let them know if I saw anything at all while they were down below. From my place at the wheel with the only noises I could hear being the surf breaking on the shore and the faint exhaust noises coming from astern as the exhausts with the baffles on dipped in and out of the water. I had a good view along the coast, on both sides of the boat. Away to starboard, I could see in the distance and coming down the road towards us, a lorry with shaded or very faint headlights on, and when it got to a point directly ahead of the *177*, it stopped, and my eyes being used to the dark picked out what I took to be an officer climbing out of the cab of the lorry. The reason I say this is because whoever it was had a torch in his hand and it shone on leather jackboots or gaiters. He went round to the back of the lorry and I saw the back-board drop down, then out came man after man. All this I could see very clearly, as I still can when I close my eyes and think about it.

They were soldiers of course I could see that, and I noticed that there were red lights going on in or near the gun emplacements, so I decided the time had come to call the skipper back to the bridge. All this had happened within a minute or two of them going below; as I bent down to bang on the pilot house door a searchlight came on and shone right on us from right ahead; it was like daylight and as if the sun had come out suddenly. I stood up straight and as I did so rifle and machine gun fire came from the direction of the beach. Without waiting for the two officers to get on deck I put the wheel hard-a-port and the three engine throttles which were in front of me on the top of the pilot house, I pushed up as far as they would go. The officers had just got on deck when she started to spin round, and the first air-bursts from 88mm guns, made the sea around us sizzle as the white hot shrapnel exploded into it.

For a few minutes the *177* sped away from the beach, then slowed and stopped in her tracks, the skipper took the wheel off me and above the noise of the gun fire and the sound off the bursting shells, I heard him shout for me to run aft to make smoke by turning on the taps on the two smoke cannisters on the stern. This I did and as the acid hit the water, clouds of smoke arose from the surface of the sea, making a thick wall of fog between us and the shore, the beam of light from the searchlight which had been fixed on to us, now hit the smoke and the beam 'bent' up towards the sky. Our Bofors gun had been shooting back all this time, and suddenly the searchlight went out as I felt my way back along the now dark deck to the engine room hatch, to find out what had made the engines peter out, for that was the second thing that the skipper had shouted to me as I left him.

Getting down onto my stomach, I shouted down the hatch and asked what the trouble was. The chief motor mechanic, who was pumping petrol by hand into the centre engine, answered, 'What silly b-----d pushed the throttles up like that; the engines are starved of fuel. Tell the Skipper we shall be OK in a few minutes'. This silly b-----d was of course, myself. As I stood up to make my way back to the bridge, I was blind through staring into the light of the engine room, and at my first or second step I fell over our four passengers who were laid flat out on the deck trying to get what cover they could from flak that was still flying about. As I got onto my hands and knees and preparing to stand up, the skipper turned round and saw me, and shouted, 'Get up, Coxswain, what the hell are you doing down there like that?' I explained the circumstances of what had happened, but I am not sure to this day whether he believed me. I can only guess that he gave me the benefit of the doubt as he did not mention it again.

By this time the stern had started to tuck itself down into the water as the engines picked up revolutions again and we were soon doing forty or forty-five knots, the water boiling up astern of us. The air-bursts were still going off from the 88mm, but thankfully due to the smoke screen and the fact that we had been stopped for a few minutes, they were some distance ahead of us and about ten feet above the surface of the sea. We were soon out of range, and we had no damage or casualties at all. At some point about this time we went through another smokescreen which had we found out later been laid by the American PT boat, but there was no sign of him in the near vicinity, so the skipper gave me a course which would take us back to Golfe Juan.

Several miles from Ligurie, we managed to contact the PT boat on the radio. He told the skipper that from the action that he had seen taking place from inshore, he surmised that the *177* had been sunk and that we had all been wiped out. He was now on his way back to the area to see if there were any survivors who had managed to get away in the boats or dinghies that he knew we carried, after having second thoughts on what he had seen. On the way back to base, we passed close to the port of San Remo, and had some more shots fired at us from there. It was reported to us over the radio that there were some radio controlled explosive motor boats, suspected to be working from there and very active, but we saw nothing of them.

Arriving back at Golfe Juan we received a great welcome from the Yanks who provided both their own PT boat's crew and our own, with a great hot meal, after which we turned in for the remainder of the night or what was left of it, only to be awakened by the watch on deck, and asked to come and see what was going on, on the pontoon. The crew of the PT boat which had been our partner on the previous night were all lined up in their best uniforms, and were being given Citations for the brilliant cover which they had given MGB*177* on their mission the night before. After some breakfast in the American mess, we got on with our daily chores, cleaning up, and on that day we re-painted the deck with non-slip paint, after we had returned all the equipment which we had failed to put ashore on the previous night. It was while we were doing this that we were told that the operation had been betrayed; the Germans had a reception committee waiting for us to appear at Ligurie. We talked then of the old man in the black Homburg and the young woman who showed herself off, for it could have been those two who had shopped us, but we never found out.

Christmas 1944 saw us in Leghorn again. We had developed a duff engine while at Golfe Juan, but apparently there was considerable difficulty in getting the American base to let us have a new one. Somehow this news got mentioned to General Eisenhower by some

devious means, and it was put to him that we were the only boat in
this theatre of war which was trained for the job of putting people
ashore on enemy-held shores. This must have made all the
difference, because we had without warning a crowd of American
Navy engineers roll up one day just before our tea time; they brought
a new engine with them and lifting gear, and worked throughout the
night taking out the old engine and putting in the new one. It was
from them that we heard about 'Ike's' hand in this. Orders had been
urgently transmitted to them that this work had to be done or heads
would roll, so it was done.

The very last bit of work that we in the *177* did was to go to Savona,
a small port on the Italian Riviera. We were sent there to see if the
Germans had left or withdrawn from there. It was in May 1945, and
broad daylight when the Skipper Brian Smith edged gingerly in
towards the coast, making for the harbour, which we did not enter,
the anchor being dropped just clear of the mole on the starboard side
of the entrance. A rubber dinghy was put over the side, and the first
lieutenant and two ratings went ashore to the beach, to speak to some
people who were standing there watching us with some interest.
Hardly had he stepped ashore than he was on his way back, urging
the two lads with him to pull like mad; coming alongside he shouted
that the boat had anchored on top of some magnetic mines, and that
the locals ashore had been waiting to see if we touched one off.
Fortunately we did not, and moved immediately to a more
comfortable spot which those on the beach had told the first
lieutenant about. They had also told him that most of the Germans
had left Savona, but there were one or two still left. They might have
been having a last fling for some one was sniping at us with little
success, but we could do nothing about it. After another excursion to
the beach for more information, the first lieutenant and the two men
clambered onboard pulling the dinghy up with them, and we set off
to return to Leghorn. We had not got very far when the Mistral
began to blow, the wind that came sweeping over the Austrian Alps
and funnelled itself through the Brenner Pass, then vented its fury
over the Tyrrhenian Sea. We had to heave to and put out a sea
anchor on the end of a cable, and somehow we survived the night
hanging onto the end of it. What a rough night it turned out to be.
Though we suffered no damage to the boat, our bodies were bruised
in many places, and we were very hungry to boot.

The wind dropped away with the coming of daylight, and the
skipper estimated that we must have been blown back towards the

coast again, so he decided that we would put back and make for a small fishing village showing on the chart. We arrived and entered a small natural harbour, somewhere not far from Savona. We entered between two cliffs and saw ahead of us a sort of pathway of floating timber. Keeping to this path we made our way to a stone built jetty, with shops and cafes at the back of it. As we moved slowly between the lines of timber, looking down into the water we could see that each piece of it was made fast by rope, to an ordinary sea mine which due to the motion of the water seemed to be waving about. The water was so clear that we could almost see the sinkers on the bed of the harbour, holding the mines in place.

By the time we had reached the quayside quite a crowd of people had gathered there watching us approach, some pointing to a place where we should make fast to. When we had done so, one of them who spoke English shouted that if we went onshore, we must keep clear of the tins which were perched on the top of the bits of wood which were stuck in the ground. These we could see were situated about the road and the square which was surrounded by the shops we had seen. He told us that under the tins were German land mines, laid before they had pulled out. The mines in the harbour had been marked by some of these men on the jetty in the event of a boat such as ours coming in, and they had made a good job of it.

We were allowed to go ashore for a look round by the skipper, and I and several others made our way towards a cafe to see if we could get a drink. As we went in through the open door, we got the shock of our lives – it was full of the local Partisans, both men and women. They must have been living rough for ages for they were burnt brown by the wind and sun. The women looked like young Amazons with their blouses or shirts open most of the way down their chests, their bodies festooned with guns and knives, hand grenades hung from their waistband belts, and bandoliers of ammunition hung around their necks and shoulders. God, what women they were, and how fit they looked. The men of course were just as well armed and looked just as fit, but it was the women who caught our eye. I myself at least had not seen anything like them before. We shook hands with many of them and they told us that the Germans (Tedesce) had left during the night, and that it was the first time some of those we were now meeting, had been down to the village for many months.

It cost us nothing for drinks when they found out what our particular war effort on their behalf had been, and it was an effort for us to get ourselves back onboard the *177*, until these fine people started to get excited over something or other that was not our concern, and began waving guns about and playing with the grenades at their belts. It was then that we decided to leave them and return to the boat for something to eat. What a sight it had been for us to see, I wished that I had got a camera with me as I would never in my life have another chance like that, to record the happiness of some people who had been prisoners in their own country for so long. And so it was that we left this happy village and made our way back to Leghorn. It was now that we started to get this feeling that at last the war was almost over but for the shouting. Those Partisans had thought so too, for their main cry had been '*Tedesce morte*'.

CHAPTER ELEVEN

War in Europe ends and Home we go

As we lay in the inner harbour at Leghorn, awaiting the word that the war to end all wars was over, or at least the one in Europe, because there was still one going on in the Pacific where the Japanese had to be fought to the death. It was generally thought by all of us in the outfit, that the ACF would be regrouped and then be sent out there to continue with the job we had been doing here in the Mediterranean. At this late moment of the war, none of us felt like going off on any sort of mission again, for there was still time for such a one to turn out to be the last, and after almost six years of sea time, I for one felt that it was time to call it a day.

The day which brought the end of the war in Europe came, and on that day there was no work done. When the news came through all sorts of pyrotechnics were let loose over Leghorn, signal rockets, Very lights and ships' sirens were blowing off. This was the day that we had waited so long for. Officers vanished going to where they all go when the pink gin is flowing; the crews were left to their own jolly devices, which meant that the rum bottles came out, every-one went from ship to ship shaking hands with people they knew and strangers alike. Soon there were bodies laid all over the jetty and on the decks of the boats, most of them stoned out of their minds, one of them being myself. I woke up some hours later laid out on the deck of the *177*, feeling half dead and perished with cold.

The last thing that I could remember was feeling the tears rolling down my cheeks, thinking about all the men that I had seen go to their deaths. Apart from Fred Powell, my shipmate and friend on the *Northern Gem* who was killed on May 8th 1940, and my uncle who was drowned around the same time, I could remember no other names, not even faces, and I thought how lucky I had been to come through without a scratch. I drained a bottle which lay near me, turned into my bunk, and promptly fell asleep again.

At first it was all so exciting, then as the days passed by a feeling of anti-climax set in with the majority of us. I think it was because that now we knew it was all over, we wanted to get home as quickly as possible. In my case I had been away from home nearly two years and I wanted badly to get home and see my parents again, but more than that, I wanted to get home to be with Gladys again, and get married, then to settle down to a normal life again, if I could remember what a normal life was.

Then orders came directing us to first to Naples, then to Ischia, an island in the Bay of Naples. According to the skipper we were going there to have extra long range fuel tanks fitted on the deck, which would give us the fuel needed to get the *177* back to England, where we would get leave before being taken onboard some merchant vessel along with the *177*, for passage out to the Far East, to continue the fight out there. This was what we had both feared and expected. At home they would think I was mad as I had already written to say that I would be home for good in about six weeks I thought, so they had to get the wedding arrangements under way. Now I had to write again and tell them to hold their horses and wait until I knew for certain.

At Ischia the fuel tanks were fitted, and we had two Royal Air Force compass calibrators come aboard, to bring the compass up to scratch; this they did and once we had put these two ashore again we set off, this time it was to be first stop Malta. This was to enable us to top up with fuel to see us to Gibraltar on the next leg for home. But again there appeared to be some doubts as to what we were to do next, and we once more had to wait for orders. Along with the other lads I had a grand time ashore there, once we found out that we were going to hand over the boats in Malta and be sent home on a troop ship, I asked Nobby Hall, who had been on one of the other boats in the Adriatic, if he would come to Hull and be my best man and he readily accepted.

It was true this time; we were going home on the next ship so I wrote home again to tell them the good news and that I should be in England in about three weeks, and that once I landed I would send them a telegram to confirm my arrival, so that plans could be put into operation for the big day.

She was one of the Castle Liners; as far as I remember it was the *Capetown Castle*, but whichever one it was, she looked lovely to us. We left Malta, bound for of all places, Naples, to pick up more servicemen who were due to return to old England and home, and when we had completed this part of the journey, we should be heading in the right direction. As I walked into the cafeteria onboard for my first meal. I got a smell in my nostrils which made my mouth water to such an extent that I'm afraid I was drooling at the mouth; it was the smell of kippers frying, I hadn't tasted them for years, and whoever put them on the menu could not have chosen a better meal as far as I was concerned. I made a proper hog of myself, when we were told that we could go round as many times as we liked with our plates, I went round three times to the best of my knowledge, for they were the kippers made from the large Norwegian herrings.

The rest of the voyage was just a happy memory; it was made without the worry of attack from marauding U-boats or aircraft, and most of our time was spent lounging about the decks in the warm sunshine for most of the day, and then either taking part or just watching one of the numerous card games which took place until the wee small hours of the morning. We arrived at Southampton, and soon a telegram was winging its way to my home: 'Arrived in England be seeing you soon'. The date was 6th July 1945.

We eventually entrained for our home bases, and I said goodbye to the lads who were going to Portsmouth and Chatham, especially to Nobby Hall, telling him that I would let him know the date of the wedding. I got two weeks leave from Lowestoft and arrived at the Paragon Station in Hull at about two o'clock in the morning. As I came down the platform I could see my father and Gladys waiting for me. I passed my travel warrant to the ticket collector for perusal, stepped through the barrier and was immediately picked up by two Redcaps, the Military Police. For several minutes we had quite an argument. They had stopped me, they said, because I was wearing a battle dress and a naval petty officer's cap and tie, and that this was not a proper uniform. They were trying to make out that this dress was illegal, but I finally got it through their obstinate skulls that I was dressed as I had been for the last two years, and that my travel warrant had been handed to me at HMS Europa after spending two years in the Mediterranean. Finally they decided to let me go.

What a welcome home that was, but the next one was much better. Gladys was dressed in her WAAF uniform, and looking as happy as I was feeling once I had shaken off these two MPs; my father shaking my hand until I thought it would drop off, and in this happy mood we got into a taxi and made our way home to where my mother and sister waited for my arrival.

Sleep was out of the question. Daylight was on us before I had even finished telling them all that they wanted to know, and of course there were so many things that I wanted to know myself, the main one being when the big day was to be. It was Tuesday the 10th July, only three days away, and I had no number one suit to wear. Before we had left Malta I had gone into Bernards, the navy tailors there, and had ordered a doeskin one, asking them to deliver it to my home address as quickly as possible, telling them what it was for, and they assured me that it would be there on time. The morning of the big day came and with it the postman with a parcel containing my new suit. Bernards had kept their word, albeit just in time, and I have been eternally grateful to them. When I tried on the suit it was a perfect fit apart from the sleeves which were a bit short, but this presented no problem. Nobby Hall arrived and at 2·30 that day it all happened.

Afterwards we had the reception and the next day we went to Grimsby for our honeymoon. One of Gladys's aunts had been kind enough to lend us her home there for as long as we wanted. As my new wife was only on one week's leave at the time she had to go back at the end of that week to the No 1 Group Lancaster bomber base at Killinghome where she now worked in the sick bay; she managed to get another week's leave out of them, at the end of which she went back to the bomber base, and I went back to Lowestoft.

It wasn't long before she was demobbed and I had managed to get us some decent rooms so we were soon together again. The Navy had not forgotten my request to sit for my mate's ticket, and I was already on the course when Gladys arrived. She helped me no end with my work and I think that she knew the rule of the road as well as I did myself. I also owe some thanks to Skipper Lieutenant Mullender whom I met once again; he took me under his expert tuition once more in his own house, where he put me through the hoop on many nights with the models of ships and buoys he had there.

I passed my examination for mate's ticket, and got my demob papers on the same day, 9th October 1945. I did not get rated up to Chief Petty Officer as I had hoped to do, but I was not unduly worried about that. I came out with group 27 after six years and three months of what should have been the happiest years of my life, our lives in fact, the lives of all the men who served throughout the war and had survived. At least we had lived through it all, and I for one would not like to think that our children would have to go through it all again. One has only to look at the war memorials in each town and village to see why. Those of us who were there can remember those who never made it back home, and when we look around the world today, we can ask ourselves what it was all about, and was it worth the loss of so many young men of that time?

We had two sons whom we managed to help through universities with a struggle. I did go back to fishing for seven trips in 1947 after 18 months out of work, but gave it up to see the lads grow up, and because I could see what my being away for three or four weeks at a time was doing to Gladys. I then managed to get a job on the Hull fish market as a filleter; within a couple of years I became manager of a small fish merchants, but the money was very low as it has been in the fish trade the whole of the time since the war ended. I would think it was the lowest paid work in the country, but at least one was not being swilled about the decks and could always be home even very late at night to sleep in your own bed.

In Lowestoft I met some of the crew off the *Northern Gem*, who had been there when I left her. Both they and the old *Gem* had come through it all to the end; the *Gem* had been released a few weeks before and was now being altered back to her original pre-war state ready to take up her old job of deep sea fishing, up in the Arctic Circle. I went onboard her once again in 1948, when she came into St Andrew's Dock at Hull to land her catch of fish having been diverted from Grimsby. As I walked around her, a flood of memories came back both happy and sad, but I was pleased that we had met again, for the last time as it turned out, for not long afterwards she was sent to the scrapyard to be broken up.

She was considered obsolete; in substance maybe, but *never* in my own memory.

Epilogue

The Sparrows Nest was originally a country estate; it was taken over by the local authorities to be used as a park for the public at large in Lowestoft. In 1939, it consisted of amenities such as a concert hall, some conservatories, and an open air stage amongst other things. Elsie and Doris Waters were appearing there when the war broke out, and the Sparrows Nest then became HMS Pembroke X. It was to become the rallying ground and the base for men of the Royal Naval Reserve and later Hostilities Only men, all to be classed as the Royal Naval Patrol Service, an assembly point for all the brave men who were to be sent on their various drafts, to many parts of the world, to ships, depots, and all the places that were to come into contact with, and to be used for war purposes.

The Sparrows Nest, eventually became HMS Europa, and was so until the end of the war when both the Germans and the Japanese were beaten and all the 'Sparrows' were demobilized and sent home for good.

In October 1953, a memorial was unveiled by Admiral of the Fleet Sir Roderick McGrigor; on its base were 17 bronze panels bearing the names of some 2,385 officers and men of the RNPS, the Royal Naval Patrol Service, who died at sea in action, and have '*No Known Grave but the Sea.*'

On October 6th 1979, I went back to the 'Nest', 34 years after I last saw it, to be at the Memorial Service there held beneath this lovely tall column of gleaming white stone. At its peak a replica of the *Golden Hind*, shining brightly in the sun of that early winter day. Reading the names on the bronze panels of the many men who did not come back, here and there I found the names of some of the lads I had sailed with in pre-war days of fishing; there were also two I had known on the *Northern Gem*, it was a sad but very moving occasion and many memories came back.

One happy thing happened on that visit to Lowestoft. A meeting took place between my wife and me, and Tim Coleman and his wife Lily. It was the first time that we had seen or spoken to each other for 34 years, and it all happened by chance. As we walked around

Lowestoft, we passed a telephone kiosk and I said to my wife, 'Just let's have a look at the phone book in there'. Selecting a 'Coleman' from the group of 8 or 10 on the page, I dialled the number. It was Lily who answered the phone, and I then spoke to Tim, who thought I had come back from the dead. He sent his daughter whom we had nursed on our knees all those years ago, to pick us up in her car, and when we arrived at his home, they were waiting for us at the garden gate. The meeting was similar to the *This is Your Life* programme on the television. We kept in touch by phone and letter after that, and he told me that it was weeks before he got over the shock of hearing my voice, and stopped shaking.

I'm sorry to say that he has since passed away, and to the best of my knowledge, there are only two of the old crew left, myself and Charlie Keen who was the *Gem*'s signalman, and the longest serving member of her I believe. We keep in touch by phone and by letter, and one of these days before it gets too late, we shall meet for the first time since 1945, we shall have a lot to talk about. I have not been able to trace any others of her crew, it is possible that some are still around. If they are and they happen to read this, I say *Dosvi Danya*.

Sid Kerslake
Fleetwood 1983

Appendix A

A/S Escorts for Convoy P.Q.17

Ship	Commanding Officer	Code Word
Keppel	Commander J.E. Broome RN.	Candid
Douglas	Lt. Cmdr. B.S. Tennent RN.	Winter
Fury	Lt. Cmdr. C.H. Campbell D.S.C. RN.	Habit
Offa	Lt. Cmdr. A. Ewing RN.	Minute
Ledbury	Lt. Cmdr. R.P. Hill RN.	Stilton
Wilton	Lt. A.P. Northey D.S.C. RN.	Combat
Leamington	Lt. B.M.D. I'Anson	Hothouse
Dart		Ladder
Lotus	Lt. H.J. Hall R.N.R.	Marrow
Poppy	Lt. N.K. Boyd R.N.R.	Ticket
La Malouine	Temp. Lt. Bidwell R.N.R.	Palace
Dianella	Temp. Lt. Rankin R.N.R.	Bunny
Submarines	*P 614* and *615*	
Lord Middleton	Temp. Lt. Jameson R.N.R.	Hillman
Ayrshire	Temp. Lt. Gradwell R.N.R.	Garden
Lord Austin	Temp. Lt. Egsar R.N.R.	Wisdom
Northern Gem	Sk. Lt. Mullender D.S.C. R.N.R.	Apache
Palomares	Act. Cpt. Jauncey RN. (Retd.)	Fisher
Pozerica	Act. Cpt. Lawford RN. (Retd.)	Riley
	Fleet Sweepers	
Britomart	Lt Cmdr. Stamwitz	Tarter
Halcyon	Temp. A/Lt/Cmdr. Harding	Mallet
Salamander	Lt. Muttam RN.	Kitten
Empire Tide	C.A.M. Ship	Bonnet
	Rescue Ships	
Zaafaran		Competent Stretcher
Zamalek		Competent Stretcher
Rathlin		Competent Stretcher

Convoy Captain
Commodore J. Dowding DSO RD RNR *River Afton, Penway*

Survivors List Convoys PQ 14 and PQ 17

Picked up by H.M.T. Northern Gem Commanding Officer SK. Lt. Mullender DSC, RNR
Out of the Water   HMS *Leda A.M. 20th September 1942*

R.F.Green	P.O.	C/JX 130618
W.R.Fogwill	A.P.O. (Ty)	P/JX 143034
J. Young	Yeo	C/JX 131436
B.R.Potts	E.R.A.	C/MX 45643
J.W.Usher	P.O.Ck. (0)	C/MX 49632
H.A.Stride	A.B.	C/JXI27721
W. Hampson	A.B.	D/JX 237885
H.D.Benson	A.B.	C/JX 259319
C.A.Rowton	A.B.	C/JX 219104
T.A.Beck	A.B.	C/SSX 30882
J.H.Turner	A/L/Sig. (Ty)	C/JXI49239
R.Sewell	Tel.	C/SSX30697
S.W.Wood	O/Sea(RDF)	P/JX288642
H.F.Hadley	A/L/Sto (Ty)	C/KX96956
L.Burgess	Sto.I.	C/KX99710
S.Seary	Sto.I.	C/K66779
J.D.Pilmer	Sto.I.	C/KX 105324
B.W.Barber	Steward	C/LX 23986
L.J.Prendergast	Wireman	C/MX96088
J. Pengally	Lieut.RN.	Discharged *Rathlin* PM 20th
N.R.Lambrick	Lieut.RN.	" *Seagull* "
H.C.Aall	Lieut.RN.	" *Rathlin* "
D.B.Mather	Sub Lieut RNVR	" *Seagull* "
H.L.Champion	Warrant Eng. RN.	" *Rathlin* "
A.E.Croft	P.O.	P.M. 20th Discharged Dead
H.T.Cook	S.P.O.	—Ditto—
C.C.Spence	O/Sea	—Ditto—
W.J.Crockett	C.P.O.	S.S. *Rathlin* PM 20th
D.Hutchinson	P.O.Tel	—Ditto—
E.J.Yard	S.P.O.	—Ditto—
A.E.Pilkington	Ch.Stoker	—Ditto—
W.J.Banfield	Ch.Stoker	—Ditto—
T.Garside	O.A.	—Ditto—
F.T.Taylor	Motor Mechanic	—Ditto—
V.Johnson	A/P.O. (Ty)	—Ditto—
L.J.Wamond	L/Radio Mechanic	—Ditto—
J.Stringer	Sto.I.	—Ditto—
W.Maskell	Sto.I.	—Ditto—
R.I.Heaton	A/L/Sto (Ty)	—Ditto—
F.W.Bullen	Sto.I.	—Ditto—
T.Ward	L/Cook (0) (Ty)	—Ditto—
G.E.Phillips	Sto.I.	—Ditto—
E.W.Grubb	L/Sig.	—Ditto—
O.N.Peacock	O/Sig.	—Ditto—
J. Brown	A/L/Sea (Ty)	—Ditto—

J.M.Docherty	A.B.	—Ditto—
A.J.Wesley	A.B.	—Ditto—
T. Fuller	A.B.	—Ditto—
F.W.Knapp	A/L/Sto (Ty)	—Ditto—
S. Petts	A.B.	—Ditto—
H.C.Ellis	A.B.	—Ditto—
J.H.Jackson	A.B.	—Ditto—
R.C.Smith	O/Sea	—Ditto—

. . . . . .

HMS *Leda* Passengers From PQ17

3rd Engineer	Alex L. Sutherland	Ex SS Navarino
Able Seaman	Ivor Hanford	Ex *SS River Afton*
Able Seaman	Adam O'Hagan	—Ditto—
Fireman	Robert Taylor	—Ditto—
Able Seaman	Gilbert White	—Ditto—
Able Seaman	George Jamieson	—Ditto—
3rd Officer	Macdonald	Ex *Navarino* Transferred *Rathlin*
3rd Officer	Docherty	Ex *River Afton* To *Rathlin*
3rd Officer	De Coste	Ex *River Afton* To *Rathlin*

RFA Gray Ranger Survivors picked up A.M. 22/9/42

H.D.Gausden	Master
D.L.Hood	Chief Engineer
P.Cawley	Seaman Gunner P/JX268468
W.St.Clair	Seaman Gunner D/JX366355
P.Reilly	Seaman Gunner C/JX336867
R.Harvey	Seaman Gunner C/JX311287
A.Mayfield	Seaman Gunner C/JX334561
G.Bright	Leading Gunner P/JX165000
C.B.Fletcher	Able Seaman P/JX203928
G.Palmer	Able Seaman C/JX177999
S.Curry	Donkeyman Greaser
J.W.Gallagher	Donkeyman Greaser
G.Rosie	Donkeyman Greaser
L.Hussen	Donkeyman Greaser
J.B.Cowan	Carpenter
W.Alloway	Assistant Steward
A.Sharp	Galley Boy
A.Gibson	Able Seaman
P.Cowie	Able Seaman
T.Madison	Electrician
D.Bradbury	Pumpman
R.Lawless	Seaman Gunner P/JX336911

SS Bellingham — Survivors picked up — 22/9/42. A.M.

H.Cook	Able Seaman
H.Lunt	Able Seaman
C.Ohlson	Able Seaman

J.Moore	Chief Cook	
W.Davis	Messman	
L.W.Kroeger	Gunner	
L.Hall	Gunner	
A.L.Pierce	1st Engineer	
I.Hall	2nd Engineer	
J.D.Hawkins	Water Tender	
E.H.Boyd	3rd Mate	
R.Stout	Water Tender	
J.Merkel	Ordinary Seaman	Ex- *Pan Atlantic*
J.A.Jones	Wiper	—Ditto—
V.Kallisma	Fireman	—Ditto—
J.R.Nash	2nd Engineer	—Ditto—
W.Jacques	Chief Officer	—Ditto—
R.E.Hernandez	Able Seaman	—Ditto—
R.R.Ellebracht		Ex-*Pankraft*
K.Asch	Radio Operator	—Ditto—

SS Troubador . . . Passengers embarked Archangel on N.Gem 13/9/42

A.Kieff (British)	Fireman
M.Moyse (British)	Fireman
D.A.Waters (American)	Watertender
L.Kellor (American)	Trimmer
G.Dickinson (American)	Trimmer
R.Johnson (American)	Able Seaman
P.Riorden	Fireman
L.Dussak	Trimmer
G.Shether	Trimmer
A.Larson	Fireman
W.Johansen	Fireman
A.Cordeiro	Fireman
J.Novak	Messman

Merchant Ships lost on Convoy PQ17 July & August 1942

Alcoa Ranger	5116	tons	US	Sunk	
Aldersdale (oiler)	8402	"	UK	"	
Azerbajan (tanker)	6114	"	USSR		
Bellingham	5345	"	US		
Benjamin Harrison	7191	"	US		
Bolton Castle	5203	"	UK	Sunk	
Carlton	5127	"	US	"	4 Killed
Christopher Newport	7191	"	US	"	3 Killed
Daniel Morgan	7177	"	US	"	3 Killed
Donbass	7925	"	USSR		
Earlston	7494	"	UK	Sunk	
El Capitan	5255	"	Pan		
Empire Byron	6645	"	UK	Sunk	18 Killed
Empire Tide (Cam)	6978	"	UK		

Fairfield City	5686	"	US	Sunk	6 Killed
Hartlebury	5082	"	UK	"	37 Killed
Honomu	6977	"	US	"	19 Killed
Hoosier	*5060*	"	US	"	
Ironclad	*5685*	"	US		
John Witherspoon	7180	"	US	Sunk	1 Killed
Navarino	4841	"	UK	"	1 Killed
Ocean Freedom	7173	"	UK		
Olopana	6069	"	US	Sunk	6 Killed
Pan Atlantic	5411	"	US	"	26 Killed
Pankraft	5644	"	US	"	2 Killed
Paulus Potter	7168	"	Dutch	"	
Peter Kerr	6476	"	US	"	
Rathlin (Rescue)	1600	"	UK		
River Afton (Comm.)	5423	"	UK	Sunk	23 Killed
Samuel Chase	7191	"	US		
Silver Sword	4937	"	US		
Troubador	5808	"	Norwegian		
Washington	5564	"	US	Sunk	
William Hooper	7177	"	US	"	3 Killed
Winston-Salem	6223	"	US		
Zaafaran	1559	"	UK	Sunk	1 Killed
Zamalek	1567	"	UK		

American P.T. Boat Squadron 22 Based Golfe Juan 1944/45

Commanding Officer., R.J.Dressling Lt Commander USN, at the time of the MGB 177's involvement.

Numbers	Names of Boats	USN PT Boat
302	Dock Trotter	"
303	Hogan's Goat	"
304	Cherry	"
305	Sudden Jerk	"
306	The Fascinating Bitch	"
307	Sad Sac	"
308	La De Dah!	"
309	Oh! Frankie	"
310	Alcyone	"
311	Wanderer	"
312	The Stray Lamb	"
313	Sea Wolf	"

Index

Index

54, 55, 56, 57, 58, 60, 62, 63, 65,
66, 67, 68, 69, 70, 71, 72, 73, 74,
75, 76, 77, 78, 80, 81, 83, 84, 85,
86, 90, 91, 92, 93, 96, 97, 98, 99,
100, 101, 102, 103, 104, 106, 108,
109, 110, 112, 113, 114, 116, 117,
118, 119, 120, 121, 122, 123, 125,
126, 127, 128, 129, 130, 131, 132,
133, 141, 147, 154, 165, 169, 171,
172, 175, 176

Northern Pride, HMT: 15

Northern Spray, HMT: 15, 18, 20, 22,
24, 28, 29, 30, 36

Northern Wave, HMT: 15, 19, 123

Northern Patrol: 16

Northern Lights: 55

Norfolk: 135

Norfolk HMS: 70

Northey, Lieut A. P., DSC, RN: 175

Norway: 4, 8, 17, 36, 37, 39, 41, 43,
44, 47, 54, 67, 75, 89, 167

Novak, J.: 178

Nova Scotia: 131

Novaya Zemblya: 79, 82, 87, 91, 93

Obdurate, HMS: 109, 117, 118

Obedient, HMS: 109, 116, 117

Ocean Freedom: 80, 81, 82, 84, 179

Ocean Voice: 101, 102

Oerlikon: 37, 41, 47

Offa, HMS: 175

Ofot Fiord: 17, 19, 21, 22, 36

O'Hagan, A.: 177

Ohlson, C.: 177

Olopana: 179

Onslow, HMS: 109, 112, 117, 120,
121, 122, 123

ONS5: 126

Order of the Patriotic War: 151

Oribi, HMS: 109

Orwell, HMS: 109

Ostvaagoy: 38

Outer Hebrides: 109

P 614 (submarine) HMS: 175

P 615 (submarine) HMS: 175

Paani (bread): 87

Pacific: 165

Palmer, G.: 177

Palomaris, HMS: 71, 80, 81, 89, 175

Pan Atlantic: 101, 179

Pankraft: 101, 179

Paragon Station: 105, 167

Partisans: 163, 164

Patriksfiord: 70

Patuskas (potatoes): 87

Paulus Potter: 179

Peacock, O. N.: 176

Peake, Harry: 30

Pembroke, HMS: 171

Pengally, Lieut J., RN: 176

Peter Kerr: 179

Petts, S.: 177

Phillips, G. E.: 176

Phoney War: 16, 17

Pickering Road: 133, 134, 136

Pierce, A. L.: 178

Pilmer, J. D.: 176

'Pleasurer': 7

Plimsoll lines: 68

Polar Medal: 144

Pooley, Ordinary Skipper: 46, 48,
50, 51, 97, 112, 132

POPS: 152

Poppy, HMS: 80, 175

Porter Street: 106

Portsmouth: 167

Potts, Basil: 100

Potts, B. R.: 176

Powell, Fred: 22, 23, 24, 30, 31, 36,
165

Pozerica, HMS: 71, 80, 86, 89, 175

Pram dinghies: 142

Prince Eugen: 54, 56

Prendergast, L. J.: 176

Puffer boats: 19, 22, 23

Purser's peas: 88